The Magnificent Soul

The Magnificent Soul

The Art of Living in a World Founded on Consciousness

George Walter Chyz

Final Revision

Disclaimer:
The author is not a healthcare professional and no part of this book is to be regarded as medical advice. This book offers insights and information from the author's personal perspective; in the event the reader uses any of the information in this book for themselves or others, the reader assumes full responsibility for their understanding, actions and the results.

ISBN-13: 978-1986106290

ISBN-10: 1986106292

Dedication

To my beloved Soul
Thank you for blessing my life
I love you

Acknowledgments

I'm most grateful for the infallible guidance from my Soul.

I'm also deeply grateful for my parents Harold and Cynthia.
They truly loved me and were always there for me.
Although they passed on, I'll always love them and be
grateful for all of their love, encouragement, and support.

My brother Grant has been a pillar of integrity, who I love and respect.
Thank you for your loving support and wise advice.

A very special beloved taught me how to love beyond what
I imagined possible. Thank you, radiant one.

Adrienne Poremba, Taylor S., Heidi Erhardt, and Axl Axelrod helped me
to make this book into a gift that I am proud to share with the world.
Thank you all for the valuable guidance, editing and proofreading.

Thank you Milan Param for the illustrative artwork.

I'm also very grateful for the help of: Jessica Abelson; Alison Armstrong;
Eden Ahbez; Alenka; Daddy Bray; Janie Comito; Deva; Drew and Oceania
Castellini; Kirstie Carlson; David Chalmers; Eona; David Cory Frankel;
Bach Goetz; Bridget Gregory; Brian Gottschalk, James Herrington; Michael
Hickey; Benjamin Hoff; Home; Kayon; Dr. Ernst Katz; Rakhal Kincaid;
Sherrie, and Tulsi Klappert; David Lopez; Lilith; Hopi Elder Martin;
Marjola; Miracle; Madeleine Migenes; Jeffery Munoz; Angel Masi;
Charlynn Medeiros; Xena Miranda; Wayland Namingha, Jr.; Anthony
Natividad, Indigo Ocean; Michelle and Mackenzie Quarton; Mark Reese;
Robin; Tim Schoenhorn; Tim-i; Serenity; Dr. Zhi Gang Sha; Sky;
Sophianada; Ruby; Rudolf Steiner; Todd Swan; Jeffrey Turnbull; Jonathan,
Susan, and Marie Walczak; Stephanie Wichenhouser; Rick Yamashiro and
so many others who through conversations, books, editing, etc. have helped
me develop and clarify what is shared in these pages.

Throughout my life, I have been touched by people, movies, books, nature,
plants, animals, and circumstances. My heartfelt gratitude goes out to
everyone and everything that has helped me to learn what is shared herein.

A very special thank you goes out to all of the people who have loved me!
I know that I haven't been the easiest person to love. Therefore, I'm
especially grateful for everyone's patience and all of the intimacy we shared.
Thank you one and all.

To the One-Who-Is-All, I'm eternally grateful for everything!

Table of Contents

Glossary

All words or phrases included in this glossary appear in the text using the capitalization shown here. When a term or phrase is first introduced in the body of the book it is italicized as shown here. Once introduced normal type is used but the capitalization is retained to help you know that it's a glossary word or phrase.

Now that you know this Glossary is available for your reference if you need it, you're welcome to skip over it and begin with the Chapter 1.

Beneficence of the Quintessential Core
A feature of *Triality* in which the balanced blend of qualities found in the *Quintessential Core* are notably beneficial, conducive to life or general health.

Consciousness-Origin Cosmology
A theoretical story that includes the purpose, cause, and outline of the primary events of our universe. This cosmology begins before the beginning of time and proceeds to the end of time.

Creator
A portion of the *One-Who-Is-All* that is assigned the task of forming the *Grand Illusion*.

Age of Individuation
The current age in which civilization grows and individualizes humanity. This age appears to be nearing its end.

Age of Love
The emerging age, which is predicted to be dedicated to the full blossoming of love in a peaceful and prosperous world.

Evil's Silver Lining
The notion that positive results emerge from incidents that appear to be awful or "evil" when they get started.

Feebleness of Incompleteness
A principle predicting that something missing an important component, exhibits feebleness due to its incompleteness. For example, a car without an engine is feeble. This principal is the corollary to the *Supreme Power of Wholeness* principle.

Grand Illusion
A label for our reality that implies it's some sort of elaborate illusion. Chapter 5 discusses the *Grand Illusion*.

Heart-Center
The physical region where the heart is located.

Heart-Opening Breath
A breathing technique that brings the practitioner into balance and opens their heart to achieve a state-of-mind similar to being in love.

Similarity of Opposites
A feature of *Triality*, in which extreme polar opposites are found to be unexpectedly more similar than different.

Liberating Your Genius
A principle that reveals how to bring forth masterful skills. This principle is shared near the end of Chapter 18: Following Your Heart.

Maleficence of Extremes
A feature of *Triality* in which extreme polar opposites tend to be destructive or divisive.

Original-People
Pre-civilized people who have not been influenced by civilization.

One-Who-Is-All
The one and only consciousness that existed before this universe began. This consciousness is the foundation of everything. The *One-Who-Is-All* is the driving force behind everyone and everything.

One
An abbreviation for the *One-Who-Is-All*.

Pragmatic
A person who has turned away from their *Soul*, and by doing so, has inadvertently cut themselves off from their *Soul's* intuition, which includes one's conscience.

Quintessential Core
The central wholeness of a *Triality*. The *Quintessential Core* lies in the middle, between the opposite extreme endpoints that constitute a duality. This is the key ingredient that transforms a dualistic spectrum into a *Triality*.

Romantic
NOUN – A person who lives with their heart open, following the intuitive guidance of their *Soul*. These people tend to be relatively humble.
ADJECTIVE – Characterized by a sense of wonderment, magic, inexplicably perfect timing, joy, and/or love.
The negative connotations of romantic are shown to be misunderstandings.

Soul or Superconscious-Soul
A godlike consciousness that resides in each human's *Heart-Center* and acts as a divine guardian that is dedicated to guiding a person from conception to death.

Soul-Magic
The way *Souls* work independently or together to orchestrate miracles and serendipitous synchronicities—mystical experiences that make one's life extraordinary.

Soul Mate
One's *Soul Mate* is their *Soul* arranged ideal beloved. For people who are into polyamorous relationships, *Soul Group* is a more appropriate label.

Supreme Power of Wholeness
A principle that notices how wholeness provides extraordinary power, one that exceeds the sum of the parts. This idea proposes that when the important components of something are properly assembled into a complete whole, a magnificent power is obtained. In the case of the *Soul*, its consciousness is comprised of balanced portions of emotion and intellect, giving it godlike powers which are commonly labeled divine or Holy. This principle helps to highlight the important qualities of wholeness, especially in comparison to incompleteness. The corollary to this principle is the *Feebleness of Incompleteness* principle.

Triality

Triality
A model similar to duality; however, a *Triality* includes a pair of extreme opposite endpoints, a spectrum that spans from one endpoint to the other, and a central wholeness named the *Quintessential Core*. See the diagram on the right.

True-Self
The *True-Self* is the fullest expression of who a person is. This full expression of one's personality is contained in a person's *Soul* and can reveal itself when one's heart is open.

Way-of-the-Heart
A life path in which a person is dedicated to following their *Soul's* guidance. The three key elements are opening the heart, following the heart and opening to love.

Chapter 1
The Soul Resides in the Heart

"What your heart thinks is great, is great.
The soul's emphasis is always right."
—Ralph Waldo Emerson (1803–1882) philosopher and poet

A CONSCIOUSNESS IN THE HEART

Although most people believe that the brain produces consciousness, this chapter shows that the most important portion of human consciousness, the soul, resides in the physical heart.

The late neuropsychologist Dr. Paul Pearsall specialized in assisting heart transplant recipients and their families with the psychological issues that arose when a new heart was placed in a person's chest. In his book *The Heart's Code*, Pearsall shares astonishing stories that imply an important part of human consciousness literally inhabits the heart organ.

In one case, a woman received a donor heart from a murder victim. While she expected to simply receive a muscular pump to help circulate her blood, she also received **memories** of the heart donor's demise. Those memories included the murderer's identity.

The subsequent police investigation, using her leads, recovered the murder weapon and convicted the murderer. In order for this to be possible, the heart must have contained **real memories** from the murder victim. Evidently, these memories were not stored in the brain, but in the physical heart that was placed in this woman's chest.

In another example, a heart transplant patient who detested Mexican food received a donor heart from a Mexican man. After the transplant, the recipient became very fond of eating Mexican food. He also changed his sexual style, and other personality traits.

According to Pearsall, these types of unexpected changes would take place when a person's heart was removed and a heart from someone else was placed in their chest. Pearsall claims that heart transplant patients commonly undergo significant personality changes. His book, *The Heart's Code*, provides numerous examples that exhibit substantial changes in sexual, dietary and musical preferences, sleep patterns, and communication style, as well as other personal habits, such as cigarette smoking.

In an unusual "domino transplant," a patient with failing lungs is given a new heart and lungs from a deceased donor. Then the healthy heart that was removed from the heart-lung recipient is donated to a third person, Fred, who's heart was failing. When the process is complete two men are alive. Fred has a new heart that was donated by the other living man who received the heart-lung combination from the deceased donor. Dr. Pearsall had the rare opportunity to discuss post heart transplant personality changes with the two living men and their wives.

After the heart-only recipient, Fred, described his new personality with the living donor and his wife, they confirmed that those personality traits existed in the donor before the transplant took place. Then, at the end of the meeting, Fred's wife exclaimed, "My Fred received a personality transplant."

So, when a heart transplant is performed, the donor's persistent behavior—what I'm calling personality—appears to relocate with the heart organ even though the conscious-mind in the recipient's head remains untouched.

In his book, Dr. Pearsall offers many examples supporting the age-old idea that one's personality resides in their heart. These well documented heart transplant cases disprove the modern theory that "it's all in the head," and revive older theories about the heart.

THE PRECOGNITIVE HEART

Researchers at the HeartMath Institute of Boulder Creek, California discovered that the heart, or something in the heart, also appears to know the future.

In a well-documented scientific study,[1] researchers placed human test subjects in front of a computer screen one at a time. On each subject's chest, just above their heart, the researchers placed a few Electro-Magnetic Field (EMF) sensors, to monitor the EMF signals that had been found to emerge from the heart. Blood pressure and heart rate were also monitored.

An application running on the computer randomly selected one image at a time and displayed it on the computer screen being viewed by the test subject. The computer database contained two types of images: disturbing images and calming images.

As these two types of images appeared on the screen, the sensors near the observer's heart received two significantly different EMF signals. One type of signal corresponded to the subject viewing a disturbing image, while the other type of signal corresponded to viewing a calming image. These results confirmed the researcher's theory that the heart was involved in the person's reaction to the images.

This conclusion is quite reasonable, however while analyzing the data, an unexpected and much more fascinating phenomenon was discovered. The researchers noticed that the heart began reacting to the image three to five seconds **before** it appeared on the screen.

Remarkably, the heart began its reaction **before** the random image selection application had selected the corresponding image. This astonishing result indicates that the heart, or something in the heart, is aware of the future!

Additional research conducted at HeartMath[2] found that the heart's EMF output in these emotionally-charged situations induce glands in the brainstem to release chemicals that cause the person to feel particular emotions. This means that something in the heart has the power to control how we feel about things we encounter.

According to HeartMath's Director of Research, Rollin McCraty, the results of these studies have been duplicated in labs around the world, ensuring their validity and accuracy.

THE INFALLIBLE VOICE IN THE HEART

In addition to all of that, two research projects conducted at Stanford University support the proposition that our source of intuition resides in the heart.

The Stanford researchers investigated human test subjects that had developed an ability to place themselves into a trance state. In this state-of-mind their brains where measured to be in delta or theta brain wave frequencies, the brain's two lowest frequency ranges. While in the trance state, the subjects remained awake and aware, yet their conscious-minds stopped having thoughts or ideas that are normally discussed inside one's head using their "inner voice." In other words, no internal dialogue takes place while a person is in a self-induced trance state.

Even so, people with this ability have discovered that they occasionally hear their "inner voice" make a statement, seemingly on its own. When the researchers were made aware of these mysterious statements emerging within these people, they devised a way to investigate and analyze the statements themselves.

The researchers asked the test subjects to enter into their trance and wait for the voice to speak on its own. Then, after the voice spoke, each subject was instructed to tell the researchers exactly what the voice said. The researchers recorded the statements as they were retold by the test subjects.

Upon investigation, and after fact-checking each statement, all the statements were found to be true. Surprisingly, some information seemed to be impossible for the test subject to be aware of at the time of the test, making the findings particularly intriguing. In the research report's conclusion, the mysterious inner voice was named:

"the infallible voice"[3] to acknowledge its accuracy.

Inspired by these results, follow-up research was devised to determine where the infallible voice was coming from. In the second research project, the same test subjects were placed, one at a time, into a small room that was outfitted with sophisticated EMF sensing equipment. This offered the ability to monitor the EMFs within the room, including those located within the subject's body. Additionally, the subject was provided a way to indicate when the infallible voice was speaking and when it was not speaking. Once situated in the room, the subject entered their trance state-of-mind.

During the periods of time when the infallible voice was speaking, the researchers discovered that EMFs ranging from 250 to 1,000 cycles per second emanated from the top of the subject's heart, and beamed up into the middle of the subject's head. Furthermore, the beam of EMFs only appeared when the voice spoke. Based on this, the researchers wrote in the second research report's conclusion:

*"...the **infallible voice** comes from the **heart**."*[4]

These two research projects persuasively indicate that infallible knowledge is transmitted from the heart up into the head.

Albert Einstein, the celebrated physicist, supports this idea:

"The state-of-mind which enables a man to do work of this kind [theoretical physics], is akin to that of the religious worshipper or the lover; the daily effort comes from no deliberate intention or program, but straight from the heart."

"The intellect has little to do on the road to discovery. There comes a leap in consciousness, call it intuition or what you will, and the solution comes to you and you don't know how or why."

THE SUPERCONSCIOUS-SOUL

Combining the implications of all that has been presented so far, it becomes clear that an important portion of consciousness must be located in the heart region. My intuition has guided me to believe this consciousness is what has been referred to as the soul:

soul: noun;
The spiritual or immaterial part of a human being or animal, regarded as immortal.
• A person's moral or emotional nature or sense of identity.[5]

Due to the infallibility and knowledge of the future possessed by this portion of consciousness, I've decided to name it the *Superconscious-Soul*. Most often, for brevity, I'll simply use *Soul*.

HOW THE SOUL INFLUENCES OUR PERSONALITY

While considering the results of the HeartMath image study that showed something in the heart has knowledge of the future, and the associated glandular chemical release study, I was intuitively offered the following insight:

Knowing an emotionally-charged image is about to be viewed, it is actually the Soul residing in the subject's heart that sends a specific EMF signal up to the head before the image appears. This EMF signal is sent to induce corresponding glands to initiate the process of injecting chemicals into the cerebral cortex. The timing is synchronized to cause the feelings that are generated by the chemicals to emerge when the image appears.

In order for a person's emotional response to correspond to an unexpected event (such as seeing a disturbing image), the glands that produce and deliver the chemicals must be induced to begin their activities slightly **before** the event takes place. Otherwise, the person's emotional response would be noticeably delayed. However, because the Soul has knowledge of the future, it can take advantage of the available time gap that exists between its foreknowledge of the emotional event and the actual occurrence of that event. During the interceding moment, the Soul has the opportunity to choose which EMF signal to send up to the glands located in the brainstem. The signal determines the amount and type of psychoactive chemicals that are released into the brain. This arrangement gives the Soul control over which feelings arise in the individual, propelling the individual to act accordingly, thereby influencing their personality.

Thus, the divine knowledge of the future and the ability to induce glandular activity in the brainstem gives the Soul control over a person's likes, dislikes, and even how strong those feelings are. The real-life heart transplant cases presented earlier support this theory by showing that something in the heart effects one's personality.

Throughout the course of my life, I've become aware that I can't control my desires. They are what they are. Sometimes, I might have an idea as to why I have certain desires, still in most cases, my desires are inexplicable. Additionally, I've found that I can't intellectually choose to like something other than what I currently desire confirming that human desires aren't controlled by the conscious-mind.

Most people presume our subconscious-mind is responsible for our desires, however I've come to believe that the Superconscious-Soul wields the power to control desires. If this is correct, then the power to influence who a person is and how they react to their surroundings is placed in a portion of consciousness that knows the future and resides in our hearts.

SCIENTIFIC PROOF

As you can see, scientific research has provided compelling support for the idea that we have a Soul in our heart. However, it's important to remember that all theories are, by definition, theoretical. Human beings are so complex that it's beyond our ability to take into account every possible detail. Even on a purely physical basis, theories regarding the operation and workings of a human being remain open to debate.

Moreover, the statistical math that is used to compute the confidence of scientific experimental results require an infinite number of tests to achieve 100 percent *confidence*. Therefore, the scientific method can provide *support* for theories, but not definitive proof. This support can very strongly indicate that a theory is nearly certain to be true, still scientific **proof** is a misconception.

At any time, a specific example that shows how an existing theory fails to fit reality can crop up. A single example of failure to fit reality is enough to discredit a theory, proving it false. So even though positive proof is impossible, proving a theory false only requires one solid example showing that theory fails to fit reality. There are numerous cases in which respected theories have been turned into myths, or in other cases the use of a theory is restricted to be used only within the conditions that have been verified to fit the theory.

With this important scientific reality accounted for, the research shared so far provides strong support for the theory that some sort of divine super-consciousness appears to reside in the heart.

SPIRITUAL SUPPORT

The following excerpts from the world's most popular spiritual scriptures point to the heart in ways that support the idea that a divine consciousness resides in the heart.

In Judaism's Old Testament, Psalm 37, King David claims that the law of God is located in the heart of the righteous:

> [29]*The righteous shall inherit the land and dwell upon it forever.* [30]*The mouth of the righteous utters wisdom, and his tongue speaks justice.* [31]*The law of his God is in his heart; his steps do not slip.* [6]
> [Source: Psalm 37, English Standard Version of the Holy Bible]

Also, in Ezekiel, the Lord places a new spirit in the heart:

> [26]*And I will give you a new heart, and a new spirit I will put within you. And I will remove the heart of stone from your flesh and give you a heart of flesh.* [27]*And I will put my Spirit within you, and cause you to walk in my statutes and be careful to obey my rules.*
> [Source: Ezekiel, chapter 36, English Standard Version of the Holy Bible]

Then, from Christianity, in chapter 17 of Luke:

> *{17:20} Being asked by the Pharisees when the kingdom of God would come, he [Jesus] answered them, "The kingdom of God is not coming with signs to be observed, {17:21} nor will they say, 'Look, here it is!' or 'There!' for behold, the kingdom of God is in the midst of you.*
> [Source: Luke chapter 17, English Standard Version of the Holy Bible]

Midst is defined as "in the middle point or part," while "middle, center, heart and core" are listed as synonyms for midst; therefore, midst means center, and is a synonym for heart. Thus, according to Jesus, the kingdom of god is in your heart!

In another passage, Jesus' disciple John directs his followers to their inner God:

> *{4:4} Little children, you are from God...for he who is in you is greater than he who is in the world. ...*
>
> *{4:12} No one has ever seen God; if we love one another, God abides in us and his love is perfected in us. {4:13} By this we know that we abide in him and he in us, because he has given us of his Spirit.*
> [Source: 1 John, chapter 4, English Standard Version of the Holy Bible]

Next, from Islam, the Quran reveals how the heart is a portal connecting a person to the divine consciousness identified as God:

> *[6:125] Whomever God desires to guide, He spreads open his heart to Islam; and whomever He desires to misguide, He makes his heart narrow, constricted, as though he were climbing up the sky.* [7]

Later, the Quran points out how this portal can be sealed to prevent divine guidance as follows:

> *[40:35] Those who argue against God's revelations, without any proof having come to them–a heinous sin in the sight of God, and of those who believe. Thus, God seals the heart of every proud bully.* [8]

This passage indicates that an arrogant or proud person can become disconnected from their Soul. The Quran has 15 passages that claim God places a seal or veil over some people's hearts. Later this blocked condition will be discussed in detail.

Also, in Hinduism's Bhagavad-gita, Krishna explains that he is the Supreme Lord, a "Supersoul" residing in everyone's heart:

[8:4] Physical nature is known to be endlessly mutable. The universe is the cosmic form of the Supreme Lord, and I am that Lord represented as the Supersoul, dwelling in the heart of every embodied being. [9]

Finally, from Taoism, the adept Bruce Frantzis explains:

"The middle tantien [focus of essence] is located near the heart on the central channel. It governs all relationships, including how you connect to your essence and the Tao." [10]

The Tao is essentially equivalent to the consciousness commonly called God in the western world. A primary difference is that Taoists don't personify the Tao. Moreover, Taoists claim the nature of the Tao cannot be adequately defined nor fully understood. Taoists refrain from expounding on the Tao, knowing that words would diminish its ineffable magnificence.

I decided to label that which is often called God, the *One-Who-Is-All*, or simply the *One*, for brevity. This name avoids gender bias and the appearance of aligning with a particular spiritual path. The fact that all the major religions meet in the heart supports the idea that all religions share the same ultimate source. Even though each religion identifies that source with a different name, or in Hinduism with many different names, all these labels appear to ultimately point to one source that humans can access in their hearts.

Amongst the popular spiritual paths, the only exception to the Soul in the heart connection is Buddhism. Unexpectedly, the Buddha categorically denied the existence of a Soul. Because Buddhism includes reincarnation, many consider it to be a spiritual path. Nonetheless, careful investigation reveals that Buddhism is more of an intellectual philosophy that advocates particular beliefs and practices. In short, the Buddhist practitioner is encouraged to use their intellectual conscious-mind to suppress their natural personality and desires (that I'm claiming arise from the Soul) and chart a course half way between the extremes of sensual abandon and strict asceticism.

Later, once this book's thesis has been more completely shared, I'll show how Buddhism helps an enormous number of people to alleviate their suffering and improve their lives.

In spite of the Buddhist exception, the spiritual passages presented earlier reveal how the human heart provides a common thread linking the world's major religions together.

Even though the passages referenced indicate that the One resides in all of our hearts, or is somehow linked to us through our hearts, most religious people choose to worship an external deity. It's quite common for people to look outside themselves in an attempt to connect with their concept of a gigantic deity outside of themselves. This is likely due to the popular teachings offered by clergy who strictly avoid mentioning the personal heart connection to the One. If this inner connection became popular, no clergy would be needed, thus job security could be why the inner connection to the One is ignored by clergy. Additionally, most of the scriptures identify the One as an external deity.

Be that as it may, I've shown how this magnificence, no matter what one may choose to call it, is connected to each of us in our hearts. Thus, the divine presence of the One-That-Is-All is closer than most people have been able to imagine.

THE KEY TO THE TREASURE IN YOUR CHEST

In addition to the great spiritual paths coming together in the heart, the scientific research shared above indicates that our hearts are where science and spirituality unite.

Once I acknowledged my Soul's existence and its divine nature, a relationship began to grow. This inner God became my greatest ally, physician, guide, and beloved guardian. I discovered that my Soul is the elusive source of intuition, conscience, genius, love, happiness, miracles, and more.

Then, reviewing my life, I realized this inner divine presence had been with me all along. Furthermore, it became quite clear that the Soul is the most precious part of who a person is.

> *"Ordinary riches can be stolen, real riches cannot.*
> *In your Soul are infinitely precious things*
> *that cannot be taken from you."*
>
> —Oscar Wilde (1854–1900) author

To unlock this "treasure chest," it's helpful to open one's mind to a perspective that places consciousness at the foundation of the universe. The next chapter explores this re-emerging view of reality.

Chapter 2
Turning Reality Right–Side–Up

For as long as we've known, humans have endeavored to explain the experience of life and the tremendous universe where it takes place. All around the world, cultures have stories that attempt to explain why reality is the way it is, and how it came to be that way. Many explanations are viewed as myths, others as viable theories. Still, the search continues.

Physicists dedicate their lives to discovering the truth about the universe. In spite of that, there are evermore theories resulting in more confusion than ever before.

Why is the truth about reality so elusive?

THE GRAND ILLUSION

The answer for some is that reality is a *Grand Illusion*. Many leading scientists and enlightened spiritual masters have come to agree that physical reality is some sort of elaborate illusion.

An illusion is defined as something that is likely to be wrongly perceived or interpreted. Accordingly, if reality is an illusion, then the truth about the universe is going to be difficult to pin down.

After personally experiencing several transcendental adventures, I came to believe the illusion theory of reality. The type of transcendental journey I refer to is when a person's conscious-mind exits the physical realm and finds itself immersed in pure consciousness. In that alternate reality, one encounters an unmistakable sense of being home. Those who have explored the realm of pure consciousness are familiar with this profound feeling of being home.

Upon returning to the physical realm, the explorer has the opportunity to compare the two realms. Unexpectedly, the physical realm seems artificial in comparison to the realm of consciousness. Consequently, most people who have transcended often come to embrace the theory that the physical realm is an illusion.

In addition to feeling one is home, the transcendentalist also experiences a knowing that they are one with everything. Then upon returning to the physical realm, that sense of oneness fades.

Eventually, these journeys led me to believe that the Grand Illusionist is the Oneness that is encountered in the realm of consciousness. Accordingly, this illusionist fashioned the physical realm out of Itself. After arriving at this conclusion on my own, I further discovered that this idea is as old as humanity.

A FOUNDATION OF CONSCIOUSNESS: PANPSYCHISM

A word that approximates this idea is panpsychism:

Panpsychism: noun;
the doctrine or belief that everything material, however small, has an element of individual consciousness. [11]

This word contains the Greek component pan, which means all, and the Greek *psych*, which originally meant *"Soul, breath, and life."* Therefore, panpsychism is a philosophy that claims everything contains a Soul or portion of consciousness.

In alignment with this ancient idea, modern scientists have been developing theories that place consciousness at the foundation of reality.

Max Plank, the world-renowned father of quantum physics, may have been the first modern physicist to speak quite clearly in support of consciousness being the foundation of reality. In 1931, *The Observer*, a weekly British newspaper, reported that Plank said:

"I regard consciousness as fundamental. I regard matter as derivative from consciousness. We cannot get behind consciousness. Everything that we talk about, everything that we regard as existing, postulates consciousness."

Just four years later, in 1935, quantum entanglement was introduced by Albert Einstein, Boris Podolsky and Nathan Rosen. This popular mystery has remained unsolved by matter-based physics to this day. Despite that, this important conundrum is easily explained by placing consciousness at the foundation of the universe where it becomes a medium for instantaneous communication between the distant particles that are entangled and have been shown to exhibit "spooky action at a distance." Sadly, Plank's view on consciousness was not taken seriously when he offered it.

More recently, the age-old panpsychist perspective has been gaining evermore prestigious proponents.

The famous stem cell biologist Dr. Robert Lanza, was ranked the third most important scientist in the world by *The New York Times*. A *U.S. News & World Report* cover story called him a genius and likened him to Einstein. In 2010, Dr. Lanza wrote a book entitled, *Biocentrism: How Life and Consciousness Are the Keys to Understanding the Nature of the Universe*. In his book, Lanza proposes that life and consciousness are fundamental to the entire universe. Biocentrism claims that **consciousness creates the material universe, not the other way around.**

Additionally, David Chalmers, professor of philosophy and co-director of The Center for Mind, Brain and Consciousness at New York University, presented a TED Talk in which he thoroughly and unapologetically discusses this issue. In the TED Talk, he states that he strongly supports **"...consciousness being the foundation of everything!"**

MATERIALISM

Even though the consciousness foundation concept of panpsychism is immemorial, the more popular idea that matter is the foundation of reality began to take hold just 330 years ago. In 1687, Sir Isaac Newton published *Principia*. This important book introduced calculus to the field of mathematics, supercharging it. Then, Newton used his powerful invention, calculus, to derive his famous *laws of motion*. These laws were also introduced in *Principia*. Subsequently, Newton's equations have enabled engineers to accomplish countless technological advancements. These powerful mathematical tools are still used today.

Other mathematical equations were developed by Nicolas Carnot, who published *Reflections on the Motive Power of Fire* in 1824, making him the "Father of Thermodynamics." Combining the *laws of thermodynamics* with Newton's *laws of motion* engineers became able to predict forces, power, and motion to harness energy and propel physical devices. This led to amazing inventions like steamers, trains, cars, sawmills, airplanes, etc.

Another huge leap took place in 1865, when James Maxwell introduced what are commonly called, "Maxwell's Equations." These equations embodied Maxwell's classical theory of electromagnetic radiation, also called Electro-Magnetic Fields, or simply EMFs. Before Maxwell, light, electricity, and magnetism were considered separate phenomena. Maxwell's partial differential equations brought light, electricity, and magnetism together in a way that was unified and, most importantly, predictable. Maxwell's exceedingly useful equations enabled inventors to develop radio, television, cellphones, remote controls, blue-tooth, WI-FI, and much more.

All of this, plus countless contributions from numerous physicists, scientists, and engineers shifted humanity's view of reality by focusing our attention on matter and energy. Accordingly, our viewpoint was diverted away from the age-old consciousness concepts that revered gods and goddesses—huge portions of divine consciousness, each with particular responsibilities. Those old ideas were cast aside by the belief that matter and energy were the foundation of reality.

Then, in the 1800s, compulsory schooling systems were established in industrialized nations. These schools taught the materialistic theories that had been adopted by science, making those ideas the prevailing point of view in the developed world.

With the materialistic model of reality firmly established, the idea that the human brain is some sort of biological machine that produces consciousness emerged. Thus, reality was turned upside-down; matter and energy became the new foundation, while consciousness became something produced by a biological machine—the human brain. Today, most people believe this machine-brain theory to be true. In spite of that, it's easy to conclusively prove that theory false.

PROVING THE MACHINE–BRAIN THEORY FALSE

One simple way to prove the machine-brain theory false is by considering the implications of well-documented near-death experiences. A familiar example involves a patient expiring on the operating table. Their heart and brain stop functioning. The physicians revive the heart, and the person is brought back to life.

Afterward, the person recalls observing the physicians working to revive their body from up above, near the ceiling. In documented cases, the previously dead person correctly recalls what was said and done, even while their brain had ceased activity and they were documented as clinically dead.

If the physical brain is a machine that generates consciousness, these real documented cases would be impossible. Specifically, if the machine-brain theory is true, the conscious-mind must remain in the head, and stop functioning when the brain stops functioning.

To accomplish what has actually occurred, the conscious-mind must exit the head, hover up above the body, and watch what is taking place from outside of the brain. For the conscious-mind to exit the brain and continue to function, the mind's existence and operation must be independent of the physical brain. Thus, the conscious-mind can't be produced by the brain's electro-chemical activities.

The cardiologist, Pim van Lommel designed an extensive research project to investigate this phenomenon under the controlled environment of a cluster of hospitals with a medically trained staff. Over the course of more than 20 years, van Lommel and his fellow researchers systematically studied such near-death experiences in a wide variety of patients who survived a cardiac arrest. The results were published in the renowned medical journal, *The Lancet*.

Van Lommel's book, *Consciousness Beyond Life: The Science of the Near-Death Experience*, published in 2007, provides evidence that the near-death phenomenon is an authentic experience that cannot be attributed to imagination, psychosis, or oxygen deprivation. Based on his extensive research van Lommel shows that our consciousness does not always coincide with brain functions and that consciousness can even be experienced separately from the body!

This proves the materialistic machine-brain theory false, making it a myth. By failing to fit reality, modern science requires the machine-brain theory to be discarded or revised.

According to the modern scientific method, all that is needed to prove a theory false, is to find **one** example showing that the theory fails to fit reality. Here we have 20 years of systematically documented examples. In spite of this, most scientists turn a blind eye to these facts which prove the machine-brain theory false while they continue to support the machine-brain myth.

REINCARNATION CLOSES THE CASE

Another way to prove the machine-brain theory false is by considering the meticulously well-documented cases of reincarnation catalogued by Jim Tucker, M.D. and Ian Stevenson, M.D. During 50 years of investigation, these two men compiled 2,500 validated cases of reincarnation.

The process begins by carefully interviewing a young child who claims to remember a previous life. Then, an in-depth investigation uncovers facts that corroborate the detailed memories. Tucker's book, *Return to Life: Extraordinary Cases of Children Who Remember Past Lives*, shares examples and theoretical explanations for the clear implication that the child's physical brain could not contain memories of events that took place before the child was conceived. Something other than the brain must have held those memories. Since these children aren't descendants of the people they recall being, DNA can't be involved in the memory transfer. Something apart from the physical aspects of reality must have carried those memories into a new life.

A database containing the details of over 2,000 cases has been uploaded onto the internet for researchers to examine for themselves.

This tremendous wealth of information proves, without a doubt, that consciousness exists beyond the physical experience we call life. The physical brain of a child can't possess specific details of an actual departed person's life; their residence, profession, relatives, and actual events that took place. Therefore, that deceased person's memories must have survived their death and relocated into the mind of the unrelated child who has the memories. A few cases could be brushed off as coincidental, however 2,500 cases most certainly drives the proverbial final nail into the coffin of the machine-brain theory.

Let's not forget that the machine-brain theory was a recently introduced idea. Furthermore, the machine-brain theory has never offered a plausible explanation of how the physical brain produces consciousness or holds memories.

Given all of this information, one may wonder why consciousness is still viewed as a product of the physical brain—and matter continues to be seen as the foundation of reality.

INDOCTRINATION, DENIAL, AND TIME

One reason the materialistic view of reality remains in place is because nearly all schools throughout the world teach a curriculum that presumes a matter-based reality. Additionally, science-fiction stories and pseudoscientific documentaries present the machine-brain myth along with countless other matter-based theories, as if they're proven facts. The phrase "scientific proof" is used quite often, even though science can only prove that a theory is false. Positive proof that an idea is true is not scientifically achievable. This limitation of the scientific method was explained in Chapter 1.

Thus, the indoctrination achieved by schooling, science-fiction, documentaries, periodicals, and the magnificent illusion of a material reality that appears unquestionably solid, all help to keep the antiquated idea that matter is the foundation of reality alive and restrains people from adopting a new perspective.

"The greatest obstacle to discovery is not ignorance—

it is the illusion of knowledge."

—Daniel J. Boorstin (1914–2004) historian

In addition to indoctrination, denial is a powerful primal method used by people to hold their position on issues that have been clearly disproven. So, even though materialistic myths have been formally debunked—by actual events and the rational scientific conclusions that those events infer—most scientists remain in denial of these advancements. Without doubt, people prefer to remain on course with what they have come to believe rather than turn their perspective of reality upside-down, or in this case, right-side-up.

Rupert Sheldrake has identified ten materialistic core beliefs that most scientists take for granted. Here's his list:

1. Everything is essentially mechanical. Dogs, for example, are complex mechanisms, rather than living organisms with goals of their own. Even people are machines; 'lumbering robots,' is Richard Dawkins's vivid phrase, with brains that are like genetically programmed computers.
2. All matter is unconscious. It has no inner life or subjectivity or point of view. Even human consciousness is an illusion produced by the material activities of brains.
3. The total amount of matter and energy is always the same (with the exception of the Big Bang, when all the matter and energy of the universe suddenly appeared).
4. The laws of nature are fixed. They are the same today as they were at the beginning, and they will stay the same forever.
5. Nature is purposeless, and evolution has no goal or direction.
6. All biological inheritance is material, carried in the genetic material, DNA, and in other material structures.
7. Minds are inside heads and are nothing but the activities of brains. When you look at a tree, the image of the tree you are seeing is not 'out there,' where it seems to be, but inside your brain.
8. Memories are stored as material traces in brains and are wiped out at death.
9. Unexplained phenomena like telepathy are illusory.

10. Mechanistic medicine is the only kind that really works.

In Sheldrake's books, *The Science Delusion: Freeing the Spirit of Enquiry*, and a U.S. edition, *Science Set Free: 10 Paths to New Discovery*, he shows how all these core beliefs or dogmas falter under well-thought-out scientific scrutiny. Still, Sheldrake is pro-science:

> *"I want the sciences to be less dogmatic and more scientific. I believe that the sciences will be regenerated when they are liberated from the dogmas that constrict them."*

The published discoveries offered earlier support Sheldrake's position. In particular, consciousness functions outside of the brain proving that matter isn't the foundation of reality. Still, the myths or dogmatic beliefs prevail, leaving reality upside-down for most.

To see why science is stuck in the physical, it's important to step back and notice that we're at the beginning of a new chapter in the development of humanity's catalogue of knowledge. Although popular theories have been debunked, and several popular dogmatic beliefs have been proven false, it will take considerable time for a new set of theories and beliefs to be accepted by the scientific community. To begin with, a convincing alternative must be provided to take the place of the antiquated theories that have become dogmatic beliefs.

So far, none of the new models have become widely accepted. When a new model of reality grabs the interest of a large enough number of scientists, then the current perspective will shift.

> *You never change things by fighting the existing reality. To change something, build a new model that makes the existing model obsolete.*
>
> —Buckminster Fuller (1895–1983) inventor, designer, and author

In the meantime, there's agreement that the scientific method works well. While matter may not be the foundation of reality, many material-based theories also work quite well. The countless successes of the modern materialistic model support this with exceptional confidence. So, even when a consciousness-based model takes hold and our beliefs regarding the foundation of reality change, physical reality will continue to operate as it always has. Engineers and scientists will continue working with physical matter without any significant changes. On the other hand, what will undergo tremendous change is our understanding of consciousness which will reach beyond the brain and quite likely extend throughout the entire universe.

PSYCHOLOGY

The branch of science most closely associated with consciousness—psychology—was dragged into the materialistic view of reality. To align with the rest of the scientific community, which had adopted the myth of materialism, psychologists were pressured to formally reject the idea of the Soul around 1930. This change took place even though psychology originally meant, "study of the soul."

This transformation progressed in stages. To begin with, in 1910, the Greek term *psych* was altered from the original Greek definition, "soul, breath, and life," to instead mean "mind." Incremental changes of this sort enabled psychologists to gradually move away from the Soul, and align their beliefs with the materialistic view of reality that modern science had adopted.

Despite that, a highly respected Austrian psychoanalyst, Professor Otto Rank, published a classic book entitled, *Psychology and the Soul: A Study of the Origin, Conceptual Evolution, and Nature of the Soul.* This book appeared in 1930, right at the moment when the Soul had been completely discarded from psychology.

This book was translated into English for a second time in 1998. The first English translation appeared in 1950. The title and timing of this book begs the question: If the Soul is no longer part of psychology, then why was this book recently translated into English again?

On the back-cover jacket, Esther Menaker explains that the book, "...is important for our time of transition from a materialistic determinism to a more spiritual view of reality..." Certainly there are some people involved in psychology that believe in the idea of a divine consciousness that resides in the human heart—the Soul.

Professor Rank explains how the Soul is beyond science:

"Contemporary psychology may be a science, but its basis, the soul, can-not be explained by science. The psyche is neither brain functions, as modern neurology believes, nor sublimated biological drives, as Freud conceived it." [12]

In spite of Rank, materialistic psychology marched on.

THE BIRTH OF NIHILISM, DEPRESSION, AND MATERIALISM

When scientists mistakenly placed physical matter at the foundation of reality, they caused a new belief system to arise.

Unfortunately, the resulting materialism can include a detachment from emotional values that can eventually lead to depression.

After accepting this fundamental flip of reality, some people developed the idea that life is meaningless, and named their philosophy "nihilism." This idea developed during the 1800s when it grew out of the rational materialism that had become prominent when matter was placed at the foundation of reality. Coincidentally, this was happening at the same time that the field of psychology was discarding the Soul.

The nihilistic perspective that arises when reality is thought to be a soulless machine, eventually comes to see people as soulless robots and finally life becomes meaningless.

A meaningless life is considered to be one of the most common causes of depression. Billions of people worldwide are fighting depression, and many are losing the battle. The World Health Organization estimates that approximately one million people commit suicide each year. That's one suicide every forty seconds.

Another problem that snowballed when physical matter and energy became glorified as the foundation of reality, was that a larger portion of humanity began striving for material wealth more excessively than ever before. Unfortunately, the perpetual struggle for material wealth fails to improve the emotional happiness of the people who embrace materialism.

Over 2,300 years ago, the disconnection between happiness and material wealth was already known:

"Happiness is a quality of the Soul, not a function of one's material circumstances."

—Aristotle (384 BC–322 BC) philosopher and scientist

These words of wisdom suggest that a resurgence of consciousness—and the Soul that is the essence of human consciousness—could be just what we need to pull humanity out of the tailspin of depression that has reached pandemic proportions.

THE RESURRECTION OF CONSCIOUSNESS AND PURPOSE

In the following chapters, I'll share a consciousness-based cosmology that's in alignment with the up-and-coming consciousness movement. I even offer an explanation of how consciousness forms the illusion of matter. More importantly, this particular cosmology

24

shows how the Soul is of pivotal importance for all of humanity. Even above all of that, the cosmology begins by explaining the purpose of the universe, and humanity's critical role in achieving that purpose.

With purpose and Soul in hand, nihilism is vanquished. Shifting one's perspective to a reality founded on consciousness sets the stage for rekindling and deepening one's relationship with their Soul.

By knowing that my Superconscious-Soul resides in my heart, I've been better able to nurture the most intimate of all relationships. The interplay between my conscious-mind (in my head) and my Superconscious-Soul (in my heart), has become the most important relationship in my life. This relationship provides a fountain of happiness, joy, and intuitive guidance. Additionally, serendipitous synchronicities, orchestrated by my Soul, fill my life with countless reasons to be grateful for the miraculous life I am so blessed to live.

AN INTIMATE RELATIONSHIP WITH THE SOUL

Cultivating the intimate spiritual relationship between my conscious-mind (in my head) and the Superconscious-Soul (in my heart) has been the most powerful practice of my life. This divine guardian, my Soul, has filled me with the blessings of wisdom, love, honor, respect, kindness, sincerity, joy, miracles, and more. The three key steps to developing this supernatural relationship have been to: open my heart, follow my heart, and open myself to love. Each step has led me to surrender deeper and deeper to my magnificent Soul.

This relationship is depicted in the classic painting shown below.

Jesus Christ's right hand is positioned to signify, "the home of God," while his left hand is pointing toward his heart with all five fingers indicating that the heart is God's home. Flames rising from the top of the heart depict the transmission of divine guidance. This is consistent with the scientific research offered in Chapter 1, which concluded that the infallible voice emerges from the top of the heart as EMF radiation.

Finally, the halo indicates that Jesus is being enlightened by guidance from the God in his heart.

On the right side of that same image, Mary is shown to have a similar relationship with her heart, indicating that this divine connection is available to people who are not purported to be a god or goddess. In this instance, there's a sword in Mary's heart signifying that her heart aches having lost her son. Despite that, her halo asserts that she has remained receptive to the divine guidance from her heart.

Similarly, in the image on the left, the Hindu demi-god Hanuman is depicted opening his chest. There, where a heart would be found, are the images of Rama and Sita. Hanuman is the faithful servant of Rama, who exemplifies the ideal man. Sita is considered to be the ideal woman. Thus, this image indicates that opening the heart and following the divine guidance that emerges from within, leads the follower to being the most ideal human they can be.

My Soul has guided me to notice how these images provide encouragement for each of us to remain attentive to the intuitive guidance of the Superconscious-Soul residing within. In Christianity, this divine consciousness is labeled the Holy Spirit. In Hinduism, it has been named the Atman.

I've discovered that following my heart is the most important practice in my life. Accordingly, this book has two primary purposes:

- ♥ To help you discover this relationship, if you haven't already;
- ♥ To provide tools and encouragement for you to deepen this vital relationship.

Everyone is blessed with a Superconscious-Soul that is their personal divine guardian, an inner god devoted to unfolding the grand plan of the One-Who-Is-All. Consciously developing a relationship with one's Soul and fostering love for this magnificent part of oneself is the simple answer to what many people are seeking.

In the following pages, you'll find tools, techniques, encouragement, and examples from my personal journey that you may find helpful on your unique adventure.

26

Chapter 3
How I Discovered the Soul in My Heart

"There is something sacred that is more powerful than anything else on Earth—The Holy Grail is the Soul."

—Suzanne Ward (born 1933) author

THE BLACK WIDOW SPIDER

In 1964, when I was just 4-years-old, my life was profoundly affected by a terrifying encounter with a black widow spider.

Myself, my brother Grant (age seven), and our friend Steven (age eight) were exploring an empty lot in our Detroit neighborhood, when we discovered a black widow spider under some debris. The red hourglass on her abdomen made it easy for us to identify her.

We captured the spider in a jar and took it to Steven's house, where we placed her in a wooden box with a screen door. Once she was safely inside the box, my brother and I went home for dinner.

The next day, Grant and I were eager to go to Steven's house and check on the black widow spider. The three of us looked through the screen door, but no one could find her. We opened the door, yet there was no spider to be found. My brother and Steven came to the conclusion that she had escaped through a narrow crack located along the bottom edge of the box.

This crack was half the width of the black widow's shiny abdomen, which I intuitively knew to be hard and therefore not able to squeeze through such a narrow opening.

Wooden Box

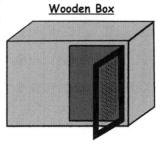

An illustration of the box is shown on the right. As you can see, the left portion of the interior can't be seen through the door, so the spider could have been located in that hidden area.

I explained to the older kids that the crack was too small for the spider to escape. Therefore, it must be hiding in the corner that we couldn't see from outside of the box. They disagreed, and reiterated their belief that the spider had escaped through the narrow crack.

I further noticed that the doorway was big enough for a person's head to fit through it, so I suggested that one of them put their head inside the box to view the hidden area and find the black widow.

They countered that I ought to put my head in the box.

Since they didn't believe the spider was in the box, I argued that they should be willing to put one of their heads in to check.

One of them convinced me that I needed to put my head in the box to prove to them that I was right.

Being only 4-years-old, I was quite naïve. Plus, I wasn't aware of how truly dangerous a black widow could be. Most importantly, my ego wanted to convince the older kids that I was right. I foolishly accepted the challenge and picked up the box, raising it above my head with the front of it facing down. In this position, gravity swung the door open, and I lowered the box over my head.

Once inside, I couldn't see much at all. My eyes needed time to adjust to the darkness. As they adjusted, the spider came into focus and appeared directly in front of my nose.

A bolt of terror shot through my body. I reacted quickly, throwing the box up and away as I let out a loud scream. A deep primal fear of this lethal spider shook me to my core. I recall crying and twitching uncontrollably for some time. This experience exposed me to the most extreme feelings of terror that I've ever encountered. Luckily, I wasn't bitten by the deadly black widow.

The power of this event affected me in multiple ways.

THE UNEXPECTED SILVER LININGS

Looking back on my life, I believe this incident had at least two unexpectedly positive effects on me:

I knew intuitively that the black widow spider was in the box. I was also aware that it was dangerous to place my head in the box. Even so, my ego viewed the situation quite differently.

My big brother and our older friend Steven believed the spider had escaped through a tiny crack, however my infallible intuition informed me otherwise. With this knowledge, and the other kids' encouragement to put my head in the box, my ego saw an opportunity to obtain respect from the older kids.

To do so, I needed to act in defiance of the intuitive knowledge that a dangerous spider was in the box. The opportunity to gain prestige was so important to my ego that I chose to risk a venomous bite.

As a result, I was sternly punished for my ego's defiance of my Soul's wisdom in an attempt to gain prestige. This scorching incident branded me with two beneficial lessons:

- ♥ Honor the inner voice of wisdom.
- ♥ Restrain your ego's yearning for recognition.

With this terrifying incident locked in my emotional memory, I became unconsciously afraid to venture far from my Soul's guidance. Throughout my life, whenever I veer away from my intuitive guidance, self-inflicted reminders steer me back to center, reinforcing the original lesson involving the black widow.

I don't recall making a conscious choice to follow my intuition; it seems I was maneuvered into following it. Without any intention on my part, the black widow incident seemed to train me to make choices that honored my intuition. Eventually, I discovered the infallibility of intuition and chose to follow my inner guidance consciously.

One might imagine that this may have restricted my life causing it to be uneventful. On the contrary, I've found the intuitive path of following my heart to be filled with marvelous blessings, making my life extraordinarily delightful in unexpected ways.

FOLLOWING MY HEART

When I was in school I didn't know I was using intuition. In fact, I remember believing that I didn't have intuition. By confusing intuition with premonition, I thought intuition was knowledge of the future. Despite that misunderstanding, I unwittingly used intuition to remain on the Dean's List throughout most of my school years.

A memorable example of using my intuition took place when I was a senior in high school. My American History teacher gave our class a standardized test with numerous questions. The teacher explained that this test wouldn't affect our grade. Instead the results would be used by the U.S. Department of Education to compare the quality of American History education amongst high schools across the nation.

The teacher further explained that the test was timed, and that anyone who finished early could bring their completed test up to his desk and leave the classroom.

The test included a booklet and a multiple-choice answer sheet with ovals to be filled in with a pencil. I opened the booklet and found the first two pages filled with text to be read. I turned the page and found more written material, followed by multiple-choice questions. I quickly flipped through the booklet, to discover lots of written material. With my slow reading pace, I estimated that I wouldn't have time to complete all the reading, let alone answer the questions.

Given this situation, I thought to myself, "What should I do?"

The answer that arose from within was: "Skip the reading and simply answer the questions."

Since this test wasn't going to affect my grade, that idea seemed reasonable. With that strategy, I'd be able to complete the test.

I read each question and the associated multiple-choice answers, then quickly picked the best answer without giving it a second thought. With my notoriously slow reading, it still took me about thirty minutes to complete the test. When I was done, I got up, placed my test on the teacher's desk and left.

A couple of weeks later, while entering that class, the teacher stopped me and asked, "How did you cheat on that test?"

"What test?" I inquired.

"That big standardized test you took a couple of weeks ago. You were the first one done. You left the class twenty minutes early and you got a perfect score! How did you do that?"

"I guessed," was my simple reply.

Guessing may have been what I thought I was doing at that time, despite that I've discovered that I was following my Soul's intuitive guidance.

Beyond that specific example, I was using a similar method on all my tests. I skipped the reading assignments and homework unless the assignment was graded. Back in the 1970s and early 80s, where I went to school, homework was provided for the student to practice. Without really thinking about it, I simply avoided doing what wasn't specifically required. Although some teachers applied pressure encouraging me to do the homework, they weren't forceful enough to change the pattern that I had developed.

Even though I wasn't doing the recommended studying, my Soul was guiding me to receive outstanding grades. I continued using the same strategy throughout college, where I received awards and more high grades. Finally, I completed my formal education with a Master's of science in mechanical engineering at MIT. There, I obtained a research assistantship that took care of tuition and provided a stipend that was enough to cover all of my living expenses.

During all of this I behaved childlike, partying nearly every night and avoiding the process of growing up. Even now, at fifty-nine, I still feel young at heart. Some appreciate that, while others wonder if I'll ever grow up. The reason I'm sharing this is to provide an example that shows how attentively following my intuition made my life so easy that I was able to be successful without needing to grow up and become overly serious.

On one occasion, I disagreed with an MIT professor who was the author of the textbook and a leading expert in the subject of the class. In my usual childlike way, I didn't take these important considerations into account. In spite of this man's reputation, my pugnacious nature popped out, and I foolishly claimed he was wrong during class. After a little back-and-forth, the professor tabled the argument to be discussed after class.

Once class concluded, we walked to his office together. He led me to his chalkboard, where I drew diagrams of two examples that would expose the point of contention. He advised me to redo the exercise using one of my examples, claiming that I would discover for myself that he was correct. Although I was compelled to share what appeared intuitively true to me, I didn't feel the need to prove it. I suppose my habit of avoiding homework also pressed me to let it go.

The following day, this respected professor spent the first half-hour of class solving one of the examples I drew in his office. Unexpectedly, he proved himself wrong to the entire class and announced, "George was right." I was shocked and very impressed with this man's integrity. He had obviously done the work. Then, in spite of the results, his dedication to truth pushed him to share his findings.

Later, I wondered, how could I, a young student of this recognized authority, best him in his field of expertise? Especially in this advanced class, where the level of math was reaching my outer limits.

Eventually I discovered—it wasn't me, or more precisely, it wasn't my conscious-mind in my head. The divine Soul in my heart intuitively advised me. And when it did, I reacted from the traumatic black widow encounter, speaking out in defiance of this man's well-established authority.

In hindsight, this incidence and others that revealed to me how accurate intuition is, prepared me to write this book. The black widow spider encounter caused me to listen to and follow my Soul's intuitive guidance more than most people.

My childlike antics and lazy approach to school seemed rebellious and fun when I was in school. In spite of that, afterward, I could hardly read. By avoiding the reading assignments and studying in general, I was still reading at a sixth-grade level at 25-years-old! I actually had a reading expert test me. She couldn't believe I had obtained a Master's degree, especially one from MIT.

After the reading test revealed how poor my reading skills were, I reviewed my reading history and could only remember reading eight books from cover to cover! The expert told me that I simply needed practice. Now, after reading many books, I'm a much better reader, though I'm still slower than most.

The positive view of my poor reading skills is how I've come to know for certain that my intuition provides an infallible source of knowledge that I can depend on.

In support of this, Albert Einstein once said:

"The intuitive mind is a sacred gift and the rational mind is a faithful servant. We have created a society that honors the servant and has forgotten the gift."

Given the praise I've found for intuition, plus my personal experiences, I've come to believe that the black widow spider incident enriched my life. That encounter helped me remain a faithful servant to the sacred gift of intuition. As a result, I exceled in school even while limping along with a sixth-grade reading ability.

Beyond school, my Soul helped me excel in many other ways. Throughout my life I've discovered how to achieve outstanding results with little or no practice. Even though it doesn't work for everything, there have been many situations when I've surprised myself by doing things that I didn't know I could do. An observer would suspect that I had trained for years to have such masterful skills. The age-old idea of putting your heart into it, to achieve the best results, has enhanced my life in countless ways.

Despite my shyness, poor reading skills, and a childlike approach to life, by unwittingly living in alignment with my Soul's guidance, my life has been filled with an abundance of blessings and serendipitous synchronicities.

Eventually, I noticed that most people don't employ their intuition with the regularity that the black widow spider and my brother helped me to. Thus, Einstein's claim that our society has mostly forgotten the gift of intuition appears to be true. I hope this book helps to reverse that trend.

INTUITION IS FROM THE HEART

Once I became aware of how unusual my life was, I began to investigate the source of intuition by pondering the question, "Where do all of these answers come from?"

The intuitive answer that arose was: "Your heart."

At the time, that didn't make sense to me. Having been taught that my heart was a pump, not a source of knowledge, I was perplexed.

Then, after going through a roller-coaster romantic relationship, I became aware of an interesting phenomenon. While I was deeply in love, everything appeared to be wonderful. Even things that normally upset me seemed just fine. Yet, when I was heartbroken, life seemed loathsome.

In 2001, I decided to see if I could discover why this change in perception took place. To do so, I ventured out into nature and away from people. Once secluded, I asked: "Why is it that when I'm in love the world is wonderful, yet when I'm brokenhearted, it's awful? And what does my heart have to do with this phenomenon?" Then, I laid down on my back, closed my eyes, and relaxed very deeply.

Soon, the following answer was presented to me:

The heart is the balance point.

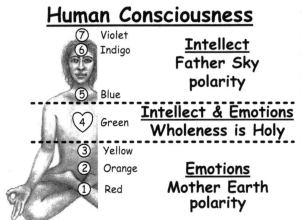

Human Consciousness

⑦ Violet
⑥ Indigo
⑤ Blue
④ Green
③ Yellow
② Orange
① Red

Intellect
Father Sky
polarity

Intellect & Emotions
Wholeness is Holy

Emotions
Mother Earth
polarity

Skyward from the heart is the intellectual, masculine ego-polarity that culminates in Father Sky. The upper three chakras (foci of essence) are blue, indigo, and violet—colors of the Sky. This part of human consciousness is commonly referred to as the conscious-mind.

Earthward from the heart is the emotional, feminine memory-polarity that culminates in Mother Earth. The lower three chakras are red, orange, and yellow—colors of the Earth. This portion of human consciousness has been named the subconscious-mind.

In the center, the heart chakra is green, the color of plants. Plants send their roots into the Mother Earth while their branches reach up into the Father Sky. The beneficent plants draw the opposite polarities together to form all that is needed for life on Earth. In a similar way, the Soul in the heart combines the intellect from above and the emotions from below to form a divine genius that's whole, or Holy. The wholeness of this portion of consciousness enables it to access the wisdom of the universe—the One-Who-Is-All.

Moreover, when a person is in love, their heart opens and their Soul shares its Holy perspective with their conscious- and subconscious-minds. With this divine perspective, one comes to know that everything is perfect. From this balanced and Holy state-of-mind, all of life becomes beautiful. Everything seems to move in perfect time with the rhythm of the One. As long as the open-hearted person follows their Soul's divine guidance, life flows with less effort.

Alternatively, when one falls out of love, their heart closes, and the divine holistic perspective is lost, leaving the person to view reality from the polarity they're accustomed to.

From the upper, intellectual, masculine view of reality, one questions their Soul's guidance and may choose to follow their intellect. Life loses its beauty and luster as the masculine polarity becomes confused and frustrated by the emotional feminine aspects of reality—aspects that confound the intellect. Due to the distortion that develops from a strictly intellectual perspective, this one-sided half-perspective fails to see the perfection that actually exists.

Alternatively, from the emotional feminine perspective, a person becomes biased and confused in a similar but opposite way. From the feeling end of the spectrum, one becomes agitated by the cold, logical aspects of reality that lack emotional depth. This half-perspective fails to see the perfection of reality due to the distortion that develops from a strictly emotional vantage point.

When experiencing life from either the masculine or feminine polarity, one falls out of step with nearly half of reality—the portion that's aligned with the opposing polarity. Either polarity causes the individual to step out of time with the rhythm of divine wholeness, and leaves one in a state of feeble confusion.

Only from the holistic central perspective of the Soul can a person understand and embrace the entire spectrum of reality, in a balanced way, that reveals the perfection that always exists.

When in love, the heart opens to reveal eternal perfection. When brokenhearted, the heart closes hiding that same perfection. Thus, it's always best to live with one's heart open.

The last message that came through during this "vision quest" was that the Soul shares its infallible genius more clearly with open-hearted people by providing infallible answers to the questions they contemplate via intuition.

Needless to say, I was very surprised to receive an explanation that included a three-part arrangement of human consciousness: an unusual model that was clearly incompatible with what I had learned in school.

This took place in 2001, when I was 41-years-old. At the time, through many years of schooling and lots of real-life experiences, I had found my intuition to be impeccably accurate. I also recalled how the idea that intuition comes from the Soul in one's heart fit the age-old adages; "open your heart," "listen to your heart," and "follow your heart."

So, regardless of how unconventional this concept appeared to my scientifically-trained mind, I began sharing the idea that inner guidance may come from a consciousness located in the human heart.

A NEW VIEW OF REALITY GRADUALLY EMERGED

After discussing this with a dear friend, she lent me two books that supported the idea of a Soul in the heart. The heart transplant information and the Stanford research that identified an infallible voice in the heart presented in Chapter 1, came from those two books.

Encouraged by the support and confirmation I found in those books, I continued to use my intuition to explore this phenomenon and how it related to my experience of life. This adventure into consciousness became my personal hobby. Along the way, I discovered tools that deepened my connection with my Soul.

One very simple example is how pondering a question in the conscious-mind provokes an intuitive answer. Often, the answer arrives instantly, however in some cases, the answer comes later, often the next morning, or when the conscious-mind is quiet.

It was in using this method of inner inquiry, in addition to more elaborate methods, that I was able to uncover an alternative perspective of reality: one based on consciousness. Over several years, via vision quests, personal encounters with people, books, transcendental experiences, and countless intuitive messages from my Soul, I've found the scattered pieces of a fascinating jigsaw puzzle. In some cases, the pieces were literally placed in my hands, like the books with the research reports my friend had loaned me. Gradually, my intuition guided me to assemble these puzzle pieces, bringing into focus an alternative view of reality; a reality that contains far-reaching implications for each of us.

It seems the source of innovative ideas always has been the Superconscious-Soul, via intuition.

"Intuition is the source of scientific knowledge."
—Aristotle (384 BC–322 BC) philosopher and scientist

The most celebrated architect of the twentieth century agrees:

"The heart is the chief feature of a functioning mind."
—Frank Lloyd Wright (1867–1959) architect

The three quotes from Einstein presented earlier further support the claim that intuition from the heart is the ultimate source of scientific discoveries and technological innovation.

My career as an inventor began when I was a child. Countless experiences revealed to me how the cognition of new ideas comes from the Superconscious-Soul. In creative endeavors, I often receive new ideas in the morning when I'm waking up. It seems all creativity is influenced by a creative assistant, muse, or afflatus:

afflatus noun formal
A divine creative impulse or inspiration. [13]

BOOK LAYOUT

To share the details of what I've learned in an organized way, the rest of this book is arranged into three parts:

Part 1: A New Model of Reality

In the first of the three parts, I share a consciousness-based model of reality that resolves issues that have remained unsolved by materialistic science. By shifting to a foundation of consciousness and weaving in a demystifying cosmology, the perspective that emerges is shown to fit reality in ways that deliver a deeper understanding of humanity and our role in the grand play we call life.

Part 2: Future Predictions

In the middle part of this book, I show how an unexpectedly simple plan can resolve the growing chaos taking place today. Miraculously, this plan offers a truly beneficial and compassionate way to take care of everyone. This future resolution is based on the *Consciousness-Origin Cosmology* that is woven into the book's narrative.

Part 3: Tools and Techniques

Finally, in the last part of this book, I offer tools and techniques, including the *Heart-Opening Breath*, Soul-Healing, *Liberating Your Genius*, Soul Love, and more. Each technique is presented in detail so you can use it in your life. These tools, and the tips that accompany them, can help you to enrich your life in remarkable ways.

At 59-years-old I don't have any physical pains or psychological issues that I'm aware of. Just two years ago, I couldn't say that. By using the Soul-Healing technique I finally resolved some physical and psychological issues that had persisted for over thirty years.

My personal happiness has increased to a healthy level and stabilized. I'm more content than ever before and more easily satisfied. I often laugh at myself and the quirky absurdities of life. When I do get upset I'm able to let go of the issue quickly and come back to center easily. All in all, I'm healthy, happy and have a positive outlook.

To close the book in an interesting way, in Chapter 23, I share some very intriguing support from the Hopi and Hawaiian cultures. That chapter also provides a glimpse into the intuitively driven investigative adventure that led me to uncovered evermore compelling support for what is shared throughout this book.

To begin **Part 1,** the next chapter presents a fundamental model that consciousness uses as a building block to fabricate the Grand Illusion. It's a simple but crucial upgrade to duality that my Soul guided me to name Triality.

Part 1: A New Model of Reality

Chapter 4
Triality: The Illusionist's Magic Wand

In this chapter, I'll begin with the well-known concept of duality, then by adding a third component, *Triality* will emerge.

Duality is the quality of being dual, a term that comes from "duo," which simply means "two." Today, the term "duality" is commonly used to imply a high degree of difference between two things, often a pair of opposites. Some people tend to think in terms of dualistic opposites, like black versus white. In mathematics, computer science, geometry and philosophy, binary duality has specific utility.

Dualistic Spectrum

In spite of that, in world of nature, shades of gray capture the gradual transition that spans between the two polar opposites. An example that spans from past to future is illustrated on the right.

Past and future can be thought of as a duality; however, we all know that a range exists between the recent past and the distant past. This also holds true for the near future and the distant future. Shades of gray s-t-r-e-t-c-h from past to future, forming a spectrum, or range of time.

Gradual Transition of Time

Future

Past

THE QUINTESSENTIAL CORE

In 1989, my Soul revealed to me a mostly unnoticed, yet supremely important feature, which can be found in the heart of all dualistic spectrums. This central component is shown in the diagram on the right. In this example, using time, the present moment is located in the middle. I was guided to name this third component the *Quintessential Core* to emphasize its importance.

Time Plus Quintessential Core

Future

Present Moment

Past

We may have great memories of the past, and exciting hopes for the future, still we all know that the marvel of life occurs in the present moment. By adding the extraordinarily vital present moment to the clearly incomplete dualistic spectrum, a realistic model of time is produced. It's interesting to notice that the most important ingredient of time was completely ignored by the oversimplified dualistic model.

Triality

Masculine

Quintessential Core

Feminine

TRIALITY

My Soul advised me to name this more complete model of reality *Triality*. A generic Triality is depicted on the left. It contains two opposite polarities labeled "Masculine" and "Feminine." These opposites are joined by a spectrum with the all-important Quintessential Core in the center.

Now that this Triality model has been introduced, I'm going to use the time example to show how the Quintessential Core, in this case the present moment, forms the Triality of time then fades into the background, leaving behind what appears to be a dualistic spectrum. The process is broken into five steps that are depicted in the following diagram.

1. First, the present moment is the original wholeness, or Quintessential Core.

2. Then, the Core forms two opposite polarities by bisecting its own nature into opposites that begin to extend outward and away from one another. This birthing of two from one is depicted using the ancient Mandorla symbol.

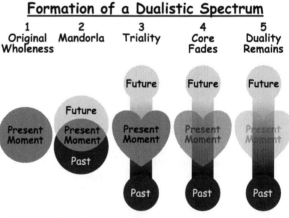

Formation of a Dualistic Spectrum

| 1 Original Wholeness | 2 Mandorla | 3 Triality | 4 Core Fades | 5 Duality Remains |

3. Next, the Triality is complete: The Quintessential Core, the spectrum, and the two opposite endpoints are all clearly defined.

4. Mysteriously, the Quintessential Core begins to disappear.

5. Finally, a dualistic spectrum, a gradient between polar opposites, is what remains obvious to the casual observer. The barely noticeable present moment indicates how the present moment nearly disappears to people who focus mostly on the past and future.

As you'll see in the examples that follow, Quintessential Cores have an elusive quality that causes them to be mostly unnoticed by people who are more focused on the extreme opposite polarities, thereby ignoring the magnificent wholeness that resides in the center. Beyond that, it seems that the extreme opposite polarities have an alluring quality that draws people's attention away from the more important central component. Nonetheless, with careful examination, the elusive Quintessential Core can be discovered and appreciated for its exceptional qualities.

Once the necessary groundwork is laid, I'll explain why Quintessential Cores are intended to be elusive. For now, I'll focus on discussing the Triality model's features, to show how the sequence of events depicted above fits reality. On top of that, I'll show how this more complete Triality model significantly enhances one's understanding of reality.

Continuing with the example using time, let's not forget that most people tend to place their attention on the past and future. Memories of the past and hopes for the future are reasonably stable. Conversely, now's ever-changing nature makes the present moment flit by in an elusive way.

This is because now can't be paused for careful examination. The present moment slips by like a wisp of air carrying a subtle though clearly noticeable fragrance—a curiously wonderful aroma that disappears as quickly as it arrives. The mental memory of the intriguing scent remains in one's mind after the currents of air have carried the fragrance away.

In a similar way, as the present moment drifts by, we capture memories of important events as they take place. Each memory is recorded when the actual event was taking place. Then, after that moment has passed, our memory retains a record. These memories of the past, like frames of a movie, can be carefully analyzed for the rest of our lives. The long-lasting nature of these memories make them seem more tangible than the present moment which remains in motion.

Additionally, the relatively stable nature of memories makes them convenient to contemplate and share with others as stories. Even so, memories aren't as powerful nor as fulfilling as the actual experience. Recalling a memory is less exhilarating and also less authentic than the actual experience that took place in the present moment that has become the past.

Step 2
Mandorla

This careful examination of how our memories of the past are formed clarifies how the past is actually produced during the present moment. This is depicted in step two of the five step Formation of a Dualistic Spectrum diagram. That step is shown again on the left.

Just as the past is shown to emerge from below the present moment, the future is similarly extending up above the present moment predicting that our hopes and dreams are also formed in the present moment.

As predicted, we conjure up our dreams and store them in our memory banks during the present moment. By storing our hopes as memories, they become unexpectedly similar to memories of the past, even though the past and future are polar opposites.

The ancient Mandorla symbol presents this important formational step in a clear yet simple way illustrating how the polarities are opposites of one wholeness that resides in the middle.

The central almond-like shape, turned on its side, is traditionally used to frame pictures of Holy personalities like the Mother Mary, Jesus, etc. An example with Jesus is shown on the left.

This central part of the Triality, the Quintessential Core contains the original wholeness, which is Holy.

My Soul guided me to see how this Mandorla symbol can be art-

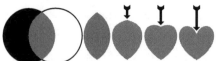

fully modified into the modern heart symbol as depicted in the progression of images shown on the left.

By pushing the top vertex of the Mandorla downward, as indicated by the arrow, that protrusion is transformed into a dimple. The resulting heart symbol contains a feminine valley at the top and a masculine protrusion at the bottom.

These dualistic features of the heart symbol retain the union of opposites concept that is lost in the older Mandorla symbol. Because the two-in-one wholeness concept is important, and because love is a key feature of this book, I chose to use the heart symbol to represent the Quintessential Core.

Continuing with the process of how the duality of time is formed, the polarities that emerge in Step 2 move further apart to become the more well-known dualistic spectrum that spans from past to future. Meanwhile, the Quintessential Core remains in the central balance point which, in this case, is the present moment. Thus, Step 3 is a complete Triality.

Then, to cause the core component to nearly disappear, a type of parlor magic, called misdirection is employed. Even though the past and future don't actually exist, these intriguing memories distract people's attention, drawing the observer's focus away from the most important present moment.

In some magic tricks, mirrors are used to distract the observer's attention. Even though the reflection in the mirror is not an actual object, it's intentionally designed to be glamorous and often shimmering so it will capture the observer's attention and provide the distraction needed to pull off the illusion.

In a similar way, the past and future are not actual experiences; they're mental pictures that pale in comparison to the fullness of life that exists right now. Despite that, our mental pictures of past and future draw our attention forming an illusion that makes time appear to be a dualistic spectrum.

Once the past and future are captured in our memory, we can think about those moments and discuss them with our family, friends, and business associates. Human beings spend a lot of time discussing these phantoms of time. Meanwhile, the present moment is ignored as it meanders along. It's as if the present moment is less important than the memories, even though now is the only time when we can effect change, make decisions, and act.

Curiously, people who are in a rush to get a project done often get distracted by looking ahead to see what is left to do, how much has been completed, and what the next steps might be. Conversely, staying focused on the current step, the one that's taking place in the present moment, will get the project finished fastest.

You may have noticed how common it is for people to fritter away the most precious present moment. Eckhart Tolle's bestselling book *The Power of Now: A Guide to Spiritual Enlightenment,* is focused on the importance of the present moment. So is Ram Dass' landmark book *Be Here Now.*

Even though this time example has been very useful in introducing the Triality concept, time is tricky to discuss. Its fluidity makes it especially slippery. Therefore, I'll present another example, a solid everyday object that's simple to relate to and easier to discuss:

a copper penny.

THE HEADS VERSUS TAILS TRIALITY

When making a copper penny, the minting process begins with a blank, a copper disk with two smooth and virtually identical sides. This blank is placed in one die that has a relief design on it. Then, a second die with a different relief design is forcibly pressed down onto the exposed side. The high pressure squeezes the blank between the two dies, embossing the copper disk with two different relief designs. This alters the smooth surfaces of the copper blank to produce a penny with a "head" and a "tail." These embossed surface designs make the coin identifiable and help to insure its authenticity.

The copper coin contains intrinsic value—the copper that it's made of is a commodity that has a known price per pound. This material and its value is the Quintessential Core of the coin: the original essence that was later stamped to form a coin with a heads-versus-tails duality. Thus, one blank was transformed into a two-sided coin.

Coin collectors focus on the specific details of the embossed surface designs, which are features of the heads-versus-tails duality. The quality of those images determines the grade of the coin. One grading system includes ratings of poor, fair, almost good, good, very good, fine, very fine, extremely fine, almost uncirculated, uncirculated, brilliant uncirculated, and gem uncirculated. Another system contains seventy different grades.

Even though the value of the copper was the reason the coin was minted in the first place, none of the grading systems consider the value of the copper in the middle. Some coin collectors have become so focused on the heads versus tails duality that one paid $82,500 for a single 1943 copper penny!

Of course, the rarity of the coin is what drives the value for serious coin collectors. Even so, the rarity is based on the date, mint mark, and the surface quality, which are all details of the heads-versus-tails duality. None of this has anything to do with the intrinsic value of the copper in the middle.

Here, we find a different way in which the dualistic polarities draw people's attention away from the Quintessential Core which has effectively disappeared, even while remaining in plain sight.

Today, American pennies are made of aluminum with a thin copper plating on the surface. The copper in the older, solid copper pennies is worth more than a penny these days. Other U.S. coins are also made of cheap metal with plated surfaces.

The older coins, which were made of copper, nickel, silver, or gold, will always maintain real value that's based on the type and amount of metal that they contain. This intrinsic value remains reasonably stable because the value of the metal is dependable. These metals are used in ways that employ their specific properties, including conductivity, toughness, hardness, ductility, etc. The reliable value of these useful properties resides in the core of the older coins.

On the other hand, the coin collectors' value, based on the surface design, is the dualistic polar opposite value. This value varies widely, and is based on collectors being interested in owning something that's rare. The rareness is based on the date, mint mark, and grade of the coin's outer surface. All of these factors are part of a facade, a mask that has no real value at all. This value is an illusion. All pennies look essentially the same. It's unrealistic for one penny to be worth one cent while another penny is worth $82,500. That's over eight million times the face value of the coin.

Coin collecting reveals how people can become so focused on the dualistic polarities that they ignore the valuable Quintessential Core, the metal in the heart of the coin that provided real value when coinage was originally introduced as a medium of exchange.

Even when the Quintessential Core has obvious value, the duality still garners more attention. For example, a solid gold coin is valuable without question. Nevertheless, on July 30, 2002, a very rare 1933 Double Eagle twenty-dollar gold coin was purchased for 7.6 million dollars! Gold was valued at $313.29/oz. in July 2002, making this purchase more than 24,000 times the value of the gold in that coin.

When casually viewing a coin, a person may only notice the two sides—the dualistic heads versus tails. Yet, a more thorough examination reveals a Quintessential Core that is the original source of the entire coin. The surface designs are formed from this metal. Most importantly, the coin's dependable value lies in its Quintessential Core.

The fact that new coins are made of cheap metal with a thin plating on the outer surface indicates that the truly valuable, yet little noticed Quintessential Core has been discarded. Somewhat like a magician's slight-of-hand, the surface facade has distracted people from the truly valuable Quintessential Core—the metal in the heart of the coin. In this coin example, the duality is composed of two simple pictures, nonetheless some people seem to be captivated by them.

It's quite common for the central cores of Trialities to be ignored—causing reality to appear dualistic to most.

To further expose this phenomenon, I'll investigate a real-life dualistic spectrum, then identify the Quintessential Core hidden in the middle. Once the central core is revealed, you'll easily see that this dualistic spectrum is actually a Triality. More importantly, you'll notice how simply looking for the Quintessential Core uncovers it, exposing reality to be inherently balanced and whole, in spite of the divided illusion of duality that most people focus on.

ELEVATION

One of the primary dualistic spectrums of our precious home, the Earth, is elevation. The extreme upper polarity of the Earth's surface elevation is the top of the tallest mountain, Mount Everest. The lowest extreme polarity of elevation lies down at the bottom of the Pacific Ocean, in the Mariana Trench.

The deep trenches of the ocean and the towering mountaintops beckon to us in a powerfully seductive way. These opposites draw our attention so strongly that they've obtained truly famous recognition. So much so that most people are familiar with their names.

These extreme dualistic endpoints of the Triality of elevation are so inhospitable that most forms of life would quickly die in the environments that exist at these polar extremes. The only living organisms found to live in these extreme locations are quite fittingly named extremophiles—highly specialized organisms, usually microbes, that have been found to thrive in physically or geochemically extreme conditions. The extreme cold and lack of oxygen at the top of Mount Everest makes it unable to support most forms of life. Similarly, down in the Mariana Trench, at the bottom of the ocean, only extremophiles have been discovered.

The Quintessential Core that gave birth to these polarities is the middle elevation of sea level. As some portions of the Earth's surface rose and other portions fell, deep depressions and vaulted mountains developed over time. Volcanic activity, earthquakes, tectonic plate movement, meteorite collisions, and other activities fashioned the polarities out of what was originally a smoother surface.

The coastal regions found in the Quintessential Core of elevation are host to a remarkably diverse variety of life forms. Additionally, the undulating dynamic dance of water, land, and air produce a lively and complex reality that's especially enjoyable to play in. The playful surf and sandy beaches make this middle region of elevation much more wonderful than either of the extreme polarities, which are both terribly inhospitable.

The characteristics of both polarities—water on one hand and land on the other—are both present along the coastline. This wholeness contains a primal enlivening power that's missing in the extreme endpoints.

The flourishing abundance of life that's found in coastal regions is indicative of what I've been guided to name, the *Supreme Power of Wholeness*, a power that emerges from the balanced wholeness contained in all Quintessential Cores. The Supreme Power of Wholeness is meant to identify the way a thing that contains all its important parts has a power that exceeds the simple sum of the parts. In this example, the coastline combines water, earth, and air to produce a spectacular environment—one that summons our childlike wonder from deep in our hearts.

Even with this supreme power, the glorious aspects of the coastal regions are somehow overshadowed by the elevated mountain peaks and deep ocean trenches. In a mysterious way, these extreme polarities draw our attention and garner the dualistic opposites more notoriety than a fair evaluation would assign them.

This discrepancy of value becomes apparent when most Trialities are carefully analyzed. The wholeness of the Quintessential Core is consistently superior, yet the extreme opposites tend to draw more attention. This feature of the Triality model exposes a deeper understanding of reality.

Once one is aware of the magnificence of the more easily accessible middle, the common tendency to reach for the stars to discover glorious experiences can be replaced with the greater wisdom of opening one's heart to recognize the precious nature of the present moment, the coastline, and all Quintessential Cores that are balanced, whole, and easier to access than the extreme polarities.

Accordingly, the Triality model will be used to uncover important Quintessential Cores that are often overshadowed by the extreme polarities that require deliberate effort to reach. Gratefully, the more accessible cores offer more happiness and satisfaction.

Moreover, I'll show how the holy consciousness in our hearts provides the feelings of happiness and joy when someone appreciates simple things like the present moment. Conversely, what follows will also show how the people who reach toward extremes fail to obtain the happiness that they hope to find out at the dualistic polarities that are disappointing despite their seductive alluring appearance.

As you're probably realizing, Triality offers you a more realistic way to view reality. It's a game-changer that includes the mysteriously powerful, yet elusive, Quintessential Core.

Now that you're aware of Quintessential Cores, your life may begin to change. The Supreme Power of Wholeness hidden in the middle of each and every duality will begin working its way into unexpected aspects of your life causing you to perceive reality differently.

With an awareness of the elusive central core, happiness will be more accessible than you ever imagined possible. You'll be able to let go of the belief that you need to reach for extremes now that you have discovered that the most magnificent aspects of reality reside close at hand, in the Quintessential Core.

Tools, like the Heart-Opening Breath shared in **Part 3**, will provide you with ways to be more balanced and aware of the present moment so you can enhance your life with the blessings that are available within your heart.

SIMILARITY OF OPPOSITES

Ever-guided by my Soul, I was shown the illustration on the right and informed of how the opposite endpoints of a Triality circle around to find their way back to one another. This feature of Triality illustrates how the furthest extremes of the two opposite polarities are unexpectedly more similar than different.

For example, consider the copper penny discussed earlier. Both sides of the coin are stamped by dies to create embossed images, making them the same apart from the details of the image.

Dualistic polarities often develop similarities as they approach their outer limits, still they don't become identical. Even so, at their extremes, the opposites may have similarities that overshadow their differences, making them unexpectedly more similar than different.

To show how prevalent the *Similarity of Opposites* is, let's consider the duality of light versus dark. These opposites seem as if they could never be similar, especially out at their polar extremes. Even so, extremely bright light is blinding, as is total darkness. Thus, the blinding nature of extremely bright light is surprisingly equivalent to that of extreme darkness, in either case nothing can be seen.

Between these extreme opposites, a middle level of light enables a person to see quite well. Since light is a key ingredient for seeing, extremely bright light and absolute darkness are equally ineffective. Conversely, the middle level of light is a powerful ally that best supports one's ability to see with exceptional clarity. This makes the Quintessential Core in the middle unquestionably superior and unexpectedly quite different from both of the extreme opposites.

BENEFICENCE OF THE QUINTESSENTIAL CORE

The Quintessential Cores presented so far were shown to possess beneficial properties that outperform their associated polarities in practical and dependable ways. This beneficent nature becomes most pronounced and obvious when the Quintessential Core is compared to the extreme opposite polarities. I've named this property of the Triality model the *Beneficence of the Quintessential Core.*

Happiness is a place between too little and too much.

—Finnish proverb

51

MALEFICENCE OF EXTREMES

The Buddha was well aware of the malefic nature of extremes. He developed his well-known middle path based on the suffering he found to be rooted in the way many people reach for extremes.

Additional analysis of the Triality examples offered above reveal how polar opposites tend to contain maleficent qualities. In other words, when taken to their theoretical ends, the polar opposites tend to express a destructive or maleficent nature. The example of light and dark illustrates this quite well. Very bright light and extreme darkness are both blinding. Accordingly, I've named this feature of Triality the *Maleficence of Extremes.*

The case of the copper penny illustrates both of these qualities. Today, pennies are made of aluminum with a thin copper plating. By focusing only on the extreme outer surface, and ignoring the beneficent value of the coin's Quintessential Core, the intrinsic value of United States' coins has been destroyed.

The gutting of the core value of United States' coinage by using cheap metal in their cores has left Americans with coins that are merely symbolic, and equivalent to paper fiat money. In comparison, the solid coins we had in the past possessed real value. The gold in a $20 gold coin is worth over $1,000 today. Inflation wouldn't have been so severe if our money had remained backed by gold or silver.

By focusing on the heads-versus-tails polarities, and removing the core value of precious metal, our monetary system has been compromised in accordance with the Maleficence of Extremes principle.

Meanwhile, some countries are bolstering their money with gold. For instance, the yuan, a gold-backed international currency from China, is becoming a popular alternative to U.S. dollars in international trade. Additionally, some countries are reissuing gold dinar, an Islamic gold coinage that was originally issued around 700 A.D. These solid coins that contain their Quintessential Cores are considered amongst the most stable investments.

Another example of the Maleficence of Extremes is provided in the elevation example presented earlier. In that example, the top of Mt. Everest and the Mariana Trench were shown to be malefic to life. Only extremophiles are able to live in those challenging environments. Conversely, the coastlines at sea level, in the Quintessential

Core, are teeming with a multitude of life, demonstrating the beneficence of the middle level of elevation.

As a final case in point, let's consider people who hold extreme viewpoints. These people tend to provoke conflict and routinely incite destructive activities. At the same time, moderate people, who reside in the central core that lies directly in-between the extremists, tend to be tolerant of others, even if those others have extreme viewpoints. Moderates are better able to reach out from the center to comprehend a larger variety of perspectives that extend out in many directions from their centrist perspective.

Conversely, extremists are so far out in their chosen polarity that they can't relate to those who chose the opposite polarity. So, even though the Similarity of Opposites exists, and therefore all extremists share similarities, they also maintain a bone of contention that remains unresolved as both sides fanatically maintain their position.

The standoff is not because the differences are unresolvable. Rather, the opposing sides remain divided because they're made up of people who have excessive single-minded zeal. Fanatics are found at all extreme endpoints. The fanatical nature of zealots is their similarity, however rather than drawing them together, their inflexible zeal keeps them separated.

A HIDDEN DUALITY

By considering these examples, a hidden duality has been exposed: the Maleficence of Extremes versus the Beneficence of the Quintessential Core. The clear gap that exists between these features of Triality is found to be an important property of reality. Difficulties emerge at extremes, while the balance point is where the Supreme Power of Wholeness provides happiness, and health.

> *"The greatest art is to attain balance, balance between all opposites, balance between all polarities. Imbalance is disease and balance is health. Imbalance is neurosis, and balance is well-being."*
> —Osho (1931–1990) Indian guru

When reality is viewed from a polarized dualistic perspective— the healthiest option, balance, isn't even considered.

For instance, in an official debate the two sides argue to convince the judges that their side is best. Meanwhile, the balanced alternative that incorporates the advantages of both polarities is outlawed by the rules of debate even though balance is always the best option.

In spite of that oversight, both sides must have worthy features or debates would be completely one-sided.

So, with two sides that both have worthy features, Triality offers the opportunity to merge the virtues of both sides forming a blend that's better than either single side. Thus, the wholeness of the Quintessential Core is always superior to either polarity.

A LITTLE EXTRA FOR INTELLECTUALS

Consider the integers: $-\infty$ ...-3, -2, -1, 0, $+1$, $+2$, $+3$ ... $+\infty$

In this number line, infinity symbols are used to illustrate the endless nature of the set of integers.

The definition of infinity is: "a number greater than any assignable quantity or countable number." Consequently, no matter how far one ventures out toward positive or negative infinity they won't be able to reach infinity. By definition, infinity will always be further.

In spite of this limitation that is found at the outer limits of the polar extremes, zero has the unique power to conjure up the infinite.

For instance: $1 \div 0 = +\infty$, while $-1 \div 0 = -\infty$

Thus, the Quintessential Core's supreme power is clearly demonstrated with mathematics by showing that the central zero is a magical portal to the otherwise unreachable infinity.

More importantly, in the next chapter I'll show how dropping into one's center, the zero point in the heart, is a portal that leads into the foundational realm of reality—pure consciousness.

As you can see, there are numerous features of the Triality model that are realistic, empowering, predictive, and enlightening. The Quintessential Core is an essential feature that has remained missing from the oversimplified duality model. With the core included, duality is upgraded to Triality which offers a more complete and accurate model of reality.

The next chapter offers an explanation of how consciousness uses Triality to form the Grand Illusion.

Chapter 5
The Consciousness–Origin Cosmology

"See that the imagination of nature is far, far greater
than the imagination of man."

—Richard P. Feynman (1918–1988) celebrated theoretical physicist

As you probably know, cosmologies are theories that offer an explanation of the origin and development of the universe.

A NECESSARY LEAP OF FAITH

All cosmologies begin with a leap of faith. To demonstrate why, let's consider the two possible beginnings:

> ➤ Nothing existed when the universe began.
> ➤ Something already existed at the beginning.

In the first case, if a cosmology claims that nothing existed, then we're asked to believe that the universe emerged out of nothing. This gives rise to the unanswerable question: "How could something emerge out of nothing?" Allowing that question to remain unanswered requires a leap of faith.

In the second case, if a cosmology claims something already existed when the universe began, then we're asked to believe that some original thing existed. This results in the unanswerable question: "Where did that original thing come from?" Allowing that question to remain unanswered also requires a leap of faith.

For example, consider the popular "Big Bang" theory. Some propose the Big Bang emerged out of nothing, or what mathematicians call "a singularity." Acceptance of that requires a leap of faith.

Others claim that a previous universe collapsed. They propose that the implosion of the old universe rebounded to cause the Big Bang, which then produced the current universe. Even if that's true, we still don't know where the previous universe came from. Presuming the existence of a previous universe requires a leap of faith as well.

Thus, all cosmologies require a leap of faith in which the initial premise must be tacitly accepted. This is an unavoidable characteristic that all cosmologies share.

Once one goes beyond the initial leap of faith, there are two important criteria that can be used to evaluate cosmologies:

1. How well does the cosmology fit reality?
2. Does the cosmology contain helpful insights that bring forth a deeper and clearer understanding of reality?

These criteria determine the validity and usefulness a particular cosmology. Throughout this book, I'll point out numerous examples of how the *Consciousness-Origin Cosmology,* that's introduced in this chapter, fits reality remarkably well. I'll also show how this cosmology provides important insights that offer a more comprehensive and accurate understanding of reality. Moreover, this cosmology answers unsolved questions and rectifies many common misconceptions about reality and humanity's purpose. All of this will support the potential validity and tremendous value of this cosmology.

Earlier, in Chapter 2, I explained how consciousness is being returned to the foundation of the universe. For instance, Dr. Robert Lanza, who was ranked the third most important scientist in the world by *The New York Times*, proposed that life and consciousness are fundamental to the entire universe. He even proposed that **consciousness creates matter, not the other way around.**

Even if we adopt a consciousness-based model of reality, there are two key questions that ought to be considered:

1. Where did the consciousness come from?
2. Why would this consciousness choose to create the universe?

The following two sections answer these questions.

THE CONSCIOUSNESS-ORIGIN COSMOLOGY

The Consciousness-Origin Cosmology claims that one formless consciousness existed before the physical universe was formed. Though formless and singular, this consciousness was able to have feelings and thoughts. Moreover, the One's ability to feel and think was so expansive, that its enormous capacity is beyond a human's ability to imagine a consciousness of such immensity causing humans to presume that this enormous consciousness is infinite.

The origin of this One colossal consciousness is not known; therefore, a leap of faith is needed. You must be willing to consider the idea that an enormous consciousness existed prior to the formation of the universe. Fortunately, more and more people, even celebrated scientists, are choosing to presume that consciousness came first.

THE PURPOSE OF THE UNIVERSE

Being a singular consciousness, the One explored all sorts of interesting things that it could accomplish as a single consciousness. Then, once the One had experienced all the interesting adventures available to a single organism, the One wondered,

"What would it feel like to meet a mysterious other?"

In other words, the One contemplated the idea of meeting some sort of other being that it didn't know. More precisely, the One wanted to know how meeting a mysterious other would feel emotionally.

Unfortunately, since the One was the only thing that existed, no other being was available to meet. Having only itself to work with, the One devised a way to create a number of personalities out of itself.

To do this, the One condensed the essence of its own enormous consciousness into numerous small portions. Each mini-consciousness was a typical sample of the One—a mini-One. To ensure each mini-One had a unique personality, the One placed slightly different proportions of its own characteristics into each mini-One.

Once it had produced a multitude of unique mini-One personalities out of itself, the One experienced what it felt like for these little portions of itself to interact with one another. The One quickly discovered that the personalities inherently knew they were part of the One. Then, through the One's continuum of consciousness, they were able to connect to each other empathetically and telepathically providing all of the mini-Ones with knowledge of the feelings and thoughts of all the other mini-Ones without needing to "meet them." Therefore, the mini-Ones were too tightly interconnected to find the others mysterious. Lacking sufficient separation, the mini-One personalities failed to discover how it feels to meet **mysterious** others.

To overcome this snag, the One devised a plan to separate the personalities from one other. The first step was to fabricate a universe out of the only thing that existed—consciousness.

HOW THE ONE-WHO-IS-ALL CREATED THE UNIVERSE

The project of constructing the universe was assigned to a very large portion of the One-Who-Is-All that will be referred to as the *Creator*. To make the Creator whole or holy, the One used equal amounts of emotions and intellect plus proportionally appropriate quantities of all the other aspects of consciousness. Then, based on the Supreme Power of Wholeness principal, the Creator is able to function as a <u>divine</u> Quintessential Core that's capable of forming an enormous Triality with the well-known physical realm as one polarity and the mysterious astral realm comprising the other polarity. In the diagram on the left, all three realms are illustrated as if they're separate, however they actually overlap throughout the physical realm producing a semi-parallel universe with a foundation of consciousness woven throughout everything.

Triality of Realms

The dictionary definition of "astral" is:

astral: adjective;
of, connected with, or resembling the stars: astral navigation.
· of or relating to a supposed nonphysical realm of existence to which various psychic and paranormal phenomena are ascribed, and in which the physical human body is said to have a counterpart.[14]

The bold portion of this definition applies in this instance.

To deal with all the details of forming the Grand Illusion, the Creator made smaller portions of consciousness out of itself and assigned each a specific duty as a subcontractor. The creation process is subdivided all the way down to indivisible components such as subatomic particles. Each portion of consciousness manages their part of the Grand Illusion. Examples include; a galaxy, a solar system, a planet, the weather, a tree, a person, an organ, a cell, etc. Each portion has an appropriately sized portion of consciousness assigned to form and manage it. At all levels, Triality is used to form what appears to be a dualistic reality but is actually an illusion with consciousness imbedded in each Quintessential Core.

The remainder of this chapter describes each of the three top level realms; consciousness, physical and astral.

Let's begin with the original realm of pure consciousness—the foundation of everything.

THE REALM OF PURE CONSCIOUSNESS

Although consciousness is the foundation of everything, support-ing everything and connecting everything together, we can't measure or even locate consciousness because it's formless. Even while con-sciousness has intrigued philosophers and scientists for thousands of years, exactly what consciousness *is* remains unclear. With my Soul's assistance, I offer the following assessment of consciousness.

We all experience awareness, feelings, memories and thoughts as essential properties of our consciousness. Still, we don't have any tools or instruments that can detect or measure these properties. Despite that limitation, some people have discovered how to drop inward and allow the Grand Illusion to dissolve, thereby exposing the eternal realm of pure consciousness. Many methods have been developed, documented and taught. Even without training or practice, this in-ward adventure back to pure consciousness can occur accidentally.

The journey begins by dropping one's point of awareness into the Quintessential-Core or zero-point that's located in the human heart. Once there, total surrender allows reality to disintegrate or flip inside-out to reveal a void—a small dark space which is perceived by one's conscious awareness. At this point the physical body has disappeared.

Next, an expansion occurs. It could be explosive, undulating or in some other way expansive. Regardless of how the enlargement pro-gresses, the explorer's point of awareness eventually finds itself in a gently illuminated misty space that appears endless in all directions. Once situated in this realm of consciousness, one has an opportunity to experience pure consciousness apart from the Grand Illusion be-cause the later has completely disappeared.

Even though the physical body has vanished, delightful sensa-tions of warmth and bliss are unmistakably felt. A remarkable sense of peace is also present. What's more, this realm feels inexplicably timeless. While the infinite expanse is viewed from a single point in the center, one clearly knows that they are the entire endless space that surrounds their point of awareness producing a sense of oneness that replaces the normal feelings of individuality and separation.

Finally, an unexpected sense of being home is very clearly felt.

While in this foundational realm of pure consciousness, one's awareness of these emotional feelings and the associated thoughts that arise regarding the extraordinary nature of such an adventure are quite clear and undeniable, demonstrating that our awareness, emotions and thoughts are all properties of pure consciousness.

Although some claim vibrations or energy are the basis of reality, neither of those exist in the inner realm of pure consciousness, therefore vibrations and energy must be features of the Grand Illusion.

While on such adventures, I've contemplated questions regarding life in the physical realm. These inquiries have been answered instantly with clear responses that usually arrive as thoughts and/or emotions. In some cases, 3D illustrations appear to clarify the answer. Some of the most important features of this book came to me while I was visiting the realm of pure consciousness.

For instance, when I was experiencing the deepest and most profound inward adventure of my life, I remembered the original impetus that provoked the One-Who-Is-All to form the Grand Illusion. In that journey into consciousness, the blissful sensation included juicy orgasmic undulations propagating outward as expanding spherical waves that ballooned beyond my ability to fathom. This made the expanse that surrounded my point of awareness an endless cascade of orgasmic bliss. The feeling of these spherical waves pulsing ecstatically as they surged outward from my point of awareness was more pleasurable than anything I have ever experienced. I recall thinking that this sensation might be the most marvelous feeling of all!

Soon, an intuitive thought offered an unexpected insight; once I had become accustomed to this glorious sensation it would eventually normalize and then I would choose to explore something else.

Next, a memory of the distant past arrived; before the Grand Illusion was formed, the One-Who-Is-All had already experienced this glorious orgasm. Beyond that, the One had explored all of the interesting opportunities that a **single organism could explore on its own.** With nothing of interest left for the One to investigate as a single organism, the One hatched a new idea; what would it feel like to go beyond oneness and explore multiplicity? With numerous entities interacting, many new and interesting opportunities would become available. As that memory crystalized, a vision appeared. I saw a crowd of human beings milling about as I instantly knew that humans are fulfilling the One's desire to explore multiplicity.

Finally, I recalled how this concept was the basis of the Consciousness-Origin Cosmology that had been shared with me ten years

60

earlier. As explained earlier, that cosmology proposes that the One chose to explore how it feels to meet **mysterious** others. To accomplish that, the One formed the Grand Illusion and human beings out of itself to investigate meetings that require separate individuals.

With that original purpose still in my mind, I noticed that my physical body was reforming. Then, once back in my body, I noticed a delicious sweet nectar, amrita, dripping down the back of my throat. When I opened my eyes, I found myself lying next to my beloved. We had just completed the final session of a seven-day tantric lovemaking adventure. The red tantric techniques that we had practiced for seven days triggered the most profound inward adventure I have ever experienced. I'm eternally grateful to that very special woman.

While on that adventure, I discovered that it's possible to feel more ecstatic sensations without a physical body. For instance, a human body can't feel an orgasm that is much larger that itself, but without a body I had become an infinite orgasm.

Even though we don't need bodies to feel sensations, our bodies help us explore how it feels to meet mysterious others. Meeting others can't be experienced in the realm of pure consciousness because Oneness is inescapable there. Conversely, in the physical realm, our separate physical bodies make meeting others effortless. To continue experiencing those meetings, the inward adventure ends when the person finds themselves back in their unique human body.

Once back, it's common to notice that the physical realm feels as if it's an elaborate illusion. Even though the physical realm is solid and that solidity feels and appears real, the realm of pure consciousness feels distinctly more real than the physical realm. This strong sense of certainty that the inner realm is the bona fide actual reality can form such a strong and lasting impression that many who drop inward, come to believe that they've discovered their true home—consciousness. These pivotal experiences can affect the course of a person's life.

After several inward adventures, many come to the conclusion:

An endless oneness exists, and I'm part of that oneness!

Even though that may be an ultimate truth, being an individual amongst other individuals is the human experience of life that we encounter in the physical realm. This paradox of oneness being true—while individuality also <u>appears</u> to be true—means that it's impossible to meet the One. Just as your nose can't meet you, because it's part of you, you can't meet the One-Who-Is-All because you're an integral part of that oneness. Thus, the inward journey leads the practitioner out of the illusion of being an individual and back to true oneness.

REFLECTING ON ALL THE ASPECTS OF CONSCIOUSNESS

During my inward journeys back to pure consciousness, I've experienced: awareness; sensual and emotional feelings; intellectual thoughts; epiphanies and memories indicating that these are all aspects of pure consciousness. None of these features require the existence of physical material, energy, light, or vibrations.

For example, a sensation like warmth that is commonly associated with the physical body, is clearly felt without a body. Emotional feelings are also present. For instance, peace and the safe feeling of being home are routinely felt during these inward adventures.

Beyond identifying the features of consciousness, an intuitive epiphany notified me that irrational emotions and rational intellect are both needed for creativity to occur. I became aware that creativity begins with an irrational emotional leap beyond what is known and even beyond what can be rationally inferred with intellectual reasoning. This irrational emotional leap offers an entirely new option for the rational intellect to analyze and possibly utilize in a revolutionary productive way. Furthermore, irrational emotions are considered feminine while the rational intellect is masculine, placing these features of consciousness on opposite poles. Upgrading that duality to a Triality, the Quintessential Core would contain a balanced combination of intellect and emotions to be blessed with creative abilities.

Emotions have been associated with creativity forever. In Greek mythology, the Muses are nine goddesses who each provide creative inspiration for a particular subject; poetry, astronomy, song, etc. The Muses are all goddesses, linking them to the feminine irrational emotions that provide the leap or spark that ignites the creative process.

When it comes to computers and AI (Artificial Intelligence) these machines have memory and they can mimic intelligence which involves rational reasoning but, beyond that, computers lack awareness and emotions, which are vital ingredients of consciousness.

Since emotions are irrational, they're incompatible with math and logic which are entirely rational. For instance, sadness can't be expressed mathematically. Depression, happiness, joy, fear, and all emotional feelings are irrational leaving them outside the rational domain of math. Since computers are computational machines, based on rational logic and math, they're incompatible with emotions. Without emotions, these machines will not be able to achieve true creativity. (Note: Math has "irrational numbers" however those numbers are not irrational based on the primary meaning of the word "irrational." Instead, irrational numbers are not expressible as a ratio of two integers, and they have an infinite and nonrepeating expansion when expressed as a decimal making them difficult to write down. Pi [π] is a well-known example of an irrational number.)

Computers also lack self-awareness which is the essence of being conscious, leaving these machines unconscious.

Comparing human consciousness to computational machines helps to reveal how important all the features of consciousness are. Since we effortlessly experience all these aspects of consciousness, it's easy to forget how essential all the aspects of consciousness are.

With consciousness discussed, I'll move on to the Grand Illusion.

THE PHYSICAL/ASTRAL SEMI-PARALLEL UNIVERSE

The physical/astral semi-parallel universe that was formed by the Creator using Triality magic is a two-in-one Grand Illusion. The physical realm is where we live our lives in physical bodies. On the other side of the veil is the astral realm. This is where our consciousness hangs out after the physical body dies. The foundational consciousness that I labeled the Creator is present throughout the entire arrangement.

Since you experience the physical realm every day of your life, you're already familiar with that part of the Grand Illusion. That leaves the mysterious afterlife astral realm to be described.

THE ASTRAL REALM

To begin with, each human being has an astral body. When a person is alive and awake, the astral body remains hidden inside the physical body. When a person's physical body dies, their astral body emerges out of their physical body. When this happens, the person's mind exits their physical body to remain located in the astral body shifting their perspective to "the other side of the veil." This is because they view reality through astral eyes that are located in the astral body.

This natural separation is well-known to take place during near-death experiences when people find their mind viewing reality from their astral body. While clinically dead, it's quite common for near-death survivors to view their physical body from above. Some notice that they're located in a second body which is their astral body.

In addition to dying, there are other ways to explore the astral realm. For example, there are Out-of-Body Experiences (OBEs) called astral projection, astral travel or simply out-of-body travel. Those OBEs are very different than dropping one's awareness inward toward one's Soul in their heart to explore the foundational realm of consciousness as a point of awareness.

Instead, to explore the astral realm, a person can use one of the many OBE techniques that are shared in numerous books. Additionally, there are several schools that teach astral travel. For instance, the International Academy of Consciousness (IAC) teaches astral travel. This organization has offices in several countries around the world with a campus located in Portugal. Other astral travel schools include: The Phase School, School of Astral Travel–Life Foundation, The Monroe Institute, etc. All of these schools teach techniques that help people explore the astral realm for themselves.

Even without using a technique, some people accidentally find themselves in their astral body exploring the astral realm. The three memorable astral adventures that I experienced were all accidental.

To learn more, I participated in a four-day intensive workshop offered by the IAC. Both of the instructors had decades of experience exploring the astral realm and both got started with accidental adventures when they were teenagers. These experts explained that when a person falls asleep, their astral body raises up and out of their physical

 body, as shown on the left. The instructors claimed they had both observed this while on astral adventures. They further explained that people who are awake, and in their physical bodies, can't see astral bodies making this condition invisible to physical people who are awake.

The instructors further explained how astral travel techniques take advantage of the natural separation that takes place while sleeping. The trick is to keep the conscious-mind awake while allowing the physical body to fall asleep.

Then, once the two bodies have separated naturally, the person can use their willpower to direct the astral body to pull away from the physical body that remains asleep. This initial liftoff is depicted below.

There are additional skills that can be used to achieve a successful liftoff, still that's the basic astral projection process.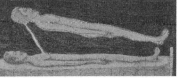

When I started the workshop, I imagined that it would be interesting to experiment with astral travel and explore the astral realm more than I already had in my accidental journeys. Then, after lots of information about the astral realm had been shared, the instructors explained that the remainder of the workshop would involve practicing astral projection methods. Intuitively, my Soul guided me to resist the temptation to explore the astral realm and instead drop out of the class. So, that's what I did.

Later, once enough information about the astral realm has been shared, I'll explain why astral travel is considered to be risky for people who are interested in following their Soul's intuitive guidance.

For now, I'll continue to share what I learned about the astral realm from veteran travelers, occasional travelers, book research, my personal experience, and my Soul's intuitive guidance.

To begin with, a person's astral body looks much like a person's physical body, but it may be a younger version that fits the person's self-image. Two important differences are how the astral body doesn't reproduce and lacks the associated genitals.

When a person's physical body is still alive, but they're traveling around in their astral body, a silver cord connects the two bodies together. That cord attaches to the astral body at the lower part of the back of the head (see illustration above). When a person's consciousness is needed back in their physical body, to deal with life, this cord instantly reels the astral body back into the physical body. When the physical body dies, the silver cord is cut, releasing the astral body.

The physical realm and our physical bodies are visible to astral travelers, but because the astral bodies are not physical they effortlessly pass through physical objects, walls, etc. Accordingly, the astral body's hands can't touch physical objects, pick them up nor move them. On the positive side, astral travelers have found that the subtle astral body is nearly weightless and can be directed to fly with one's willpower, like Superman. Many have discovered that they can leave the Earth's atmosphere and fly to distant solar systems at speeds many times faster than light! For instance, a round trip to the Pleiades star cluster and back is over 888 light years, but astral travelers claim to have made that trip in one night with time to meet "Pleiadians!"

What makes this faster than light speed travel possible is the consciousness that lies at the foundation of everything, connecting everything to everything else to provide an instantaneous expressway. In the physical realm, this same feature explains the yet unsolved mystery that Einstein called, "spooky action at a distance."

Since astral experiences can be beyond belief, the IAC has used scientific methods to confirm the validity of their adventures. For example, one of the IAC instructors described the following experiment:

At an IAC conference with many astral travelers in attendance, an unbiased man was employed to assist with an experiment. This man rented a room in the hotel where the conference was taking place. He also selected an object known only to himself and placed it in the middle of the room that he had rented. After leaving the room he locked the door and stood guard to make sure that no physical people entered the room. While he guarded the room, numerous astral travelers who had gathered in the hotel's auditorium took off on astral adventures. Once separated from their physical bodies they flew in their subtle astral bodies through the physical walls of the hotel and into the guarded room without being seen by the guard. Each traveler found and identified the object in the center of the room and then returned to the auditorium to reunite with their physical body. Once back in their physical body, each person wrote down a description of what they had found in the middle of the room. Finally, the unbiased man examined the written descriptions and confirmed that all the astral travelers had correctly identified the object!

This experiment rules out machine-brain theories that claim these astral experiences are hallucinations because everyone found the correct object in a location far from their physical bodies.

In another experiment, one of the instructors traveled thousands of miles across a great ocean to identify several objects and return to record what she had found. In less time than a physical human can make that trip, she completed the mission and returned with information that was verified to be correct.

On other occasions, people have gone on group adventures to explore the astral realm together and then, at the end of their adventure, they compare notes. The travelers confirm for each other that what they saw was also seen by the other travelers.

If you aren't familiar with astral travel, what has already been shared must seem quite outrageous. When I was first introduced to astral travel, it seemed outlandish to me. Then, once I began asking friends and acquaintances if they had heard about astral travel, I found that many knew about it. Some had actually traveled themselves. A few of those people were friends that I trusted. They helped me to accept what has been found by so many independent sources.

Although many people have experienced the paranormal astral realm, most avoid talking about it for fear that uninformed people will question their sanity. Accordingly, most astral travelers don't discuss their astral travel hobby to avoid ridicule and loss of credibility. So, if you're unfamiliar with the astral realm, consider asking your friends if they're aware of it and if they've explored it themselves. If you bring up the subject, they will open up knowing that you're familiar with the subject and interested in talking about it.

Continuing with the description, the astral realm is claimed to be quite similar to the physical realm when traveling near the surface of the Earth, or in what many refer to as the middle-Earth layer. When cruising around in one's subtle astral body, everything that is physical can be seen. One difference is how objects appear to shimmer, giving the astral realm a glamorous mystique, something like a Van Gogh painting. A much bigger difference is how deceased peoples' spirits exist on the other side where they cruise around in their subtle astral bodies. The middle-Earth layer extends beyond the Earth to include the entire physical universe so it could be labeled the "physical layer".

Exploring beyond the physical layer, experienced astral travelers have found additional layers. Most sources describe a total of seven layers with the physical layer located in the middle. The lower three layers are described as hellish while the upper three are alleged to have heavenly qualities. The further a layer is from the middle, the more hellish or heavenly the layer is purported to be.

This seven layer arrangement forms an additional Triality with the heavenly polarity above, the hellish polarity below while the physical Earth layer is the Quintessential Core in the middle.

When human spirits of deceased people are located in the middle-Earth layer they're called ghosts. By being in-between Heaven and Hell, their situation corresponds to the notion of purgatory—an intermediate state after death.

Additional features that are found when astral traveling include; the pearly gates, angels, the Father, Jesus, Zeus, Aphrodite, otherworldly spirit guides and so-called "aliens."

The review of numerous near-death accounts reveals how the outer astral layers reflect each person's beliefs regarding what occurs after death. Often, Jesus or a personally appropriate god or goddess is found in Heaven. For many, deceased relatives are encountered. Some people descend to Hell, which proves its existence for them.

A specific example that shows how astral Heaven adapts to individual beliefs comes from a man who believed the machine-brain theory. During his near-death experience, he discovered a gigantic network of spheres interconnected by long tubes. He was inside one of the tubes where he was able to view, what appeared to be, a huge neurological network. That experience supported this man's ardent belief that the brain produces consciousness, even though it doesn't.

Since it is now known that people find whatever they're looking for when exploring the outer astral layers, what is found in those outer layers can't be used to discern truth from fiction. Instead, those outer layers offer each individual lordship over their own domain where they are empowered to create their own reality.

Over thousands of years, a lot of confusion has been stirred up by people who believe that what they discovered in the astral realm provided them with a deeper understanding of "reality" that applies to the physical realm where we live. For instance, the popular theory that we create our own reality came from astral Heaven where thoughts and desires manifest a personalized domain. Despite how that occurs in astral heaven, it doesn't work that way in the physical realm.

When alive in a physical body, we all experience one reality that is essentially the same for all of us. The middle-Earth layer of the astral realm is somewhat like a bridge linking the stable physical realm with the outer astral layers that accommodate each visitor's will.

Normally, when a person is in the physically alive state, with their consciousness located in their physical body, they don't see the astral—keeping it mostly hidden. However, there are exceptions where

68

some people see into the other-side. For example, people have reported seeing a deceased relative, a ghost, some sort of fairy, elf or a so-called alien while still awake and in their physical body. While paranormal beings are rarely glimpsed by physical people who are alive and awake, those same beings are commonly encountered by astral travelers, indicating that the afterlife astral realm is their home.

A classic painting of a man viewing the astral realm is shown on the right. In the lower left corner, he's poking his head out of a star covered dome that depicts the vail. On the other side, he sees a bizarre layered realm. This image depicts a veil and layers, but fails to capture the way these realms occupy the same space— something a 2D picture can't express.

In the opposite direction, some astral spirit beings have found ways to enter people's dreams or trance-like practices. Even beyond that, there are cases in which multiple people have claimed to have seen an astral being like St. Germaine or Sai Baba while physically alive and awake, indicating that some astral beings are able to make themselves visible to physical people, even so, these cases are rare.

It's more common for a person to enter a trance state and allow a spirit to use their body as a "channel." In those cases, an astral spirit enters the channel's physical body and uses their voice to speak to people who are fascinated with that spirit's message.

A common thread found in these messages is a prediction of an impending transition to a "higher reality" that involves ascending out of the dense physical body to become a "light being" with godlike powers. While that may seem extraordinary, people who die shed their dense physical body to explore the outer layers of the afterlife realm in their subtle astral body where they obtain godlike powers. This has produced a popular belief that astral Heaven is a "better" place that leads to godhood. Various versions of this belief have existed since civilization began. Hermes was a man who traveled to Elysium, the Greek word for Heaven. There he met with deities and relayed their messages back to Earth. Eventually, he became a god himself. In Egypt he was called Thoth, while the Romans called him Mercury.

A well-known book that provides ascension details is the *Autobiography of a Yogi* by Paramhansa Yogananda, first published in 1946. Yogananda's bestselling book was influential in launching the new age spiritual movement that aligns with the astral realm and focuses primarily on the upper heavenly layers where a human can supposedly become god. This "ascension" process is detailed in *Autobiography of a Yogi* where Yogananda's deceased guru returns from the astral realm three days after his death. In that meeting he gives Yogananda instructions for ascension to godhood. The nonphysical guru actually claims that he has become god! This book's popularity indicates that many people are interested in godlike powers.

In spite of that, the Way-of-the-Heart is a humble path that leads to the full blossoming of love here on Earth while in a physical body. The details will be discussed later. For now, I'll continue describing the astral afterlife realm so paranormal issues can be addressed in a clear and demystifying way when they come up.

Today more than ever, the enticing astral opportunities for personal power are making astral travel very popular. For example, there's a fast-growing religious movement that endorses astral travel called Eckankar. It was founded by Paul Twitchell in 1965 and already has members in over 100 countries.

Spirits, Heaven, Hell and the afterlife have been key features of all religions. Even Buddhism proposes that the ultimate destination is Nirvana, a seventh Heaven state-of-being that Buddhists assert ends suffering and the cycle of birth and death.

In addition to religions, there's a very important linkage between the astral realm and hallucinogenic substance use. These controversial substances have been renamed entheogens.

entheogen: noun;
a chemical, typically of plant origin, that is ingested to produce a non-ordinary state of consciousness for religious or spiritual purposes.

In the book *Inner Paths to Outer Space*, co-author Rick Strassman, M.D., discusses his University of New Mexico study in which, Dimethyltrytamine (DMT), a well-known entheogen, was administered to human test subjects to investigate its psychological effects. When given high enough dosages, most of the subjects encountered "alien" beings just like the well-documented abduction cases compiled at Harvard University by Professor John Mack, M.D.

In Strassman's New Mexico study, the physical bodies of the human test subjects had intravenous drip needles inserted into them. Also, attendants stood watch over each test subject insuring that their physical bodies remained safe and undisturbed. Since their physical bodies were definitely not abducted, what happened?

It turns out that sufficient levels of DMT help to liberate the astral body from the physical body. Once that occurs the abductee's astral body can be spirited away by astral spirit beings who inhabit the astral realm. Because the abductee's conscious-mind is located in their astral body they experience being abducted. Meanwhile, their physical body remains undisturbed.

The 200 abductees that Professor Mack interviewed at Harvard were abducted when asleep or going to sleep. That's when the astral body naturally emerges from the physical body along with the person's conscious-mind shifting them over to the astral side of the veil.

Additional astral information comes from the South American shamans who prepare and drink "ayahuasca," a brew containing DMT. On their entheogenic adventures, they meet beings they call their "spirit brothers and sisters." Some of those shamans have drawn illustrations that depict the classic "gray aliens" and the praying mantis beings that the Harvard abductees and the New Mexico test subjects also identified with descriptions, and in some cases, drawings.

This means that peoples' astral bodies, containing their conscious and subconscious minds, are being visited and even abducted by astral spirit beings who have been mistakenly thought to be aliens. Important support that links all of these experiences to the afterlife is how many near-death survivors have met the gray aliens while clinically dead. After being revived, some share stories of meeting these curious astral spirit beings while they were temporarily dead.

When it comes to the U.S. government top-secret reports of physical spaceships and aliens, consider the documentary, *Mirage Men: How the U.S. Government Created a Myth That Took Over the World*. In this film, a government public relations expert admits that he manufactured false documents and intentionally leaked that misinformation to a well-known "ufologist." This created the famous Roswell UFO incident that successfully distracted people from discovering the real top-secret stealth aircraft development program and the associated test flight crashes that took place in and around

Area 51. Even though no physical aliens where actually involved, people continue to cite the misinformation that included fake photographs of the little gray beings being dissected.

Some people intentionally explore the astral realm to meet with spirit guides, ascended masters, angels, etc. Sufficient levels of DMT launch people into the astral realm making the transition over to the astral side of the veil easier than using astral projection techniques. The DMT molecule is nearly identical to LSD, psilocybin (from magic mushrooms), ibotenic acid (from amanita mushrooms) and mescaline (from the peyote cactus). All of these chemicals, plus others, are entheogens—substances that induce spiritual experiences.

The similarities of what has been found by people while temporarily dead, when astral traveling, and while on entheogenic trips, indicates that all of these exceptionally bizarre adventures take place on the astral afterlife side of the veil. A specific commonality that has been reported by many is the well-known little "gray aliens." Or what the ayahuasca shamans call their spirit brothers and sisters.

In the Quechua languages used by ayahuasca shamans, "aya" can mean "dead body", and "waska" means "woody vine" making one translation of ayahuasca "vine of the dead." Hence, these shamans who prepare ayahuasca must know that their brew provides people who ingest it with a view of the afterlife side of the veil. A small dose offers a glimpse, while a large dose can provide full immersion.

On the other hand, in some cases, entheogenically induced experiences can involve dropping into the foundational realm of pure consciousness. This is supported in Rick Strassman's DMT trip reports presented in his book, *Inner Paths to Outer Space*. In particular, one of the subjects reported a journey that fits dropping inward toward the realm of pure consciousness. I described the inward experience earlier when discussing consciousness. All of the other adventures that are documented in Strassman's book fit the astral type of OBE.

Adventures to the astral and consciousness realms are commonly lumped together as "spiritual" experiences despite their substantial differences. To begin with, the astral realm is found outside one's physical body via astral projection or out-of-body travel, while the realm of pure consciousness is found inside by dropping into one's center as the physical body disappears. Another clear difference is how the astral realm contains other beings; however, in the realm of pure consciousness all is One. Visions may appear in the consciousness realm to illustrate ideas but they're just 3D images, not interactive spirit beings. Finally, astral travelers have astral bodies, but dropping inward leads to becoming a single point of awareness that knows it's everything. The only similarity between the astral and consciousness realms is how they're both significantly different than life in a physical body. Having personally experienced all three realms, I'm proposing that the original foundational realm, found within, is the state of being the One—pure consciousness.

While in that realm, I've found that contemplating questions results in clear answers that can be relied on to be true. Conversely, the astral realm's outer layers accommodate each person's beliefs making those adventures fantasy. They can be fun, but they're also confusing.

So, when someone's physical body dies, that person's conscious- and subconscious-minds find themselves on the afterlife side of the veil inside of their subtle astral body. At that point, the silver cord has been cut disconnecting the astral body from the deceased physical body that decomposes back into the Earth. Later, the astral spirit being who resides in the afterlife astral realm could reincarnate into a new physical body to experience another life in the physical realm. Of course, the reincarnation process can repeat again and again...

Although horror stories portray the afterlife as a demonic realm filled with wickedly sadistic beings who have bizarrely awful agendas, the reality is that all beings are portions of the One-Who-Is-All. Accordingly, everything is working to fulfill the purpose of the universe. When it comes to us humans, the next few chapters will show how we're designed to be separate individuals so we can find out how it feels to meet mysterious others, thereby accomplishing the purpose of the universe. Although many people have aspirations to be more than a mortal human, ironically, it's ordinary gullible physical humans who are uniquely able to fulfill the One's goal for this universe.

When it comes to the spirit beings that reside in the astral realm, they work behind the veil supporting the physical play from the afterlife spirit realm. Gods, goddesses, angels, little gray spirit beings, and numerous other whole portions of the One-Who-Is-All are hidden in the astral realm where they support the Grand Illusion. For example, according to Greek mythology, Zeus was responsible for thunder and lightning. His mother Gaia was responsible for the Earth. Those divine portions of consciousness and many more can be found in the astral realm.

Conversely, our Souls are hidden within our hearts.

Although materialistic science has labeled the old theories of divine Souls and other spirits "myths," those old theories appear to be founded in truth. While mainstream materialistic science claims that random chance and physical laws are responsible for forming and controlling the universe, some courageous scientists have proposed that a creative consciousness must be behind the curtain. Physical laws may govern the physical realm in many ways, however divine beings have been found to be behind paranormal irregularities that override those laws. At a deeper level, the consciousness at the foundation of everything takes the place of random chance to insure the divine plan remains on track.

Even though humans have explored the astral realm for millennia, those astral adventures haven't yielded practical results. Instead, such adventures, have become mythical stories shared in novels, movies, mythologies and religious scriptures.

Today, astral travel methods and entheogenic substances are readily available, giving many people the opportunity to fly with gods and goddesses themselves. This accounts for the fast-growing popularity of Eckankar, the astral travel religion mentioned earlier.

When it comes to entheogens, the Santo Daime is a Catholic-style church that uses ayahuasca as a sacrament to assist with exploring the astral realm. Legal status for using ayahuasca has been obtained in Canada, the Netherlands, France, Italy, the U.S.A. and Brazil.

Additional methods that can open the doors to the astral and pure-consciousness realms include: holotropic breath work, shamanic drumming, meditation, high fever, exhaustion, etc. The astral is found outside while pure-consciousness is found within the heart.

Although the astral and pure-consciousness realms are very intriguing, this book's subject is the Soul. To provide the most complete and accurate setting for that presentation, the astral and consciousness realms have been included. Because these realms have been ignored or misunderstood by most, many common misconceptions have developed. To rectify those fallacies, where they come up, I'll refer to the astral and/or pure-consciousness realms.

After avoiding the astral realm for most of my life, I finally dug into it and realized that I needed to revise this book to include the astral realm. Still, I don't want to get overly distracted by attempting to address the seemingly endless astral details. Here's why:

THE GREAT MYSTERY

Adding the astral realm and its mysterious upper and lower layers to the already complex physical realm that we live in, produces what some have called an "unfathomable Great Mystery." Regardless of all the paranormal phenomenon taking place in the astral realm, and even though some of it bleeds over to the physical realm, living with your heart open, following your inner guidance and opening to love doesn't require an in-depth understanding of the afterlife side of the veil. Moreover, delving into the bizarre and complex features of the astral realm can easily distract a person from connecting with their Superconscious-Soul that resides in their heart.

The Soul in the heart can be embraced by anyone who chooses to acknowledge their magnificent Soul. The Soul provides the living word of the One-Who-Is-All to those who listen. That guidance is based on what's taking place in the present moment. Following that inner guidance is the Way-of-the-Heart path featured in this book.

In support of that path, the highly revered Hawaiian kahuna, Daddy Bray recommended the development of an intimate relationship with what I've labeled the Superconscious-Soul. However, what lies beyond the veil is considered a Great Mystery that is beyond human understanding. As such, Bray recommended that people resist the temptation to investigate the Great Mystery to avoid the confusion that will inevitably develop whilst exploring.

Because the outer layers of the astral realm conform to each person's beliefs and desires, using astral exploration for the purpose of learning will definitely lead to confusion. Regardless of how incorrect a person's beliefs are, the astral realm will confirm those beliefs. Then, thinking they have found reliable confirmation for their beliefs, some astral travelers share their fantastic "discoveries" in blogs, in books, on Youtube.com, and in person. Many presume that their astral discoveries apply to the physical realm even though those remarkable experiences are simply manifestations of their mistaken beliefs fulfilled in the mystifying outer astral layers. Consequently, the internet is swamped with a mountain of misinformation that originally appeared in astral experiences. Unfortunately, many people are misguided by reports of aliens, mind over matter theories, etc.

Beyond misinforming people, some warnings claim that the astral realm is a glitzy realm designed to lure people away from their Soul to instead follow external spirit guides who can be found throughout the astral realm. The divine reason for luring people away from their Souls will be explained later.

For now, to conclude this chapter, I'll introduce the Triality of Paths that have emerged due to the existence of the Triality of Realms and the ongoing play of life and death that is taking place on the physical and astral sides of the veil betwixt the two.

TRIALITY OF PATHS

Triality of Paths

Heavenly

Earthly

Hellish

The Triality of Paths is illustrated on the left.

The upper Heavenly paths and the lower Hellish paths are depicted with three dualistic spectrum ribbons. Multiple ribbons are used to indicate that there are many different paths that eventually lead to Heaven and Hell. In accordance with the Similarity of Opposites principal, the upper and lower paths wrap around and meet at their polar extremes. Later, in **Part 2: Future Predictions**, the Consciousness-Origin-Cosmology reveals how these upper and lower paths lead to the same destination, back to the One-Who-Is-All.

In the middle, the Earthly Quintessential Core represents the paths of a small portion of people, probably around 10 to 20 percent of humanity, who remain dedicated to their Soul's guidance. These people follow their Soul's love oriented path that unfolds on the physical Earth while cherishing each precious moment of life. This is the lesser known Way-of-the-Heart path.

The upper and lower paths are very enticing and well-advertised, drawing most people away from the central Way-of-the-Heart path. The upper paths are considered exalted and intellectual. Meanwhile, the lower paths are associated with emotions and debauchery. Those two polarities could be viewed as the classic good versus evil duality. One way or another, most people are drawn to follow external leadership that eventually guides them toward Heaven or Hell.

The most popular lure that is used to draw people out toward the polarities is power. For example, during one of my accidental astral adventures I was offered powers to fulfill all of my desires. I chose to pass on those powers, return to the physical realm and continue following my heart. I've met other people who had also been offered superpowers, but turned them down. You may recall having such an opportunity yourself. Maybe, in an astral dream, or possibly in your life while endeavoring to earn a living. If so, do you remember saying no to that opportunity for unwarranted power?

If you followed your conscience and remained in alignment with your inner guidance that encouraged you to resist such enticing powers, later you may have noticed that people who succumb to the lure of power end up suffering. In spite of the power they acquire, physical and emotional challenges emerge to overshadow the benefits of the power that was obtained. Classic stories like *Aladdin's Lamp* dramatize this self-governing paradox in which power-hungry people often obtain power but end up with tragic results.

In spite of age-old warnings regarding power, power seekers prefer to focus on the numerous practical advantages of being powerful.

Additionally, enticing advertisements for astral Heaven are presented by most spiritual leaders who claim that it's possible to escape all the challenges of the physical realm by ascending up to the highest layer of the astral realm. Buddhists call this exalted goal "Nirvana." Additional spiritual leaders, like Paramhansa Yogananda teach their Hindu followers that ascension to Heaven and permanent union with the One is the ultimate goal for all humans. In Judaism, Christianity and Islam, spiritual leaders also promote a heavenly afterlife existence that can overcome the physical and emotional woes that accompany power.

For people who find life aggravating or seriously painful, escaping suffering becomes a popular quest. In extreme cases, people have committed suicide hoping to escape their life of suffering. Cults that advocate suicide have existed throughout time. Since most people seek power and subsequently suffer, escaping the physical realm to ascend up to Heaven has become a particularly popular goal. Military personnel who use deadly weapons to overpower other people are known to commit suicide more than twice as often as civilians.

While many people are caught up in their lust for power and the money that provides people with power, the Consciousness-Origin Cosmology claims that discovering how it feels to meet mysterious others is the divinely ordained purpose for humanity. Sure, some of those meetings can involve pain and conflict, however friendships that involve cooperation and love can be deeply fulfilling and wonderfully enjoyable.

By following my Soul in my heart, I've experienced a mostly blessed life, one filled with fortuitous synchronicities, love, joy and happiness. Even though, a bit of suffering takes place when I stray from my Soul's guidance, life is a delightful blessing when I conscientiously follow my Soul's divine guidance. I've met many people who have also experienced blessed lives by following their Soul's guidance.

Of the people who follow their heart along the Way-of-the-Heart path, many haven't realized how supremely precious their Soul's guidance is, nor how blessed their lives are, especially in comparison to those who have chosen to seek power and end up suffering. The value and benefits of following your Superconscious-Soul are clarified throughout this book which promotes the Way-of-the-Heart path.

The remaining pages offer insights for everyone; still, this book focuses on the Way-of-the-Heart path—a Soul-guided path highlighted by intuition, humility, balance, love, and romance. **Part 3: Tools and Techniques** is especially helpful for people interested in:

- ♥ opening their heart
- ♥ following their heart
- ♥ opening to love

These are the keys to the Way-of-the-Heart path that takes place on Earth in a physical human body.

Now that the Consciousness-Origin Cosmology and the Triality of Realms have been introduced, most of what follows will focus on the physical realm where we live and our Soul's connection to the foundation of consciousness—the One-Who-Is-All.

As paranormal astral issues crop up, they will be reasonably easy to discuss since the astral realm has been included in the Triality of Realms model of reality presented here, in this chapter.

Chapter 6
The Purpose of the Universe

Popular cosmologies like the Big Bang and *Genesis* don't include a purpose for the universe. Fortunately, the Consciousness-Origin Cosmology offers a purpose: the Grand Illusion is the One's stage for exploring how it feels to meet mysterious others.

To accomplish that purpose, the Earth is a stage where meetings take place. To produce actors who play the roles of the individuals who meet one another, the One initiated the formation of life and guided the process of evolution to develop a wide variety of life forms. Humans were eventually developed to be especially well-suited to meeting one another. Our purpose is to discover how it feels to meet mysterious others. This is not just our purpose as humans—it's the purpose of the physical/astral semi-parallel universe, the entire Grand Illusion, that is founded on and by consciousness.

Whenever you interact with someone, you're discovering how it feels to meet a mysterious other. This takes place even when you interact with people you've met before. We may think we know someone; then again, as we move through life and have varied relationships, we realize that we never really know who anyone is. Surprises can pop up at any time. Even our family members and closest friends can harbor mysterious aspects they hide from others.

In spite of that, if this cosmology is true, then we aren't actually individuals at all. Everything, including you, me, and this book are parts of the One-Who-Is-All. Our perceived individuality is an elaborate illusion. The physical/astral semi-parallel universe arrangement is a Grand Illusion, a Triality of Realms birthed by consciousness.

The Consciousness-Origin Cosmology claims that our universe was synthesized by the One who made everything out of the only thing that existed, the One's consciousness. The semi-parallel universe construct and everything in those realms was designed and arranged to explore meeting mysterious others—an impossibility for the One to explore as the singular formless consciousness that it was prior to the advent of the universe.

This simple purpose may seem too ordinary for such a grand experiment. Nevertheless, if this cosmology is true, then prior to the formation of the universe, the One formless consciousness had never met another—simply because no other existed. Imagine how limited reality would be if the illusion of individuality was removed. Sure, conflict would stop, but so would friendship, companionship, competition, loving another, and countless other interpersonal experiences.

Throughout the remainder of **Part 1**, I'll point out how this purpose of meeting mysterious others fits reality, answers many questions and resolves many misconceptions. For example, let's begin by considering a consciousness-driven theory of evolution.

CONSCIOUSNESS–DRIVEN EVOLUTION

It's possible to imagine the One grand consciousness guiding the formation of more and more complex forms of life, with the goal of producing a species that's appropriate for exploring how it feels to meet mysterious others.

During this process, it may have become clear that the development of life on Earth had drifted off-track to produce creatures inappropriate for meeting one another. When that sort of situation arose, the One could have decided to make a major change in the course of evolution. To prune back the divergent growth and get back on track, a great extinction could have been instigated intentionally.

Once the deviant organisms had been removed, a new direction, one more likely to result in creatures that are proficient in meeting mysterious others, could then be taken. This scenario could explain the five great extinctions as intentional course changes of an experimental development process that we call evolution.

WHY SEXUAL REPRODUCTION?

An important unanswered question in evolutionary biology is:

"Why did the ability to sexually reproduce become so dominant in the animal kingdom?"

Sexual reproduction was never needed. Many organisms reproduce asexually. Some sharks have been found to reproduce without a mate. Several reptiles, many plants, and other forms of life can also reproduce asexually. There are four types of asexual reproduction. All these methods produce offspring more readily than sexual reproduction, which has numerous complications.

For instance, the conditions required to accomplish sexual reproduction in human beings include: the onset of menses, the fertile stage of the menstrual cycle, a healthy egg, and, finally, adequate sperm count consisting of healthy sperm. Without all of these conditions in place, human sexual reproduction will fail to produce offspring. All of this makes human sexual reproduction perversely difficult, especially in comparison to one bacterium simply dividing into two bacteria. Thus, there are many challenges involved in sexual reproduction that work against survival.

Proponents of the popular survival of the fittest theory focus on the way sexual reproduction introduces new genetic variations thereby creating more diversity which in turn accelerates the evolutionary process. Even with this advantage, and 1.2 billion years of sexual reproduction, asexual bacteria remain the most prolific. For instance, scientists have found that there are more bacteria living inside the human digestive system and on our skin than the number of cells that make up the entire human body! This must be true for other creatures as well. Therefore, asexual bacteria are by far more prolific than organisms that reproduce sexually.

Overall, sexual reproduction appears to make survival of a species more difficult and less likely. The numerous anti-survival issues are reasons that prevent evolutionary biologists from being able to conclusively answer the question, "Why did the ability to sexually reproduce become so dominant in the animal kingdom?"

Conversely, the Consciousness-Origin Cosmology's proposal that evolution was guided by consciousness to produce species suitable for discovering how it feels to meet mysterious others aligns with sexual reproduction. As we all know, sexual reproduction requires humans to **meet each other and become intimately involved**.

Thus, the answer to the question of why sexual reproduction became so dominant in the animal kingdom could be to press creatures, who sexually reproduce, to meet others of their species.

Additional factors involved in human sexual reproduction tighten the fit with the purpose of the universe. For instance, mating within the family is currently considered a **first-order taboo** across most cultures. This is because the health of the offspring is compromised through in-breeding. Therefore, humans generally seek partners from another clan. Venturing away from home to find a mate from another clan requires humans to meet truly mysterious others.

GESTATION OF THE FETUS

Let's move on to the next step of human reproduction: the gestation of the fetus growing in the mother's womb. Human fetuses require nine months to gestate in the mother's womb. Pregnancy requires larger amounts of food, compromising the mother's ability to survive. Then, during the last trimester, the mother is physically challenged by having an extended belly. Both the fetus and the pregnant mother are vulnerable in later pregnancy. For instance, the fetus could die if the mother fell on her belly. Finally, birthing complications cause some mothers and fetuses to die during the birthing process.

All these factors make it important for the father and other members of the clan to provide assistance to the mother who is carrying the future of the clan in her womb.

Therefore, the long and challenging process of human fetal development impresses on members of the clan the importance of working together to support the mother and the fetus she's carrying. These reproductive issues further support the Consciousness-Origin Cosmology's theory that humans evolved to meet one another.

HELPLESS INFANTS

Another aspect of human reproduction that's tremendously risky, from a survival perspective, is the way the human infant is completely helpless when it's born. Being so dependent on their mothers for such a long period of time after birth is a trait unique to human offspring. Many animals walk shortly after they're born. For a human baby to be as developed as a chimpanzee newborn, the gestation period in the womb would need to be extended from nine months to approximately eighteen to twenty-one months! Also, the mother's hips would need to be widened to deliver the larger baby that would result.

The way human infants are helpless when born, and the relatively slow development that takes place after birth, have noteworthy impact on the parents and other caretakers. These people become involved in the important and time-consuming responsibility of caring for the helpless infant, which binds the clan together. Therefore, human infants' need for attentive care encourages humans to develop social structures that facilitate **interpersonal relationships.**

On the other hand, bacteria never need to see another bacterium. Their asexuality grants them independence the second one splits into two. While that helps them multiply quickly and independently, it doesn't press them to meet one another. So, their simple, effective and straight forward asexual reproductive method makes them unsuitable for accomplishing the purpose of the universe.

If the Consciousness-Origin Cosmology correctly proposes that meeting mysterious others is the primary guiding principle of evolution, then one might wonder why bacteria still exist?

A simple reason for the continued existence of bacteria is that all complex life forms, including humans, are highly dependent on bacteria. They live in our guts and digest our food, helping us to assimilate the nutrients. In the soil, bacteria do essentially the same thing for plants that feed the animal kingdom. Therefore, the continued existence of bacteria is essential to nearly all complex life forms.

HOMO SAPIENS

Modern humans are now identified as Homo sapien sapien. We're the only remaining variety of the species Homo sapien. Other varieties of our species existed, but all of them are now extinct.

Homo sapien neanderthalensis existed as recently as 30,000 years ago. Homo sapien cro-magnonensis existed as recently as 10,000 years ago. Another variety, cro-magnoids, may have survived until just 4,000 years ago. Because all of these varieties are members of the same species, Homo sapien, they were all able to interbreed with each other. This means they are our ancestral relatives.

All of these varieties of our species used fire and tools. They all had large brains. The Homo sapien neanderthalensis actually had significantly larger brains than we have today. All of these relatives had larger bones and more muscle, making them tougher than us.

One important difference that we have is our more vertical forehead which provides additional space for the linguistic region of the brain. With more complex linguistics, we're better equipped to have more complex discussions and develop a written language.

Some have claimed language enabled us to develop more successful hunting methods. I would argue that an assortment of hand signals and a couple of simple sounds are all that are needed to communicate the simple information needed for hunting.

On the other hand, our weapons, helicopters, land rovers, and other technological devices have clearly enabled humans to be the most capable hunters on the planet. These tools have been developed by our consciousness which is ensuring our ability to survive in spite of our physical frailty. Without fangs, sharp claws, strong bones, or the enormous strength comparable species have, we are the species that is over-populating the Earth while creatures with more physical prowess are dying off. Our creative consciousness invented the rifle and countless other tools that empower us to dominate the Earth.

Despite this survival issue that has been handled by our consciousness, when it comes to meeting mysterious others, language and our ability to enunciate words clearly makes us better able to develop complex language. With such language skills, we're better able to share our feelings and thoughts with greater precision. To clearly express the nuances of our feelings and the specifics of our opinions, complex language is needed.

Accordingly, the Homo sapien sapien was the best equipped to make the most out of meeting mysterious others. Thus, the most successful evolutionary result, Homo sapien sapien, fits the consciousness-driven evolution theory which claims we exist to explore the feelings that arise when meeting others.

REALITY SUPPORTS CONSCIOUSNESS–DRIVEN EVOLUTION

The key point offered in the last six sections involving evolution is that the result is Homo sapien sapien—beings who are well-suited to meeting mysterious others. Our lack of physical survival features has pushed us to develop cooperative social arrangements that are important for our health and survival making the meeting of others part of our strategy for survival.

Currently, 99.9 percent of species that existed so far are thought to be extinct. The fact that humans have survived and are, in fact, displacing all other species could be viewed to indicate that we fit the purpose of life on Earth. Thus, my Soul has guided me to see how the One-Who-Is-All, through our Superconscious-Souls, has guided this process to develop humans who effortlessly discover how it feels to meet others.

RELATIONSHIPS AND MEETING THE MYSTERIOUS OTHER

Beyond simply meeting one another, most humans have made relationships a central focus of their lives.

We all know that humans are fascinated by relationships. Human relationships are an inspiration for art, music, conversation, novels, movies, games, and sports, ad infinitum. Our lives are essentially about relationships, whether it be business relationships, political relationships, familial relationships, social relationships, romantic relationships, friendships, and even adversarial relationships. Thus, the purpose of the universe, meeting mysterious others, fits the human experience particularly well.

Relationships are possible based on the separation that is provided by human individuality. We must be separate from what we're relating to. Therefore, some sort of separation is required for relationships to occur.

The physical realm provides a setting that includes physical separation between people. The space between one person and another provides the opportunity for us to relate to each other as separate individuals. Still, it's an illusion. The deeper truth is that everything is part of a seamless whole.

In spite of the seamless wholeness, each of us experience being an individual human. Finding out how it feels to meet mysterious others is simple; we do it effortlessly. This is because each of us have been fashioned into individuals and placed among other separate individuals. This makes us and our physical reality well-suited to accomplishing the goal of discovering how it feels to meet mysterious others.

An 80 year-long Harvard study recently ended. The extensive research project tracked several people throughout their lives. The results revealed that good friendships are the most important factor in obtaining happiness, health, and longevity. Additionally, in four locations around the world where people consistently live extraordinarily long and healthy lives, good friendships and lots of social interaction were identified to be the prime factors in these people's longevity.

So, it seems that good relationships actually have a powerful impact on our health and happiness.

With all of this in mind, it's quite reasonable to consider the possibility that humans and the universe may have been formed to explore relationships and discover the feelings that emerge from the variety of relationships that we encounter.

THE SIZE OF THE UNIVERSE

One detail that doesn't appear to fit the idea that this universe was formed to meet mysterious others, is the enormous size of the universe. One might wonder why the universe appears to be so large if humans are the only beings of any consequence.

It's actually quite possible that the physical universe is much smaller than is commonly believed. Current estimates are based on a key assumption that has three possibilities. The topology of the physical universe is either: open, flat, or closed.

"Open" means that physical space is slightly curved, somewhat like a potato chip. "Flat" means it's not curved at all. These two options are considered when estimating the size of the universe while the third possibility is consistently ignored.

If the topology of the universe actually fits the third option, "Closed," then the universe could be a four-dimensional sphere—a hyper-sphere that appears infinite, but could actually be small compared to current estimates. No one has found a way to determine which of the three options fits our universe, leaving this critical issue unresolved. This means that the apparent enormity of the universe could be an illusion produced by a closed topology.

Here's how that illusion might work: when an astronomer looks deep into space, their gaze would effectively trace back the light beams along a spiral that coils inward, all the way back to the origin of the universe and the beginning of time. The origin could lie in the middle of an expanding four-dimensional "balloon." The billions of galaxies that are seen could actually be a small number of galaxies that are viewed over and over again. As the astronomer's gaze travels back in time, looping around a spiral pattern, each galaxy would look different each successive time it's seen. As the astronomer peers back in time, the hyper-balloon would shrink. This is the reverse of the expansion that had taken place as time moved forward—to produce a spiraling back in time—leading the astronomer's gaze back to the beginning of time, where the hyper-balloon originally appeared.

With this arrangement, the apparent hugeness of the universe and the supposed enormous number of galaxies would be attributed to an optical illusion. By forming the universe in a way that makes it appear infinite, humans feel extraordinarily small adding to the sense that we're tiny individuals who are separated from mysterious stars and planets that we'll never approach or understand. Viewed this way, this feature of reality fits into the cosmology because our sense of separation is supported by feeling small and inconsequential.

Adding the astral realm to this arrangement, the heavenly layers could exist outside the hyper-spherical balloon while the hellish layers could be located inside of that same balloon. Of course, the volumetric hyper-surface of the hyper-spherical balloon is where the middle-physical layer would be located.

SEPARATION AND INDIVIDUALITY

Meeting a mysterious other requires separation and individuality. Both of these are essential features of the Grand Illusion that must be established before any meetings between mysterious others can take place. To construct a universe that's naturally conducive to separation and individuality, Trialities are used to form dualistic spectrums in a myriad of overlapping ways.

Even though everything emerges out of one central core, that is the One-Who-Is-All, the dualistic spectrums cause reality to appear dualistic in nature. The illusion of duality provides a context that is conducive to separation. The separation is further supported by forming separate physical bodies for each organism.

THE SOURCE OF THE CONSCIOUSNESS-ORIGIN COSMOLOGY

What I've named the Consciousness-Origin Cosmology first came from Rudolf Steiner (1861–1925), an Austrian philosopher, literary scholar, educator, artist, playwright, and social and esoteric thinker. He was the founder of Anthroposophy, Waldorf Education, Biodynamic Farming, Anthroposophical Medicine, and a new form of Eurhythmy.

Even though Steiner died nearly one hundred years ago, in 1925, his followers have uploaded onto the internet over 6,000 documents, mostly consisting of records of his lectures. He was able to bring forth deep insight into just about every known subject. Steiner claimed to obtain his knowledge by using clairvoyance. He described clairvoyance as an ability to see events taking place in whatever location and time he chose to examine.

Dr. Ernst Katz (1913–2009) was a well-known teacher of Steiner's Anthroposophy. In 1990, Katz told me that Steiner personally introduced him to the cosmology at a very early age. Then he shared with me what he had learned by presenting a detailed explanation of the cosmology which starts before the beginning of time and goes to the end of time.

Steiner's cosmology includes several key features that provide explanations for many perplexing issues humanity has been wrestling with for millennia. Once I opened my mind wide enough to sincerely consider this cosmology and its implications, I found that it made sense out of infuriating problems that humanity has grappled with for thousands of years. With an understanding of why such issues exist, I've become better able to accept reality as it is. Moreover, acceptance of life as it is, is a key to happiness.

"Happiness can exist only in acceptance."
—George Orwell (1903–1950) novelist

MY SOUL'S ADDITIONS TO THE COSMOLOGY

In addition to the details that Dr. Katz shared with me in 1990, my Soul has guided me to add to the cosmology. For example, the idea in which the One-Who-Is-All uses Triality to form the physical/astral universe came to me intuitively. Over the 29 years that have passed since Dr. Katz shared the cosmology with me, I've learned much from my Superconscious-Soul regarding the cosmology.

To clarify the source of specific information shared throughout the book, I make an effort to point out when something came from Dr. Katz's explanation of Steiner's cosmology. Especially when that particular piece of the puzzle is unusual and/or important.

Finally, the detailed explanations and discussions come from my Soul. In addition to Triality, the model of human consciousness that's introduced in the next chapter came to me intuitively.

Chapter 7
Head–Heart–Gut
Triality of Human Consciousness

During the vision quest that I shared earlier in Chapter 3, my Soul presented to me a three-part model of human consciousness. Later, via additional inquiries, my Soul provided the details that resulted in the Triality model of human consciousness presented here.

The intellectual conscious-mind in the head is our masculine polarity. The emotional subconscious-mind in the gut is the feminine polarity. The Quintessential Core of the Triality, the most important portion of human consciousness, the Superconscious-Soul, resides in the heart.

Human Consciousness
Head-Heart-Gut
Triality

Head — **Conscious Mind**
masculine polarity

Heart — **Superconscious Soul**
Divine Wholeness
masculine & feminine
polarities combined

Gut — **Subconscious Mind**
feminine polarity

This head-heart-gut arrangement of consciousness is a key part of the message shared throughout this book. Along with the Consciousness-Origin Cosmology, this arrangement of consciousness supports the thesis of the book and fits with the tools and techniques that are shared later in **Part 3**.

ANCIENT SUPPORT

The only closely aligned support I've found for the Triality model of consciousness proposed here comes from Hawaiian kahuna and the Native American Hopi people. The ancient Hopi Tiponi Tablet shown on the right offers pictorial support for the head-heart-gut model.

That sacred Tablet is kept hidden. However, after I shared an early draft of this book with the Hopi elder who kept it hidden, he retrieved the Tablet from its hiding place and placed it in my hands. I was very surprised to see the obvious head, an opening with intestines symbolizing a gut, and a center-mark that is underlined. The Hopi are dedicated to following their hearts, so the center-mark must represent the divine consciousness in the heart.

Later, in Chapter 23: Support from Hopiland, Hawai'i and Mu, I'll share much more about this Tablet. For now, I'll present some modern support for the Triality of human consciousness theory.

MODERN EMERGING SUPPORT

Eighteen years have passed since my Soul first revealed the head-heart-gut human consciousness model to me. Over those years, I've come to believe that this model is the most accurate and comprehensive theory of human consciousness available. Even though it may be far afield from the popular head-brain theory, recent progress is leading some scientists to add the heart and gut regions to their human consciousness models. Significant support has emerged while I've been investigating consciousness and writing this book. Chapter 1 contained some examples pertaining to the heart. Support for the gut is shared in the next section.

The tides are turning. Consciousness is reemerging as a foundation of reality. The gut and the heart are being reconsidered as important parts of human consciousness. Ancient wisdom is being rediscovered to hold truths that had been recklessly tossed aside when materialistic science became the dominant paradigm.

The fact that human consciousness remains open to debate leaves the door open for this head-heart-gut model to be presented, so I'll continue.

TRIALITY OF CONSCIOUSNESS INTRODUCTION

Everyone is aware of the conscious-mind in the head. Even so, I need to clarify that the Triality of human consciousness model proposes that this upper mind is intellectual and contains the ego; the conscious part of the human that thinks of itself as "I." To emphasize this, I often refer to the conscious-mind as the ego-mind, using these two terms interchangeably.

The emotional subconscious-mind is located down in the gut. This subconscious gut-mind resides in the enteric nervous system. This gastrointestinal neurological network has been found to process as many, or more, neurotransmissions as the head-brain, making the idea of a consciousness residing in the human gut quite reasonable.

In support of this, the highly respected periodical *Scientific American* published Justin and Erica Sonnenburg's article "Gut Feelings—the 'Second Brain' in Our Gastrointestinal Systems," dated May 1, 2015. The authors explain that the gut-mind influences the head-brain through bidirectional communication. This gut-mind can be physically identified as a massive neurological network, the enteric-nervous system, making it similar to the brain in the head.

A growing number of people are claiming that our emotions and gut-intuition come from this gut-mind. Beyond this, I discovered some sources that claim long-term memory is stored in the gut-mind. Even so, in my Triality model, the memories are not physically stored. Instead, the nonphysical emotional consciousness that resides in the gut holds the long-term memories.

This lower portion of consciousness is often blamed for many of humanity's challenges and difficulties. This is because society has traditionally revered intelligence while associating irrational emotions with problems. There are certainly some people who see it the other way around, but historically many of humanity's ills have been attributed to the irrational, emotional subconscious.

In spite of that, the subconscious has recently experienced a comeback, as emotional intelligence has developed into an important branch of modern psychology.

Based on the renewed respect for the emotional aspect of human consciousness, some people are making an effort to achieve balance between their emotions and their intellect. One school of thought suggests that when the head and gut work together in a cooperative way, the person is able to function more effectively and experience more joy in their lives.

Nonetheless, if a Superconscious-Soul actually resides in the heart, a more direct approach to obtaining balanced wholeness would be to open one's heart and commune with the Soul in the middle. With an open heart, one goes beyond mere balance to divine wholeness.

The third and most important part of this Triality model of human consciousness is the Quintessential Core of human consciousness—the Soul. This central component resides in the *Heart-Center* and contains both emotional and intellectual aspects of consciousness, woven together to form a divinely wise Superconscious-Soul.

In Chapter 1, the Superconscious-Soul was shown to be the most magnificent part of human consciousness. Then, in the Triality chapter, the Beneficence of the Quintessential Core principle was introduced. This feature of Triality predicts that beneficial properties are found in the central component which aligns with the Soul's divine qualities of infallibility and knowledge of the future. Additionally, the elusive nature of the Quintessential Core is consistent with the way the human Soul has eluded attempts to locate it or even determine, for certain, that it actually exists.

On the other hand, the conscious- and subconscious-minds reside in well-known neurological networks located in the head and gut, respectively. When these parts of the human body are dissected and analyzed microscopically, biologists find material and structures that have become associated with consciousness, making these portions of our consciousness more in alignment with the materialistic model that associates consciousness with neurological networks.

The way the head and gut polarities are easily noticeable while the Soul is elusive, fits the feature of Triality that predicts the polarities draw more attention than the central core. Additionally, the duality that exists between the head and gut portions of consciousness fits the Triality model.

When scientists examine the Heart-Center what they find doesn't appear to be an appropriate location for any kind of mind, let alone a superconscious-mind. Even so, it's a great place to hide the Soul—right under our nose!

WEAVING THE MODEL INTO THE COSMOLOGY AND REALITY

With this model of human consciousness introduced, the remainder of this chapter weaves together:

- the Triality model of human consciousness;
- known neurological systems;
- human fetal development; and
- the Consciousness-Origin Cosmology.

In the following pages, you'll see how all of these fit together in an astonishingly elegant way.

According to the Consciousness-Origin Cosmology, the personalities or mini-Ones portioned out before the universe was formed are repurposed by employing them as human Souls. These are the portions of consciousness that the One originally distilled out of itself. They're the mini-One personalities that were able to know all about each other through the continuum of the One by using their empathic and telepathic abilities. Those supernatural abilities enabled these powerful mini-Ones to know all about one another preventing the mini-Ones from being mysterious to each other.

Even though that initial experiment failed to fulfill the One's desire to find out how it feels to meet a mysterious other, later, once the universe had been formed and humans were developed through the evolutionary process outlined in the previous chapter, each mini-One personality was placed in a human's heart to be their divine Soul—a dedicated guardian that guides its human being from conception throughout the person's entire life.

THE SOUL'S INVOLVEMENT IN FETAL DEVELOPMENT

My Soul advised me that the Soul arrives in the mother's womb at the moment of conception. This is when the male sperm enters the female egg, and their union forms the zygote: the first embryonic stem cell. A stem cell is a generic cell that can transform into any of over 220 specialized types of cells.

Shortly after the zygote is formed, it divides into two stem cells using simple asexual cell division. This process includes making a copy of the DNA molecule. When the zygote divides into two stem cells, one retains the original DNA molecule, while the other one gets the copy. Each of these cells soon divide again producing four stem cells. This process continues to produce more and more cells that are all essentially identical to the original zygote.

Apart from any rare copying errors, all embryonic stem cells are nearly perfect duplicates with **exactly identical DNA.**

Even though all stem cells begin with the same DNA instructions imbedded in them, each one can transform into any one of over 220 different types of cells. Given this situation, biologists are left with a looming question: How does one stem cell know what type of specific cell it should become to construct a human: a skin cell, a muscle cell, or one of the other 218 possibilities?

All the cells are essentially identical, with identical DNA instructions. Therefore, something must be directing each individual stem cell to transform into the appropriate type of cell and, over time, form an organism with features fitting the DNA instructions.

So, what is guiding this process called cell differentiation?

So far, this question has remained inadequately answered by the materialistic perspective—making what drives stem cell differentiation—a biological mystery.

My Soul informed me that a mini-One Soul enters the mother's womb at the moment of conception, deciphers the DNA, and then guides the process of stem cell differentiation to construct the fetus in accordance with the DNA outline. This potentially solves the mystery of what guides stem cell differentiation.

To show how this proposal fits reality quite well, let's take a slightly deeper look into the process of human fetal development. According to the Mayo Clinic's website, the first organ to become fully developed in a human fetus is the heart. Secondly, the gut develops, and thirdly, the brain. Afterwards, the arms, legs, ears, eyes, and eventually everything else is formed.

Appropriately, the three parts of the human being that are proposed to contain consciousness develop first. Furthermore, of those three centers of consciousness, the heart is the first to be completed.

If the Soul is in charge of the process, it makes sense that it would build its home first. Additionally, if consciousness is truly the foundation of everything, it also makes sense that the other two centers of consciousness would be the second and third components to be formed and become operational during the fetal development process.

While these physical parts are developing in the womb, my Soul informed me that a parallel process is taking place in the realm of consciousness, as described in the next section.

FORMING THE TRIALITY OF CONSCIOUSNESS

First, the Soul places itself in the Heart-Center to settle into its residence.

Next, the Soul condenses the essence of its own consciousness into a small portion of itself using the same process the One used to make the mini-One Soul. Earlier, in Chapter 5, I described how the One-Who-Is-All condensed out of itself a small portion of consciousness to form each mini-One personality. Now during fetal development, the Soul produces a mini-soul.

Next, the Soul divides the mini-soul into two halves: an emotional memory-half and an intellectual ego-half.

Finally, the Soul places the emotional-half in the gut's enteric nervous system, and the intellectual-half up in the head-brain's neocortex. With all three portions of consciousness in place, the head-heart-gut Triality of human consciousness arrangement is complete.

The sequence of events that takes place in the physical realm has been well studied and documented by medical researchers. A thorough description can be found on the Mayo Clinic website (www.mayoclinic.org). Remarkably, the physical sequence of development fits the Triality development process. The central wholeness—the heart—comes first. Then, the opposite endpoints—the head and gut—emerge from the Heart-Center.

This fits the head-heart-gut Triality of human consciousness theory in which the Quintessential Core forms the dualistic polarities out of itself.

In the case of reincarnation, a Soul reuses the head and gut portions of consciousness from a previous incarnation. Between lives, the conscious- and subconscious-minds reside in an astral body waiting for and possibly preparing for a future incarnation.

It's helpful to be aware of the recent advancement in DNA research showing that DNA isn't a precise "blueprint" that dictates a specific creature. For example, we now know that a caterpillar and the butterfly that it becomes through metamorphosis both contain exactly the same DNA.

Moreover, physical brain neurology can transform in just hours when the same thoughts are contemplated repeatedly. This demonstrates how consciousness can affect genetic expression.

HOW DOES THE BRAIN FIT INTO THE MODEL?

Questions that arise at this juncture include: How does the physical brain fit into this theory? Why does the brain exist? If consciousness exists without a brain, then what's the purpose of the brain?

My Soul guided me to see how the physical brain is a complex receptacle, or a jillion pin connector, so to speak. It's similar to the multi-pin connector that a computer motherboard plugs into, physically connecting the computer's Central Processing Unit with the screen, keyboard, trackpad, hard drive, speakers, etc.

In the case of the human brain, the conscious-mind plugs in to the jillion pin connector-brain by being located inside the neocortex. In this physical location, the portion of intellectual consciousness that is the conscious-mind connects to the neurological network of the human body. Once plugged in, the ego-mind gains the ability to animate the human body and receive signals from the five senses.

In a similar way, the subconscious-mind is placed in the gut enteric nervous system to play an emotional memory role. On top of that, the gut portion of consciousness manages many of the internal bodily functions involving organs, digestion, etc.

Viewed this way, the neurological system is essentially a complex wiring harness with two very elaborate jillion pin connectors: the head-brain's neocortex and the gut enteric nervous system. Rather than using copper wires, the human body uses living neurons.

The intellectual portion of consciousness located in the neocortex of the brain becomes the rational intellectual conscious-mind, while the emotional portion in the gut enteric nervous system becomes the irrational emotional subconscious-mind. Both plug into their respective "jillion pin receptacles" to operate the body and experience being a human.

SUPPORT FOR THIS THEORY

When I was involved in an IAC astral travel workshop, the female instructor shared an important personal experience that took place when she was married.

One night when her husband was asleep next to her, she used an astral traveling method to separate her astral body from her physical body. Once flying around the bedroom in her astral body she noticed that her husband's astral body was hovering up above his physical body indicating that he was asleep. Being curious about how it would feel to have a man's body, she used her mind to fly her astral body into her husband's physical body. Once inside she could feel the sensations of being in a man's body. On top of that she explained that she could control his arms and other parts of his body using her mind.

This supports the idea that the brain is a receptacle or connector that any conscious-mind can plug into by simply locating itself in the head. Once plugged in, the conscious-mind is able to control the body and sense the sensations associated with all its parts.

NEUROLOGICAL DAMAGE

Next, let's consider the effect of physical neurological damage. If an accident, an infection, or some other influence damages part of the neurological network, then the consciousness that uses that damaged part will not be able to operate or receive inputs from the part of the physical body that's connected to the damaged portion of the network.

Consciousness is not physical; it can't be damaged by the physical realm, but the neurological receptacles, as well as other parts of the neurological system, can be physically damaged. Therefore, paralysis and other neurological issues can be caused by physical damage.

THE SOUL'S ROLE AS A DIVINE GUARDIAN

The Soul that resides in the heart is a genius super-consciousness that doesn't control the body, per se. It's a guardian that oversees the human, strategically guiding its "children," the head and gut minds, from the Quintessential Core of the Triality, the heart. The Soul doesn't need a neurological receptacle where it resides, because the head and gut minds engage and operate what they view as their human body. These two minds are plugged into the neurological control network via the jillion pin receptacles (or brains) they reside in.

On the other hand, even though the Soul is the largest and most important portion of consciousness in a human, it plays the role of a self-restrained guardian watching its "children," the head and gut minds, as they operate the body and experience being alive.

This arrangement causes the human ego-mind up in the head-brain to believe it has free will. From an operational point of view, the head and gut are in control of the body, and of the two, the ego-mind in the head is the final decision-maker. The Soul is always present, residing in the heart, although the head and gut minds don't need to be aware of the Soul's presence. The Soul can remain unnoticed, observing and guiding from within in a subtle but important way.

In this arrangement, the head and gut are made of one-half of a small portion of consciousness. The small size and, more importantly, the incompleteness of each half renders humans feeble, in accordance with the *Feebleness of Incompleteness* principle.

THE FEEBLENESS OF INCOMPLETENESS

The *Feebleness of Incompleteness* principle captures an important reality that my Soul revealed to me:

When something is missing an important component, the incompleteness makes that thing feeble.

For example, a car without an engine is feeble. The engine is an important part of the car, and without it, the car doesn't do its job very well. The car can be pushed around and steered, but it's unable to propel itself. If it had all its important parts, then, in accordance with the Supreme Power of Wholeness principle, the car would have the ability to function well. However, when the engine is missing from the car, the Feebleness of Incompleteness principle correctly predicts that the car will be feeble.

The Soul is a whole consciousness with intellect and emotions. Both of these are important components of consciousness. The conscious-mind is primarily intellectual, and lacks sufficient emotional capacity to make it whole. By being incomplete, the Feebleness of Incompleteness principle predicts that the conscious-mind will be feeble. The subconscious-mind in the gut is also incomplete; it's mostly emotional and lacks sufficient intellectual capacity to be complete, rendering it feeble, as well.

The feebleness of the two operational portions of human consciousness causes humans to be inherently feeble-minded. This assessment is based on comparing our consciousness to a whole consciousness like the Soul, or the One, which are superconscious.

An important feature of our feebleness is gullibility. Human gullibility is obvious to anyone who has spent time with young children. Young children, having very feeble minds, can be tricked into believing almost anything—Santa Claus, the Tooth Fairy, etc. When we grow up, our minds mature to become less feeble and, consequently, less gullible. Nonetheless, we can still be fooled quite easily. Con artists make fortunes by taking advantage of human gullibility.

In terms of the Consciousness-Origin Cosmology, human gullibility makes it possible for humans to be maneuvered into believing that we're **individuals**. Even though the truth is that we're all part of the One, human gullibility makes us able to buy into the illusion of individuality. Then, with an individualistic perspective we're able to accomplish the purpose of the universe—meeting mysterious others.

To set up this ruse, we have been given three separate portions of consciousness. The two operational portions are intentionally very small, and split to make us gullible enough to believe we're individuals. Then, as individuals, we're able to accomplish the purpose of the universe. Meanwhile, the Soul rides along in our hearts to guard and assist us throughout our lives.

With their Supreme Power of Wholeness, Souls are, by far, the most capable portion of human consciousness. Souls know the game plan, and are fully aware that everything is part of the One. Souls also know that the entire universe is a stage to explore meeting **mysterious** others. Their divine knowledge, wisdom, and supernatural abilities like telepathy and empathy prevent Souls from being able to experience being an individual. Instead, Souls are guardians and advisors, hidden in our hearts, while our feeble conscious- and subconscious-minds accomplish the goal of the universe.

It's ironic that feebleness is needed to accomplish the goal of the universe. Still, it's quite fitting that humanity has many stories in which a feeble underdog saves the day. In those stories, the underdog manages to arrive in the right place at the right time to be the hero. With a big heart, the hero's Soul had guided the underdog intuitively. By listening to the Soul's guidance these underdog heroes really exist.

Underdog stories often have an anti-hero who arrogantly follows his ego-mind. That character puts on a good show, but lacks the all-important heart connection. The way the underdog courageously saves the day by following their heart, leaves me with a tear in my eye and a sense that a deep truth was portrayed by the story.

THE POWER OF THE INTELLECT IS A MISCONCEPTION

In male dominated civilization, a popular misconception glorifies the masculine intellect that resides in the head. There are many sources that claim pure intellect is the most powerful form of consciousness. These deceptive sources misguide people by encouraging them to focus on their intellect while repressing the emotional gut and its sensual desires that are associated with excessive indulgence in sensual pleasures.

By using the overly simplified dualistic view of reality, the masculine intellect versus the feminine emotions are mistakenly thought to be a simple duality. This dualistic view leads to the mistake of believing that only two options exist, rational intellect on one hand and irrational emotions on the other. Since men have been in power for millennia they claim their polarity is superior. Going even further, pure intellect is mistakenly claimed to be the ideal.

By upgrading the duality of intellect versus emotions into a Triality, the Quintessential Core of balanced wholeness residing in the middle is revealed. Our central Soul possesses divine wisdom fitting with the Beneficence of the Quintessential Core principle.

Thus, humans must open their hearts and follow their hearts to tap into the divine wisdom that is provided by a whole portion of consciousness, one with balanced portions of emotions and intellect woven together—the Superconscious-Soul.

SOULS WORK TOGETHER

To facilitate the process of meeting mysterious others, Souls communicate with each other behind the scenes and guide interpersonal interactions in a coordinated way. To provide Souls with the power to do their job, each Soul has control over its human's desires.

The way this works was discussed earlier, but I'll review the theory briefly. By possessing knowledge of the future, and with the ability to induce emotional chemistry production with EMF signals, the Soul has the tools to intercede and control their human's emotional response to particular situations. The personality changes that occur in heart transplant recipients show that the new heart contains a new

Soul with its own personality. This new Soul impresses its personality onto the recipient of the heart that contains it.

By having control over human desires, Souls possess an exceedingly powerful tool that they can use to guide human destiny.

Even though ego-minds have free will to make their own decisions, those decisions are based on personal desires, which are controlled by the Souls. This gives Souls the power to collectively direct the human drama we call life.

With Souls in control of human desires, the illusion of individuality is not compromised. People simply don't know where their desires come from. We must simply accept the reality that we have the desires that we have.

Some people have developed techniques to change or control human desires. These methods are used by people who would like to change their desires. These techniques are often based on the theory that the subconscious-mind is responsible for human desires. The techniques claim to reprogram the subconscious-mind, and thereby change the desires.

In spite of that theory, the heart transplant examples shared in Chapter 1 clearly show that the Superconscious-Soul in the heart is in control of our desires. If our Superconscious-Soul is as magnificent as it appears to be, then tampering with one's desires seems inappropriate, and most likely impossible.

The feeble conscious-mind ought to follow the Soul's guidance. As Einstein put it: "The intuitive mind is a sacred gift and the rational mind is a faithful servant."

In some cases, the Soul might be willing to adjust certain desires to appease the conscious-mind. The resulting changes could mislead some people into believing that the method they're using to control their desires works.

Personally, I side with Einstein, and prefer to surrender to and serve the Soul. Aligning with the Soul is a fundamental part of the Way-of-the-Heart path.

Another tool Souls use to guide humans is intuition. By sending ideas up into the conscious-mind, Souls can provide suggestions without violating one's free will. Their advice is just that: advice. The conscious-mind can choose to accept the suggestion or ignore it. My experience has taught me that it's best to follow my Soul's intuitive guidance.

If what I've proposed above is accurate, then Souls are working behind the scenes, guiding all of humanity through desires and intuition. There may be additional ways for Souls to guide us—control mechanisms that I'm not aware of. Nonetheless, with the two methods discussed here, Superconscious-Souls have the ability to guide humans as if we are finger puppets. By endeavoring to fulfill our desires, and by following our intuition, we're playing roles that are covertly orchestrated by the divine Superconscious-Souls in our hearts.

A positive way to see our roles is to imagine humans as puppets on the fingertips of the One-Who-Is-All. As the One reaches out to explore how it feels to meet mysterious others, we're the leading-edge pioneers who meet others and have the feelings that arise.

I've found it best to accept my puppet-like role and surrender to my Soul. This makes my life extraordinarily easy and joyful. The Way-of-the-Heart is nearly effortless. Additionally, the willing follower is blessed with happiness and serendipitous synchronicities that make one's life miraculous. Being a finger puppet for the One is an honor.

Conversely, when the conscious-mind takes responsibility for every step, life becomes overwhelmingly difficult and painful.

Once I realized how often my Soul guides me out of trouble, I began noticing that my ego-mind is feebler than I would have thought possible. Several times a day I notice that I've made a silly mistake—a mistake that indicates a very feeble mind. If I didn't follow my heart, my life would be a series of blunders and I would appear to be dumb. Gratefully, my Soul has my back. With my Soul's assistance, my foolish antics appear funny, causing me to laugh at myself quite often.

Miraculously, in spite of my feeble mind, by following my Soul's guidance people often tell me that I'm a genius. I explain to them that my Soul is the genius and my ego-mind is actually an idiot. I only appear to be a genius because I open and follow my heart.

WHY QUINTESSENTIAL CORES DISAPPEAR

Earlier, when I introduced the Triality model, I mentioned that I'd explain why the Quintessential Core of a Triality is so elusive. Now that sufficient background has been shared, I can simply state that Quintessential Cores elude us to facilitate the illusion of individuality.

The opposing polarities that persist when the Quintessential Core fades into the shadows facilitates the separation needed for people to be tricked into believing they're individuals.

By helping to form the illusion of individuality, Trialities are indispensable in accomplishing the purpose of the universe. The One cleverly developed Trialities to produce billions of individual humans who effortlessly experience meeting one another as mysterious others.

IS THIS STUFF TOP SECRET?

Much of what has been presented in this chapter may appear to be intentionally hidden. You might be wondering: Is it appropriate to know about these hidden secrets? And, if so, are there any benefits to knowing about: the Triality of human consciousness; the realm of pure consciousness; the astral realm; and elusive Quintessential Cores?

First of all, the notion of a Soul residing in the human heart has existed forever. Resurrecting this ancient wisdom that was foolishly discarded by modern science isn't uncovering what was intended to be hidden. Instead, it's merely recovering what was tossed aside when reality was turned upside-down.

Returning consciousness to its rightful place, the foundation of the universe, revives our awareness of the sacred flames of consciousness that animate all life. Flipping reality right-side-up brings the One-Who-Is-All back into our lives.

Being aware of the Triality of human consciousness provides a simple map of where your three portions of consciousness are located and what characteristics each one has. This clearer understanding of yourself can help you develop a deeper and fuller relationship with your gut and your Soul. As the relationship with your inner divine guardian blossoms, your most authentic self will naturally emerge. This is because the fullest expression of your *True-Self* is contained in your Soul, and when you develop a solid relationship with your Soul, it will support you in a more authentic and fulfilling way.

Conversely, when you're not aware of the Triality arrangement, much of who you are can easily remain hidden and misunderstood. You may struggle with balance, get stuck in your head or in your gut, and fail to reveal your True-Self. Wonderful parts of your most authentic self may remain hidden in your heart. The Holy Grail of life, love, and happiness may give you clues. Still, it's up to you to tune in, notice them and follow the guidance. When you're aware of where to tune into, you can more effectively follow your Soul's guidance.

Another way that the Triality model of consciousness is helpful is in how it provides a foundation for the tools presented in **Part 3**. These tools can help you commune with your Soul, and through the connection that develops, you can bring out wonderful, hidden parts of yourself that will enable you to have a much more enjoyable life.

Most importantly, by learning to live in a more balanced way—communing with your Soul—you'll fulfill your role in the grand play of life more effectively than ever before. The process is one of slowing down the mind, being grateful, and surrendering. Certainly, you'll find it helpful to know where to direct your gratitude and what you're surrendering to.

Finally, by being aware of the realm of pure consciousness and the astral realm, supernatural and paranormal events can become reasonably easy to understand. For people who make a hobby out of investigating these types of phenomenon, having a clearer way to understand them could free up time for those people to spend on their interpersonal relationships.

Now that the Head-Heart-Gut Triality of human consciousness has been shared, the next chapter will show how all three portions of consciousness are represented in the head.

Chapter 8
It All Comes Together in the Head

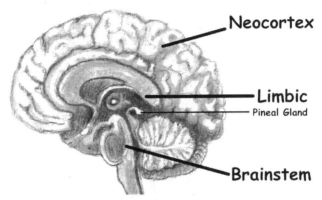

Although each of the three portions of human consciousness reside in separate locations (head-heart-gut), my Soul showed me how they all convene in the head. This part of the head-heart-gut theory is based on the three-layers illustrated in the diagram above.

Paul MacLean developed a Triune-Brain Theory that uses the same three layers. Despite that similarity, his theory was otherwise completely different.

Starting at the top, with the neocortex, I'll explain how each layer is linked with one of the three portions of consciousness. Additionally, I'll show how this three-layer system, plus a few other features of human anatomy, enable all three portions of consciousness to work together in the head.

This part of the head-heart-gut theory fits with the importance modern science has placed on the head-brain. However, by including the Soul and the gut-mind, this theory introduces essential portions of consciousness that are missing in the popular head-brain theory.

NEOCORTEX: INTELLECTUAL CONSCIOUS EGO-MIND

In this theory, the upper layer, labeled the neocortex, is the residence of the conscious-mind, which I also refer to as the ego-mind.

This portion has a rational, intellectually focused nature. Additionally, it possesses short-term memory.

This prominent portion of human consciousness is the ego-self, the component that commonly uses the word "I" to identify itself.

Because the ego-mind resides in the head while the other two portions of consciousness reside elsewhere, this upper layer is the largest of the three layers. The nonresident portions of consciousness use the limbic layer and the brainstem to communicate with the conscious-mind in the neocortex.

The ego-mind makes final decisions giving it a sense of free will. The consequences of the ego-mind's choices can have profound effects on the health and happiness of a person throughout their life.

BRAINSTEM: EMOTIONAL SUBCONSCIOUS–MIND

The brainstem is physically connected to the gut's enteric nervous system via the autonomic nervous system that travels along the spine. This neurological superhighway is a bundle of hundreds of millions of neurons that provides bi-directional communication between the conscious-mind in the neocortex and the subconscious-mind in the gut.

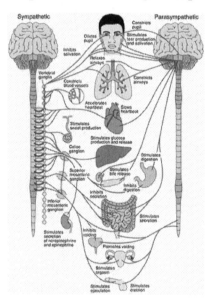

Additionally, this complex nervous system branches out along the way to connect to organs and muscles throughout the body, providing the head and gut minds with neurological connections to the entire body.

The basic idea is simple: a "wiring harness" connects the gut and head portions of consciousness together so they can interact with one another and control all the physical aspects of the body.

Some neurons branch out into every part of the physical body to provide the head and gut minds with a continuous supply of sensory information making them aware of specific sensations, including touch, sight, sound, taste, and aromas.

As a whole, this neuro-superhighway enables the head and gut to share control and awareness of the entire human body.

When awake, a person's conscious-mind (in the head) takes control of the body in many ways, while the gut-mind is always dealing with physical processes related to digestion, physical coordination, etc. For instance, it's quite fitting that many practitioners of martial arts and highly skilled athletes are aware of the gut being a focal point of physical power. By breathing deeply into the gut region, and tuning into this lower tantien (focus of essence), a person becomes able to execute physical movements more skillfully and with greater power.

Returning to the physiology, the lower layer of the brain (the brainstem) contains glands that produce psychoactive chemicals that invoke emotional feelings in the conscious-mind. To share its feelings with the conscious-mind, the gut-mind controls the production of these psychoactive chemicals via the neurological superhighway that travels up the spine.

To avoid any confusion, as discussed in Chapter 1, these glands can also be activated by the Superconscious-Soul, using EMFs. This alternate EMF remote-control pathway is similar to a Bluetooth interface that provides the Soul wireless control of the same glands.

The final issue regarding the gut is how its emotional character, and the conscious-mind's intellectual character, form a duality that can become a source of discord between these polar opposites of consciousness. When the head ignores the gut, or acts in defiance of the gut's feelings, disharmony can develop. When unresolved, the battle can grow into debilitating psychological issues.

In some cases, when the conscious-mind remains aloof, the subconscious-mind in the gut may introduce physical ailments into the body in an attempt to push the ego-mind in the head to address the emotional issue that is being ignored. Although the ego-mind has control over the waking activities of the human being, the gut-mind has more control over the internal bodily functions. Accordingly, the subconscious-mind in the gut can introduce physical ailments that interfere with the ego-mind's choices.

These internal battles can initially appear as minor annoyances. In more severe cases they can become disabling and destroy a person's life, stripping them of their health and happiness. In some cases, the conscious-mind can remain oblivious of the inner conflict. In **Part 3**, a method is provided to deal with these important, and often difficult to resolve, issues that don't appear to have a cause.

The main idea presented in this section is how the head and gut minds work together in a collaborative way, facilitated by the complex neurological pathway that travels along the spine and branches out into the entire body. Furthermore, this neurological pathway gives the gut-mind the ability to share its emotions with the ego-mind via the glands in the brainstem. This makes the brainstem the official representative of the subconscious gut-mind up in the head.

LIMBIC: SUPERCONSCIOUS–SOUL

My Soul intuitively informed me that the limbic layer is associated with the Superconscious-Soul residing in the Heart-Center.

A key component of this layer is the pineal gland (see illustration at the beginning of this chapter). This pea-sized gland is central and singular, unlike all other features of the brain, making it remarkably unique. An even more unusual feature of this gland is that it has been determined to be a small eyeball. It has a lens and receptors that are similar to the other two normal eyes. The receptors of this third inner eye are neurologically wired to the visual cortex, just like the two normal eyes on our face.

An obvious question is: What could this third eye be looking at from its concealed location in the center of the head?

In Chapter 1, I presented research that had discovered low frequency EMFs traveling from the top of the heart up into the middle of the head when the infallible voice speaks in the head. Visible light is a type of EMF that comprises a narrow range of frequencies located near the middle of the very wide spectrum of EMF frequencies. The EMF signals that come from the heart are a much lower frequency of the same form of energy. Since this third eye is much smaller in size, plus the receptors are considerably different, it could be designed to receive the low frequency EMFs that come up from the heart.

In support of that, there are ancient spiritual theories that claim the Soul in the heart is sending messages that we call intuition up into the conscious-mind in the head via the pineal gland eye. Consequently, this third eye has been called the "heart eye" by some.

Apparently, Plato agrees:

"...in every man, there is an eye of the soul, which...is more precious far than ten thousand bodily eyes, for by it alone is truth seen."

—Plato (425 BC–347 BC) philosopher

On top of that, the word "intuition" originates from late Middle English, when it originally meant "denoting spiritual insight or immediate spiritual communication." This old definition indicates that intuition originally identified communication from a spirit.

My Soul informed me that the spirit responsible for intuition is the Superconscious-Soul, the divine spirit or consciousness that resides in the heart.

Let's dig deeper into the processing of intuitive messages.

In the case of a picture, the pineal gland's receptors are wired directly to the visual cortex in the occipital lobe of the brain. Accordingly, pictures are handled by the visual cortex just as the normal eye's images are processed. When working on inventions I often see images in my mind that provide geometric solutions to difficult aspects of the invention. These pictorial answers to geometric conundrums appear when my mind is quiet, in the morning, when I'm waking up.

In other non-visual cases, once the pineal gland receives the EMF signal, the pineal gland relays the signal it received to the limbic layer of the brain. This middle limbic layer contains whatever is needed to decode the message and pass it on to the neocortex which physically touches the top of the limbic layer. Those messages arrive as an inner voice, an instructive feeling, or an inner knowing.

The pineal gland is strikingly unique in comparison to other glands and features of the brain. For example, the pineal gland has a direct supply of blood from the heart, unlike most other parts of the brain, which are shielded by the blood-brain barrier.

Another unique feature is how this gland is singular and centered, unlike all other features of the head-brain, which have a left and right hemisphere with mirrored geometry. The singular centered geometry is consistent with the Quintessential Core position the Superconscious-Soul holds in the Triality of human consciousness.

As mentioned earlier, the Soul has the ability to control the production of psychoactive chemicals that affect the emotional chemistry of the conscious-mind. The theoretical mechanism for this capability is that EMFs projected up from the heart induce the glands in the brainstem to distribute the chemicals associated with the particular signal that's issued by the Soul, as discussed in Chapter 1.

This emotional chemistry, plus the intuitive messages that the Superconscious-Soul sends up to the head-brain via the pineal gland, are two examples of divine guidance that come from the Superconscious-Soul in the heart. This theory demystifies divine guidance and makes it a physiological aspect of the human neurological system. Still, the source is an undetectable spirit—the Soul. Even so, the way our physical systems appear to fit with the spiritual components helps to confirm the existence of these undetectable portions of consciousness.

It's important to mention that there are physical, neurological connections that link the physical heart to the complex nervous system. Extensive research claims that these physical nerve connections are used to address matters such as heart rate and blood pressure indicating that this nerve pathway is used to deal with the muscular heart's blood-pumping role, and don't appear to be involved with the Soul that resides in the Heart-Center. Additional research could determine otherwise.

A final and very important part of the communication system used by the Soul is its telepathic and empathetic abilities. These supernatural abilities provide the Soul with full awareness of all the thoughts and emotions that are occurring in the head and gut minds. By remaining aware of a person's thoughts and feelings, the Soul is able to play its role of divine guardian, advising and guiding the person in a way that's timely and appropriate.

The Superconscious-Soul is able to connect with the head and gut minds via the continuum of consciousness that lies at the foundation of the universe, woven into the fabric of the entire universe. This pathway is available to the Soul because it contains a whole portion of consciousness—one that includes emotions and intellect combined. Given this wholeness, the Supreme Power of Wholeness principle predicts that the Soul possesses divine powers which include access to the continuum of consciousness. With that access, the Soul obtains telepathic and empathetic abilities.

The head and gut are both incomplete, causing them to suffer from the Feebleness of Incompleteness principle. This leaves them unable to access the continuum of consciousness directly. Without access, our conscious- and subconscious-minds don't have telepathic or empathetic abilities. In spite of that, the Soul can connect with other Souls to obtain thoughts and emotions from other people. Then, as it sees fit, the Soul can choose to share some of what it gathers with the conscious- and subconscious-minds of the human it inhabits. This can indirectly provide some people with varying degrees of telepathic and empathetic abilities.

In support of the idea that the Soul is aware of the thoughts and emotions of the head and gut minds, I've noticed that my intuition arrives in response to my thoughts and feelings instantly and appropriately. For example, when I contemplate a question in my mind, the answer to that question often pops up instantly. There are special cases involving creative ideas that take more time to arrive, but those details will be discussed later, in **Part 3**.

In addition to the way the Soul influences the conscious-mind in the head, the Soul can, at times, provide assistance in performing physical activities with masterful skill. Unexpectedly, the assistance with physical endeavors is provided through the realm of consciousness, without any physical pathway. In order to assist the head and gut minds, the Soul expands itself—growing in size—beyond the heart to encompass the head- and gut-minds and upgrade their abilities to achieve masterful results.

This occurs when a person "puts their heart into it!"

The Soul's assistance is what separates gifted masters from people with fine skills—people who have developed their abilities through practice, but don't put their heart into it. A technique for reaching beyond fine skills to achieve mastery is presented in **Part 3**.

Now that the head-heart-gut Triality theory of human consciousness has been completely shared, the next chapter delves more deeply into the divine inspiration and assistance that comes from our Souls as intuition.

Chapter 9
Intuition from The Soul

Everyone seems to have gut-intuition. At some point in your life, you've probably felt a tightness in your gut that's accompanied by a feeling that something is wrong. This intuitive gut feeling can stop a person in their tracks and cause them to change their path.

Although this type of intuition is important and real, it's not the subject of this chapter. This chapter focuses on the human experience of receiving Soul-intuition, as well as the praise that this type of intuition has been given by great minds.

To avoid any confusion, I'll identify gut-intuition by labeling it gut-intuition. On the other hand, when I use the term intuition alone, I'm referring to intuition from the Soul, not gut-intuition. When I want to emphasize that the Soul is the source, I'll use Soul-intuition.

Soul-intuition is transmitted up from the heart and into the head, delivering an idea that seems to simply pop up in the conscious-mind without being formed by conscious reasoning or emotional feelings.

Intuition: noun;
The ability to understand something immediately, without the need for conscious reasoning: we shall allow our intuition to guide us.
• A thing that one knows or considers likely from instinctive feeling rather than conscious reasoning.
ORIGIN: late Middle English (**denoting spiritual insight or immediate spiritual communication**) [15]

The spirit that's providing an insight through this mysterious type of spiritual communication is the Superconscious-Soul.

A similar word, premonition, is knowledge of the future. Based on a common mix-up between intuition and premonition, plus the fact that premonitions of future events are very rare, many people mistakenly believe that they're not intuitive, even though they are.

To clarify exactly what Soul-intuition is, I offer the following detailed explanation based on my personal experience:

Intuitive messages usually arrive as a thought or feeling.

Here's a hypothetical example: the thought that you ought to call Bruce pops up in your mind even though you hadn't been thinking about Bruce prior to the arrival of this intuitive nudge to call him. Besides, you may not have any need or reason to call Bruce.

Then, if you call Bruce, when he answers he might mention that he was just thinking about you, or that he was just about to call you. Or possibly, for some entirely different reason, your call is quite timely and well-received.

If you have Soul-Intuition then this type of guidance may be popping up very frequently, even if you hadn't noticed. If you follow the guidance, then serendipitous experiences bless your life, making it magically fortuitous. This is how one navigates the Way-of-the-Heart.

In some cases, Soul-intuition can be a feeling. To illustrate this, let's imagine you're on your way to some destination that you go to frequently. As you're traveling, a feeling arises encouraging you to take an alternate route.

If you make that change in course, it might cause you to discover something especially interesting, or it may lead you into a fortuitous encounter with someone. Perhaps you're blessed to have avoided traffic that unexpectedly piled up on the normal route. Or in some other way, a serendipitous synchronicity accompanied the route change.

On other rare occasions, the message can arrive as a voice. This voice is commonly called the internal-dialogue voice. We all use that voice to talk things out in our head.

In spite of how your inner voice is normally used by your conscious-mind in your head, on some rare occasions, this inner voice may speak on its own. You might notice that your conscious-mind didn't think the words that you could "hear" in your head. This is quite different than hearing voices from an external source, or hearing voices that sound different from your inner dialogue voice. This type of Soul-intuition uses the inner voice, that you normally use to work things out in your mind, to deliver an important message in words.

If it's just one or two words, you may not even notice that you didn't think those words yourself. On the other hand, if you are aware that you didn't contemplate those words that you just heard inside your head, the unusual experience may feel startling.

For me, the voice method is quite rare. On most occasions that I recall my intuition arriving as a voice, I was required to respond quickly. For instance, while bicycling at dusk on a road with high-speed truck traffic, I recall hearing in my head, "Get over to the right!" I swerved over to the curb and hugged it as close as I could without hitting it. Seconds later, a big truck flew by so close that I thought I was surely doomed. Fortunately, I was just emotionally shaken. My intuition had guided me to avoid a potentially fatal accident.

Another way Soul-intuition can arrive is pictorially, as an image that appears in the mind's eye. I've worked as an inventor, designer, and builder, among other things. Over the years, I've encountered difficult geometric puzzles that my intellectual conscious-mind couldn't solve. Then, the next morning, as I'm waking up, even though I'm not thinking about the geometric problem that had remained unsolved, I'll see the solution in my mind's eye.

You may be familiar with these types of intuitive experiences.

If so, then when you receive intuitive guidance and don't follow through and do what it guides you to do, then later you might think to yourself, "Darn, I knew I should have done that!"

This is because Soul-intuition is infallible. Discarding, ignoring, or postponing any activities your Soul has intuitively guided you to do is always a mistake. It's always best to follow through and do it. This is one of those very rare situations in which the word "always" is actually appropriate.

"Above all, practice being loyal to your Soul."
—John-Roger Hinkins (1934–2014) author and speaker

DO YOU HAVE SOUL-INTUITION?

If you've had any or all of the intuitive types of experiences shared above, then you have the type of intuition that comes from your Soul in your heart. Intuition and its source, the Superconscious-Soul, are key ingredients for following the Way-of-the-Heart path.

If you can't recall having these intuitive experiences, then you may not have Soul-intuition. If that's the case, then some of what's shared in this book may not fit with your experience of life.

Having interviewed thousands of people over several years, I've discovered that many people don't have Soul-intuition. This causes the lives of intuitive and non-intuitive people to have major differences that will be discussed later.

For now, I'll share the physical condition that blocks Soul-intuition in most people.

WHY PEOPLE DON'T HAVE SOUL-INTUITION

My Soul informed me that a lack of Soul-intuition is caused by calcification of the pineal gland.

In the previous chapter, I explained how Soul-intuition is sent up to the conscious-mind via EMFs that beam up from the top of the heart into the pineal gland to eventually arrive in the conscious-mind.

Given this routing, if the pineal gland is calcified, the message is blocked by the calcium deposits that obscure this eye-like gland's reception. In the next chapter, I'll share a theory that explains how this condition develops. Although the popular theory blames fluoride and diet, my Soul has provided a very different explanation that fits in with the Consciousness-Origin-Cosmology, reality, and spiritual texts.

For non-intuitive people who would like to reactivate their intuition, I provide a decalcification method near the end of Chapter 19.

As I mentioned earlier, there's also gut-intuition, which everyone seems to have. This type of intuition arrives as an unsettling emotional feeling that something is amiss, accompanied by a noticeable tightness or discomfort in the gut. The source of gut-intuition and the physical pathway it uses to reach the conscious-mind in the head are completely different from Soul-intuition.

Specifically, gut-intuition originates in the emotional gut-mind. The sensation of tightness in the gut grabs the conscious-mind's attention. Additionally, the gut-mind uses the neurological-superhighway that follows the spine up to the brainstem to cause chemicals to be produced by glands located in the brainstem. Those chemicals induce feelings of anxiety or fear in the conscious-mind. Consequently, everyone, even those with pineal gland calcification have gut-intuition which comes from the gut-mind and follows its own pathway.

Although many people recommend following gut-intuition and that is available to everyone, the gut-mind is just as feeble as the head-mind. Still, the gut-minds feelings should be taken into consideration.

What's most important is to follow Soul-intuition, if you have it.

RESPECT FOR SOUL-INTUITION

I've found that many great minds have expressed their respect for intuition, our heart, and Soul. Earlier, I shared the following quotes from Albert Einstein. His fame is so closely aligned with genius, I've chosen to present those quotes again here:

"The state-of-mind which enables a man to do work of this kind [theoretical physics], is akin to that of the religious worshipper or the lover; the daily effort comes from no deliberate intention or program, but straight from the heart."

"The intuitive mind is a sacred gift and the rational mind is a faithful servant. We have created a society that honors the servant and has forgotten the gift."

"The intellect has little to do on the road to discovery. There comes a leap in consciousness, call it intuition or what you will, and the solution comes to you and you don't know how or why."

—Albert Einstein (1879–1955) theoretical physicist

These three quotes assert that scientific discoveries are made using Soul-intuition and not intellect. Furthermore, Einstein points out that the rational mind in our head ought to serve the intuitive mind that resides in the heart. In the first quote, he specifically identifies the source to come "straight from the heart."

Others view Soul-intuition arising from the heart to be the wisest component of human consciousness.

"All grand thoughts come from the heart."

—Vauvenargues (1715–1747) author

"When the future hinges on the next words that are said, don't let logic interfere, believe your heart instead."

—Philip Robison; conductor, arranger, and music educator

"Let your soul be your pilot."

—Sting (born 1951) musician, songwriter, and actor

Several additional quotes are shared throughout this book.

If you have Soul-intuition, you may have discovered that your intuition is an infallible inner guide that deserves the utmost respect. Moreover, you may have found your intellect and your gut to be quite fallible, often leading you off the middle path of your heart.

GENIUS

"The Intuitive mind is where our genius resides."

—Angela Artemis; writer and teacher

When I read that intriguing quote from Angela Artemis, my intuition encouraged me to investigate the origin of the word "genius."

ORIGIN [of genius]: late Middle English: from Latin, **'attendant spirit present from one's birth, innate ability or inclination,'** from the root of gignere 'beget.' The original sense 'guardian spirit attendant on a person' gave rise to a sense 'a person's characteristic disposition' (late 16th cent.), which led to a sense 'a person's natural ability,' and finally 'exceptional natural ability' (mid 17th cent.)[16]

To my surprise, the word "genius" originally referred to a guardian spirit that attends a person from birth and is associated with their innate abilities and inclinations. The Soul fits this perfectly.

Thus, your Soul is your genius!

In exploring the origin of words related to intuition, I found that the original definitions are often quite accurate. Then, over time, the meaning drifted away from the truth that was captured further back in time.

Even though the recent materialistic perspective has led to many great technological advancements, those advancements appear to have actually emerged from our Souls. Meanwhile, our ego-minds have taken credit for what originally came as divine inspiration from the genius within—the Superconscious-Soul. Ironically, many modern scientists don't believe in the existence of human Souls even though they may be the actual source of scientific wisdom.

The way consciousness or spirit has been extracted from the definitions of these words has ruined their original truth.

For example, the "ORIGIN [of intuition]: late Middle English **(denoting spiritual insight or immediate spiritual communication)**" captures the way the Soul, which is a spirit, provides insights via intuition.

To emphasize the importance of that relationship, I keep pointing out how my Soul provided many of the ideas presented in this book. This may be unusual and possibly even annoying. Despite that, my personal practice is to place credit where credit is due. Citing my Soul achieves that.

On a more personal level, I thank my Soul whenever I notice that it intuitively assisted me. This occurs many times a day. The more I pay attention, the more I notice how my Soul has my back. It miraculously leads me out of fixes and into serendipitous synchronicities.

ESOTERIC VERSUS EXOTERIC

Two important words that my Soul intuitively guided me to investigate are esoteric and exoteric. To begin with here's a definition for esoteric.

> **esoteric:** adjective;
> intended for or likely to be understood by only a small number of people with a specialized knowledge or interest: esoteric philosophical debates.
> ORIGIN mid 17th cent.: from Greek esōterikos, from esōterō, comparative of esō **'within.'** [17]

The modern definition claims that esoteric refers to specialized knowledge appropriate for a small group of people, even though the origin is from the Greek root "esō" which simply means **within.**

In Ancient Greece, **Mystery Schools** only accepted small groups of students, making what they taught appear to be exclusive and therefore possibly meant for a small group of special people. The schools were known to teach esoteric knowledge, but the secret nature of the school's specific teachings left humanity with the question:

What exactly is esoteric knowledge?

Intellectual philosophers have tossed this question around so much that an entire branch of philosophy named "esotericism" is dedicated to resolving this conundrum.

The antonym of esoteric is exoteric. The definition of exoteric will help to resolve the mystery.

exoteric: adjective formal
(especially of a doctrine or mode of speech) intended for or likely to be understood by the general public: an exoteric, literal meaning and an esoteric, inner teaching. The opposite of esoteric.
ORIGIN mid 17th cent.: via Latin from Greek exōterikos, from exōterō 'outer,' comparative of exō '**outside**.' [18]

In summary, the origins of these two words are:

- ♥ esoteric originated from esō, meaning **within**, while
- ♥ exoteric originated from exō, meaning **outside**.

The current definitions of these words, plus the fact that the revered ancient Greek Mystery Schools taught esoteric knowledge, indicates that esoteric knowledge is superior to exoteric knowledge.

My Soul showed me how all of this makes sense if esoteric knowledge originally referred to intuitive knowledge that comes from the Soul which is an infallible genius residing **within** our hearts. Conversely, exoteric knowledge would refer to external knowledge from external sources like books, people, astral spirits, etc.

Throughout the remainder of this book, I'll use these terms based on their original Greek meanings, within and outside.

My personal experience of intuition has taught me some important differences between esoteric and exoteric knowledge:

Some books claim to contain esoteric knowledge even though knowledge in a book is obviously external to the reader and, therefore, exoteric. What is offered in these books may have originally come from a person's Soul as true esoteric knowledge, but once written down or spoken, the knowledge becomes exoteric.

So, why does this seemingly subtle difference matter?

When a person receives intuitive wisdom from within, the meaning may be related to, and affected by, the context in which they receive the message. The person may have been contemplating a question, or seeking guidance regarding a personal issue. When the message arrived, the setting may have helped to clarify it. These factors, and others, can affect the meaning of the message that came from the Soul—making it difficult to accurately share the true meaning of the esoteric message. Additionally, these inner ideas are usually presented as thoughts, not words—making it difficult to find the right words to share the true meaning of the message.

Finally, the interpretation and memory of the message makes people's ability to accurately share esoteric messages error-prone.

When an intuitive person is seeking a clear understanding regarding an important issue, they've been known to relocate themselves away from distractions. Doing this is called a vision quest.

Meditation can be used to quiet the conscious-mind. In some cases, fasting is used to deepen the vision quest experience. In other cases, ethnogenic substances can also be used to amplify the experience of tapping into the inner divine Soul. Tantric techniques can also be used to fortify the intuitive connection.

Some investigators have found evidence indicating that all of these sorts of tools were used in the Greek Mystery Schools to amplify the esoteric knowledge that emerges from within.

I've used many of these tools to assist in my quest for understanding. Over thirty years of experimentation, I've discovered a wide range of results, some clarifying and others distorting.

With or without employing tools to amplify intuitive guidance, esoteric knowledge must come from within oneself. When a person talks or writes about what emerged from within, the message is received by others as exoteric, simply because the knowledge is being received from outside of themselves.

Real esoteric knowledge comes from your Soul in your heart, not from a book or any external source of any kind. A book like this one can encourage you to value the esoteric guidance from within yourself. It can provide tips and tools that may help you commune with your Soul and live in accordance with its wisdom. Certainly, the purpose of this book is to encourage you to commune with your Soul and live in accordance with your Soul's guidance.

However, when it comes to living your life, this book and other books must be set aside. You must look within yourself for the guidance that comes to you from your Soul, your personal esoteric source of infallible divine wisdom.

"You have to grow from the inside out. None can teach you, none can make you spiritual. There is no other teacher but your own soul."

—Swami Vivekananda (1863–1902) Hindu sage

By retrieving the original essence of the words "esoteric" and "exoteric," the confusion that has distorted the meaning of these words is stripped away, while the important difference between these two forms of knowledge is restored. The original meaning deals with the source being internal or external. Over millennia, the meaning was turned inside-out to identify the type of audience the knowledge is appropriate for, rather than the source of the knowledge.

In modern civilization, the machine brain myth mistakenly leads to the belief that we come into this world without any knowledge. We're taught that experience, mentors, books and the internet are the only sources of accurate knowledge.

Despite that, myself and countless others have found that the knowledge that resides inside our hearts is essentially infinite, infallible and divinely predictive. Therefore, esoteric knowledge from within is superior to exoteric knowledge and it is available by simply pondering a question in your mind. Geniuses are people who have learned to listen to and accept the answer that emerges from within their heart.

On the other hand, idiots depend on their feeble intellectual ego-mind in their head and the exoteric knowledge it can access from external sources like books and the internet.

"The heart is wiser than the intellect."

—J. G. Holland (1819–1881) novelist and poet

Certainly, external sources can be handy in providing support to help validate esoteric knowledge. Quotes, examples, scriptures, scientific research and other external sources are very helpful when it comes to developing confidence. Unfortunately, the leaders who explore new territory need courage to step deeper into their hearts and trust that what emerges has merit. Then, to validate what has emerged, experimentation that tests unsupported ramifications is used to build confidence. That's how science progresses.

On the other hand, let's take a look at the well-known case of the studious intellectual bookworm who has accumulated lots of information, but lacks commonsense.

To get started, what exactly is "commonsense?"

The Soul provides infallible guidance pertaining to the present moment. By being consciously aware of this process, I've noticed that my Soul assists me throughout each and every day with countless mini intuitive nudges that I hadn't noticed for most of my life. Now, it's become very clear that my Soul is my source of "commonsense."

Moreover, since intuition arrives in the present moment to help a person deal with reality as it's taking place, the Soul's knowledge of the future makes it uniquely able to provide commonsense that facilitates a graceful life experience that is filled with precious serendipitous synchronicities.

That sort of life is quite different from how a studious intellectual can stumble through life by focusing on books and their feeble intellect.

In relation to all of this, the Triality model includes a principle named the Beneficence of the Quintessential Core. This principle predicts that esoteric knowledge which comes from the Soul, our Quintessential Core, will be beneficial. On the other hand, the Maleficence of Extremes principle predicts that exoteric knowledge from outer polarities can be destructive, especially when that knowledge is extremely far from the truth that resides in the Quintessential Core.

As we all know, libraries contain books that contradict one another. Certainly, the same is true for information found on the internet. It follows that some of the information must be close to the truth while some is further away from the truth. Some sources may even contain precious portions of the absolute truth, while others can offer complete fiction. The Maleficence of Extremes principle predicts that the more extremely false or upside-down the knowledge is, the more destructive its effect will be on those who choose to believe such falsehoods.

Additionally, the words that are written in books and on the internet, evolve over time causing their meaning to change and even reverse. In this chapter, I've shown how the words "genius," "esoteric," "exoteric," and even "intuition" have undergone dramatic changes. Their original linkage with the Soul within has been removed. In my lifetime, the word "sick" has changed from something awful or diseased to something that is awesome. At least that's how young people use that word today, and soon they'll be elders.

This means that old books which one might consider to be an accurate record of the past, could actually be very misleading today even if they originally held valid facts. This is because key words may have completely reversed their meaning since the book was written. This doesn't apply to contemporary books, but some classics are hundreds of years old. Revered spiritual texts can be thousands of years old and have been translated from archaic languages.

Some languages have more rigidly restrained meanings for their words because the meaning is based on the collective meaning of the symbols they are comprised of. Hungarian and Chinese are examples. English has a sound-based alphabet like most languages. The meaning of a word is free to change, while the pronunciation may remain the same. As you must be aware, one word can have multiple meanings that can completely contradict one another. "Sick" is an example discussed earlier.

Fortunately, an infallible genius resides in your heart. As you go about living your life in the present moment, your Soul is available to advise you. By simply pondering a question in your mind, the infallible answer may arrive intuitively. When guidance arrives, then following that guidance will offer you the most blessed life you can live. This is the Way-of-the-Heart.

Also, when considering information from external sources like books, the internet or people, you can check in with your Soul by asking, "Is this information correct?" Then listen for the intuitive cue.

Later, in **Part 3,** I offer techniques for sorting these sorts of issues out.

When it comes to gut-intuition, the source is inside and therefore, ought to be respected. Still, the Quintessential-Core is in the heart therefore, Soul-intuition deserves the most respect.

In the next chapter, I'm going to delve into how some people lose their intuition.

Chapter 10
Humanity's Pivotal Divide

If intuition is as great as many have claimed, why isn't following our intuition part of the modern education system?

Why doesn't our culture provide encouragement for us to follow our hearts?

Why is our culture so focused on the intellectual-ego-mind in our head, when great thinkers like Einstein, Frank Lloyd Wright, Aristotle and many others praise intuition and claim that the associated wisdom comes from their Soul in their heart?

My Soul informed me that the answer to all of these questions is that most people don't have Soul-intuition!

MOST PEOPLE DON'T HAVE SOUL-INTUITION

Most of the intuitive people that I've talked to about their intuition assume that everyone has intuition. Additionally, I found it's common for people who have intuition to presume that those who don't believe they have intuition...simply haven't learned to listen. Since intuition comes as an inner whisper, that's usually more of a feeling or a nudge, it seems quite plausible that some people may not notice it.

This could be the case for some people, but I've discovered there's much more to it. Years ago, I began to ask people questions like these:

> While living your life, have you noticed thoughts or feelings popping up in your head that cause you to feel or think that you ought to call someone, go somewhere, or do something, but you don't know why?
> This isn't about intuitive gut warnings that you feel in your gut. What I'm inquiring about may feel more like a nudge in your head encouraging you to take some action.
> In other words, have you experienced knowing that you ought to do something, but you didn't know why you ought to do it?

If so, then on some occasions you might be too busy to follow through and do what you felt encouraged to do. Only later, when you discovered that a problem developed as a result of not following through, you might have said to yourself, "Darn, I knew I should have done that!"

On other occasions, when you did what you had been encouraged to do, have you noticed that as a result of doing it, some sort of positive synchronistic event took place? For example, you call someone on the phone and they exclaim, "I was just about to call you," or "I was just thinking about you."

Or you go somewhere, simply because you felt you ought to go there, and after you arrive you just happen to meet someone that you end up having a great connection with. Afterward, you feel very grateful that you followed your intuition and went where it had guided you to go.

How often do these types of things happen in your life?

Some people responded, with answers like, "All the time," "That's how I live my life," or "Of course, everybody does!" People with these types of responses often share examples of intuitive experiences from their lives. These people obviously have Soul-intuition.

Conversely, other people claim they can't recall any of those things I had asked them about ever happening to them. In other cases, some people will recall and share another type of experience that's similar to intuition, but it's definitely not Soul-intuition. There are still others who change the subject and avoid answering my questions altogether, presumably because the questions don't fit into their reality which lacks Soul-intuition.

To be sure that the questions were understood, I might ask additional questions, and eventually discover that the person doesn't have Soul-intuition at all!

EVERYONE HAS GUT-INTUITION

As I mentioned earlier, I'm using the word intuition to refer to Soul-intuition. The questions presented above clarify the difference. When I use the word intuition, I'm referring to the intuition that pops up in your head, not in your gut. I'll specify gut-intuition if that's what I'm referring to.

As I mentioned in the last chapter, it does appear that everyone has gut-intuition. It's the intuition from the Soul that many people don't seem to have at all.

Because gut-intuition is included in the current definition of intuition, and because everyone has gut-intuition, the idea that everyone has intuition has been accepted. For instance, a 2014 article from *The Huffington Post* entitled, *10 Things Highly Intuitive People Do Differently,* by Carolyn Gregoire, states, "Pretty much everyone has experienced a gut feeling—that unconscious reasoning that propels us to do something without telling us why or how." She further claims, "Our intuition is always there, whether we're aware of it or not."

Then Gregoire explains that, "the first thing that people in touch with their intuition do differently [is to] listen to that inner voice."

AN IMPORTANT SPLIT IN HUMANITY

By attributing gut-intuition to the subconscious-mind in the gut and conversely assigning the inner voice to the Soul in the heart, my Soul led me to discover an important split in humanity.

Although I haven't been able to find any statistics that focus specifically on intuition from the Soul, there are statistics on pineal gland calcification.

PINEAL GLAND CALCIFICATION

Skull x-rays reveal that most adults have calcified pineal glands. This means that the pineal gland in most adults has hardened into a bonelike material that is laden with calcium—the material our bones are made of. This condition is easily identified in a head x-ray.

If the pineal gland, or third eye, is part of the pathway that Soul-intuition follows to reach the conscious-mind, then calcification of this gland would almost certainly prevent intuitive messages from reaching the conscious-mind.

This would explain why some people don't have any recollection of receiving intuitive guidance as an inner whisper, nudge, or feeling in their conscious-mind.

The incidence of pineal gland calcification in different age groups among Caucasians was reported by Wurtman et al. to be 2 percent in those 3 to 12-years-old, 46 percent in those 13 to 40-years-old, and 69 percent in those above the age of 40. [19]

Additional research has found that all but 2 percent of children have normal pineal glands prior to puberty. Then, after puberty, most pineal glands begin to shrink, and by 17-years-old, 40 percent of Americans have calcified pineal glands.

Finally, one study from 1974 found 83 percent of elderly adults' pineal glands calcified! [20]

If most adults have calcified pineal glands, then billions of people world-wide may not have Soul-intuition.

Moreover, if a large portion of the population lacks Soul-intuition, it stands to reason that our society, schooling systems, and science are mostly based on the non-intuitive intellectual viewpoint that prevails today.

Finally, if a minority of the adult population has Soul-intuition, and only people with this type of intuition were accepted to the Mystery Schools of Ancient Greece, then it makes sense that these schools had only a few students at any one time. Looking at these schools from a distance, most investigators and philosophers could have misjudged the situation, thinking the esoteric knowledge being taught was special knowledge for this select group. Despite that, the Mystery Schools could have been teaching techniques to better access one's inner knowledge that arrives intuitively from one's Soul.

The question that remains is, why would some people's pineal glands calcify while others do not?

CAUSE OF PINEAL CALCIFICATION

Although many sources claim fluoridation of water supplies is the primary cause, in 2006, only 61.5 percent of the U.S. population used water with fluoridation, with 3 percent receiving naturally occurring fluoride. This is less than the 83 percent of elderly adults who had calcified pineal glands way back in 1974 when considerably less fluoridation occurred. Therefore, it's unlikely that fluoride is the cause.

Additionally, I consumed water with fluoridation until I was 30-years-old, and I've always had intuition. Recently, I got a head x-ray confirming that my pineal gland is not calcified.

If it's not fluoride, then what's the cause?

My intuition guided me to look at the data showing that only 2 percent of people are calcified prior to puberty, while after puberty, the proportion affected increases to 40 percent of Americans by 17-years-old! This is a huge change in a very short period of time.

So, something significant must happen during puberty.

Puberty: noun;
the period during which adolescents reach sexual maturity and become capable of reproduction. [21]

Adolescence: noun;
the period following the onset of puberty during which a young person develops from a child into an adult. [22]

The hormones that accompany adolescence cause many young people to have their first romantic encounters during this transformational period, when numerous pineal glands are becoming calcified. According to the Harvard University website, testosterone, a powerful sex hormone, increases by ten times in adolescent boys!

On top of that, we all know, our romantic feelings and romantic attraction to others arrive in our minds without any intellectual reasoning. For example, the well-known concept of **love at first sight** clearly indicates that no reasoning is needed to experience the feelings of love or a powerful romantic attraction to another person.

Since a lack of reasoning is a well-known characteristic of intuition, it appears that our romantic inspirations are a form of Soul-intuition that comes from one's heart. The heart is universally associated with love and romance, making romantic inspirations from the heart—perfectly fitting humanity's age-old wisdom that links love and the heart.

The romantic thoughts and feelings that first appear during adolescence often propel teenagers into their first romantic tryst. These initial romantic encounters strongly influence one's personal position regarding love, lust, sensuality, and sexuality. One's beliefs about romantic issues are initially calibrated during the formative years of adolescence. The personality is deeply affected by these events which determine how a person views love, romance, attachment, loss, betrayal, etc. There are exceptions, but most people have their initial romantic encounter(s) during the adolescent period. These encounters don't need to include intercourse to be psychologically impactful.

It's also quite common for pivotal heartbreaking events to take place. For example, when I was just 10-years-old, the heartbreak I suffered caused me to consciously decide to avoid women for the rest of my life. Luckily, this poorly thought-out decision was abandoned about a year later, when I met Heidi. With a new relationship in hand,

I recovered from my adolescent heartbreak to face the vicissitudes of love again at a more-worldly 12.

This may seem funny, but many people get their heart broken more severely and fail to rebound. Then, to avoid further heartache, many adolescents may choose to ignore the intuitive whispers from their hearts. People may be subconsciously aware that their inner guidance led to their heartache, so choosing to ignore intuition from the heart would be the obvious way to avoid additional heartache.

Certainly, romance isn't the only situation in which people can experience heartache. Our relationships with our parents, siblings, best friends, aunts, uncles, grandparents, mentors, spiritual leaders, and others can involve love, intimacy, and heartache. For some, it could even involve a pet. The bond between a person and their companion animal can be very powerful. The death of a dear companion can be emotionally devastating.

HEARTBREAK CAN LEAD TO A HARDENED HEART

My Soul advised me that many people realize that opening and following their heart will lead to more heart-wrenching pain, and in order to stop it, they develop a **hardened heart.**

A **hardened heart** is a biblical term that refers to being unable to perceive, understand, see, hear, and, remember.

Certainly, people with **hardened hearts** are not deaf, blind, or lacking memory, so in what way have these people with hardened hearts lost their ability to see, hear, or remember? My Soul informed me that these terms are meant to be applied to the intuitive messages that arrive from the Soul in one's heart.

Messages that include romantic love-at-first-sight promptings can, and often do, lead to heartbreak, or at least heartache. Still, we know that the physical heart doesn't become hard, so what hardens? The pineal gland, the inner eye that receives the intuitive messages, hardens by becoming calcified or bonelike.

Earlier, I explained how the pineal gland receives a direct supply of blood from the heart, while most of the brain is protected by the blood-brain barrier. This unusual physical feature of this central brain gland may be intended to enable the Soul in the heart to send calcium-rich blood to the pineal gland in order to calcify it.

A calcified pineal gland will physically end romantic promptings, which are a type of Soul-intuition. Additionally, a calcified pineal gland will cut off all forms of Soul-intuition. Once a person's pineal gland is calcified, they'll no longer perceive, understand, see, hear, or remember any of the intuitive messages from their Soul.

PRAGMATICS VERSUS ROMANTICS

I'm proposing that heart-wrenching experiences cause many people to stop listening to their Soul. In turn, the Soul calcifies the pineal gland, giving the person the opportunity to pursue a pragmatic way of life: one that will protect them from the heartache of loss and rejection. Throughout the remainder of this book, I'll refer to people who fit this condition as *Pragmatic*.

On the other hand, people who remain attentive to their intuitive guidance maintain healthy pineal glands. These people continue to experience romantic promptings and all forms of Soul-intuition. I'll label these people, *Romantic*.

This pivotal divide in humanity creates a world with two different types of people:

Romantics, having maintained a connection with the Soul in their heart, these people tend to rely on their inner guidance (more or less, depending on the individual).

Pragmatics, having chosen to avoid additional heartache, disconnect from the Soul in their heart, and are left to depend on their conscious- and subconscious-minds to navigate through life.

There isn't a clear line dividing the Romantic and Pragmatic people; in fact, there's a lot of overlap.

Romantic people can act like a Pragmatic at times, and vice versa.

However, Romantics tend to be humble and generous givers while Pragmatics are inclined to be arrogant and greedy takers.

The most clearly distinguishing difference is that Romantics have Soul-intuition, while Pragmatics don't. This forms a pivotal divide that splits humanity into esoteric versus exoteric lifestyles.

Esoteric Romantics are connected to the One and its knowledge through their Soul within.

Pragmatics are left to search outside of themselves for knowledge and a connection to the One. Fortunately, the afterlife astral realm provides upper and lower paths that lead back to the One. In **Part 2** I will show how these paths are designed to accommodate Pragmatic people.

OTHER CAUSES OF PINEAL CALCIFICATION

Sadly, some children are physically or emotionally abused. Obviously, these types of situations can lead to calcification.

In addition to Romantic hardships that push a person away from their Soul, there are other pivotal experiences that can lure people away from their Soul.

For example, I recall two occasions in which I was presented with opportunities for tremendous personal power. In both cases, to obtain that power I would have had to disregard my conscience which advised me to walk away. In one of those cases, I clearly remember being aware that this important decision would determine my fate. I actually knew, intuitively, that my Soul was on the line.

If I chose to take advantage of the opportunity and go against my conscience, my ego would be using its free will to obtain more power, but my Soul would be lost. On the other hand, by following my conscience, my life would be humbler, but my Soul connection would remain intact. In both cases, the power being offered was very enticing to my ego making it difficult to remain in alignment with my conscience. In spite of that, I chose to pass on those opportunities for power—knowing in my heart that it was more important to maintain integrity with my conscience.

You may recall making a choice in which you considered disregarding your conscience. You may have even felt as though your Soul might be lost in the bargain. If so, then you know which choice you made, and also the consequences of that choice.

SEX AND RACE FACTORS

Some pineal gland research investigated differences in white versus black people. The results indicate that white men have higher rates of calcification than black men. Other studies found that men have higher rates of calcification than women.

So, it appears that black women have the lowest incidence of calcification while white men have the highest rates of calcification.

This fits with how, black people, and especially black women, are well-known to have "Soul." Especially when it comes to music and singing. On the other hand, white people and especially white men, often lack Soul and exhibit the biggest ego issues.

MISCONCEPTION ABOUT ROMANTICS RECTIFIED

If pineal gland calcification stops Soul-intuition, and more than half of the population is calcified, then Pragmatic people are the dominant portion of modern civilization. Accordingly, Pragmatics establish the popular point of view. The Pragmatic yardstick views Pragmatic people as realists, while Romantics are commonly thought to be overly idealistic, believing in fanciful ideas like true love, *Soul Mates*, honor, honesty, kindness, etc.

Unfortunately, trashy romance novels have tarnished the original sense of romance that involved heroism, chivalry, valor, trustworthiness, loyalty, etc. Open hearted Romantics still cherish those important values and often wonder if time passed them by.

Meanwhile, the selfish "taker" reality that Romantics don't belong in, continues to grow in popularity.

If intuition is as infallible as many claim, then Romantic people have maintained a connection to the deepest truth known. The Soul is our Genius that provides a divine connection to the One-Who-Is-All.

By showing how Pragmatic people are disconnected from this inner source of infallible knowledge and divine guidance, it becomes clear that Pragmatics are actually shortchanged. Their ego may have taken charge to make their life better, however they're left to fend for themselves with the feeble intellect of their ego-mind.

Steve Jobs called intuition, "more powerful than the intellect."

Thus, the popular misconception that Romantics are overly idealistic is flipped right-side-up to reveal how Pragmatics are disconnected from their divinely wise Soul. It's the Soul's guidance and its Supreme Power of Wholeness that brings miracles into one's life bestowing treasures that bless one's life in unexpectedly fabulous ways that can be beyond one's ability to imagine.

Despite that, since Pragmatic people represent the dominant portion of our culture, they establish the norm and offer their way of measuring success which tends to be based on some type of power that inflates the ego. Thus, we live in an ego-driven divisive world.

Moreover, since Pragmatics lack intuition and don't personally experience the Romantic way of life, they ridicule it often calling Romantics foolish or childish. Pragmatics who offer this sort of criticism don't notice the difference between being childlike and childish.

Admirable qualities that are childlike include a child's intuitive wisdom, their precious honesty, and their cherished wonderment. Most Romantic people retain these fine qualities while they tend to refrain from the self-centered behavior that is truly childish.

On the other hand, even though a Pragmatic approach to life may have an outward appearance of maturity, Pragmatic people follow their ego-minds which are selfish, making Pragmatics childish.

Over time, without Soul-intuition and the delightful serendipitous synchronicities that accompany a Romantic's life, Pragmatic people grow to resent what they're missing. When the miraculous blessings that accompany a Romantics life stop taking place, Pragmatics all but forget how precious it was to experience a miraculously blessed life. Then, unable to retrieve what has been lost, they often ridicule the delightfully blessed lifestyle that Romantics retain.

This poignant message is conveyed in the epic movie, *Citizen Kane*. Rosebud is a childhood sled that appears in the final scene. It symbolizes the simple, but blessed childhood that the fabulously rich protagonist was never able to regain in spite of his extraordinary financial power.

Hopefully, identifying this pivotal divide and sharing it will help Romantic people to better understand Pragmatic people and vice versa.

Beyond that, this split in humanity will be shown to serve as an important tool used to accomplish the purpose of the universe.

The next two chapters expose the monumental effect that this pivotal divide has had on humanity.

Chapter 11
Original–People

"Man did not weave the web of life, he is merely a strand in it.
Whatever he does to the web, he does to himself."
—Chief Seattle (1786–1866) Suquamish & Duwamish tribal leader

ORIGINAL–PEOPLE

There's a very small number of truly *Original-People* alive today, but some do exist. In a book compiled by Survival International, *We Are One—A Celebration of Tribal Peoples*, there were over 100 remote tribes in 2009. Most of these have been contacted to varying degrees, but some are being observed from a distance by anthropologists using binoculars, satellite images, and other devices.

Two of the most isolated tribes live on the Andaman Islands of India. The Sentinelese population was estimated to be 500 in 2015. The Jarawa population consists of approximately 250-400 people. Both of these groups have aggressively and successfully resisted all the attempts civilized people have made to visit them. Despite that, some contact has recently been initiated by members of both groups.

Just fifty years ago gigantic regions of the Amazon basin and other remote areas remained unexplored by civilized people. These areas contained millions of Original-People. Over the course of the last fifty years, many anthropologists directly contacted Original-People, and then studied those people soon after they were discovered.

Coincidently, I met an anthropologist who had lived with some newly-discovered Original-People. She confirmed that those people lived in a wilderness area that had not, until then, been explored.

I asked this anthropologist if the Original-People she had lived with **behaved like individuals**. She was quite surprised by this question, and told me that no one had ever posed that question to her.

I encouraged her to take some time to think about her experience with the Original-People she had lived with, then tell me if she considered those people to be individuals. After a moment of contemplation, she answered, "They were **definitely not** individuals."

In support of her answer, she told me that those people lived and worked together without needing to talk much at all. She further claimed that the Original-People she studied **never discussed differing viewpoints!**

I found it difficult to imagine a group of people who never discuss differing viewpoints.

Beyond that, she explained that the Original-People would get up and do a complicated group project without any announcement or discussion. The group would simply standup and do it together, as if they were **one organism.** Furthermore, they would work together and complete the project in a coordinated way **without speaking a single word the entire time!**

According to this anthropologist, the Original-People she lived with and studied were **not individuals.**

Over the next couple of years, I met two more anthropologists. I asked each one of them the same question, and got nearly the same answer. Both of these anthropologists stated that the Original-People they lived with, "were **definitely not** individuals."

To be absolutely clear about this, the Original-People I'm referring to are people who were just recently discovered, and had not experienced interaction with civilized people until these first encounters. Once civilized humans interact with Original-People, the interaction gradually individualizes those people, taking them out of the Original-People category.

Of course, the process of individuation takes time, and the degree of individuation has a very broad range. However, the fact that some of the last people who may still behave as if they are not individuals are being observed, from a distance, to avoid contact. This clearly demonstrates that our contact with Original-People is known to transform them.

Tribal people who dress and look like Original-People, but have experienced interactions with civilized people, have through those encounters, already become somewhat individualized. The people who have not been influenced by civilized people are the only adult humans who still behave as if they are not individuals.

The idea that people who have never encountered modern civilization behave as if they're not individuals may be hard to believe, but there are a multitude of anthropological observations confirming this reality.

THE ONENESS PERSPECTIVE

To help you accept this aspect of reality, I'll show how an unexpected "oneness perspective" actually makes sense. Let's begin with Chief Seattle's famous speech:

> *"All things share the same breath – the beast, the tree, the man... the air shares its spirit with all the life it supports. Man did not weave the web of life, he is merely a strand in it. Whatever he does to the web, he does to himself."*

Chief Seattle may have already been influenced by civilization when he made this speech, but it's clear that he still held a perception which viewed all of life as one organism. This point is made quite clear when Seattle explains, "Man did not weave the web of life, he is merely a strand in it. Whatever he does to the web, he does to himself."

As discussed earlier, according to the Consciousness-Origin-Cosmology, we're all part of one organism—the **One-Who-Is-All.** What we do to others, we're doing to parts of the One that we're all portions of. Therefore, we are doing those things to ourselves.

This oneness perspective is a complete reversal of what most civilized humans hold to be, without question, true. We presume that we're individuals. Beyond that, we presume that everyone and everything are individuals even though that is not true.

ONENESS PERSPECTIVE FITS THE COSMOLOGY AND REALITY

The Consciousness-Origin Cosmology, as Dr. Katz told it to me, claims that early humans were designed with the **potential to be individuals.** In spite of that, in their natural state, they knew they were part of everything, and that **oneness perspective prevented them from behaving like individuals.**

When Dr. Katz made this claim, it seemed impossible to me. How could humans lack individuality? At that time, in 1990, I believed all humans were individuals. We're obviously separate physical beings, so how could a separate human being not think of themselves as an individual? Back then, this seemed preposterous to me.

Accordingly, to test this part of the cosmology, I asked the aforementioned anthropologists if the Original-People they lived with were individuals. When all three anthropologists independently stated, "They were **definitely not** individuals," that answer unanimously confirmed Katz' difficult-to-believe claim. Gradually, I was discovering how accurate the Consciousness-Origin Cosmology is.

Over the years, I've found more support for this little-known feature of reality, the oneness perspective of Original-People:

For instance, in Jean Liedloff's classic book, *The Continuum Concept: In Search of Happiness Lost,* the author shares what she learned when she spent two-and-a-half years in the South American jungle, living with a clan of Original-People. She was especially moved by how these people cared for their children. She noted that they would hold the infant continuously for a year-and-a-half to two years. When the baby took it upon themselves to leave the mother, she would let the baby venture out on its own without concern. When that baby returned, the mother would hold it again. Soon, the baby would leave and fail to return to the mother. That ended her motherly duties.

Once on its own, the child would mimic the older people and become a contributing member of the clan. This would take place around the age of four! No training, punishment, or encouragement was needed. My Soul-intuition guided me to realize that each Original-Person's Soul guided them to do their part by imitating older members of the clan. Thus, no external guidance was needed.

In a similar way, animals don't need training, they "instinctively know" how to survive. Scientists use the term "instincts" to label countless behaviors but fail to identify the source of instincts. My Soul informed me that each creature's Soul provides what we call instincts, resolving this mystery with a consciousness-based explanation.

Returning to the Original-People observed by Liedloff, she watched them operate in an egalitarian way, sharing all the food gathered evenly amongst everyone. Even Liedloff received an equal share. This is the natural way to share what has been gathered when everyone was perceived to be parts of one organism: A single being with multiple parts that are connected through the web of life—the One-Who-Is-All.

An unusual accident that supports this idea was observed by Liedloff. In this particular instance, one boy shot an arrow that landed in another boy's chest. The mother of the shooter arrived at the scene and asked what happened. After she was informed of the details, she showed great surprise because of the unusual nature of the accident.

Oddly, she didn't blame or reprimand her son, knowing it was an accident. Everyone involved was part of the continuum, the One underlying web of consciousness. Blaming one portion of the One, the shooter, for injuring another portion of the One, the boy with an arrow in his chest, doesn't make sense.

To better grasp this point, imagine that you're using a handsaw to cut a piece of wood. With one hand, you're holding the piece of wood and with the other hand you're pushing the saw to cut through the piece of wood. As you start pushing the saw, it jumps and you accidentally cut a finger on the hand that's holding the piece of wood.

If that happened to you, would you blame the hand that was pushing the saw for cutting a finger on your other hand?

Of course not, because both hands are part of you. It doesn't make sense for you to blame or punish one hand for cutting your other hand. If you began scolding one of your hands for being careless and hurting the other hand, people would think you had lost your mind. If you went even further and punished that hand, people would be certain you had lost your mind. The fact that both hands are yours makes blame and punishment nonsense.

In a different situation, if you were holding a piece of wood for me to cut, and I accidentally pushed the saw in a way that caused it to jump and cut your finger, you might get upset and blame me. This makes sense, because I'm a separate individual.

Blame, credit, gratitude, hatred, love, and many other aspects of modern civilized reality are based on the way we behave as if each person is a separate individual.

Even though I intellectually believe that everything is One, I still behave as if I'm a separate individual. Therefore, my intellectual beliefs aren't as strong as the ingrained perspective of individuality that can be seen in my behavior. Consequently, I find myself engaging in blame even though I intellectually believe that we're all one.

On the other hand, based on the primal truth of oneness that the Original-People operate from, blame doesn't make any sense at all. That's why the mother of the boy who shot the arrow didn't blame or reprimand her son. Instead, she simply expressed her surprise at the unusual nature of the accident. Her ingrained perspective that everything is one caused her to see both her son and the boy who had the arrow in his chest as parts of one giant organism: Life, an organism connected by consciousness—the One-Who-Is-All.

This helps to explain why the Original-People are so kind, considerate, hospitable, and gentle with each other, and even with total strangers. They see everyone as parts of themselves. Even though physical separation exists, down at the foundation of reality—in the realm of pure consciousness—everything is one. The oneness point of view that comes from that ultimate truth makes Original-People's behavior difficult for us to believe, and quite confounding to our ingrained individualistic point of view.

The first three paragraphs of Howard Zinn's well-known book *A People's History of the United States* documents the type of unusual behavior I'm referring to:

> *Arawak men and women, naked, tawny, and full of wonder, emerged from their villages onto the island's beaches and swam out to get a closer look at the strange big boat. When Columbus and his sailors came ashore, carrying swords, speaking oddly, the Arawaks ran to greet them, brought them food, water, gifts. He later wrote of this in his log:*
>
> *"They . . . brought us parrots and balls of cotton and spears and many other things, which they exchanged for the glass beads and hawks' bells. They willingly traded everything they owned. . . They were well-built, with good bodies and handsome features. . . They do not bear arms, and do not know them, for I showed them a sword, they took it by the edge and cut themselves out of ignorance. They have no iron. Their spears are made of cane. . . They would make fine servants. . . With fifty men we could subjugate them all and make them do whatever we want."*
>
> *These Arawaks of the Bahama Islands were much like Indians on the mainland, who were remarkable (European observers were to say again and again) for their hospitality, their belief in sharing. These traits did not stand out in the Europe of the Renaissance, dominated as it was by the religion of popes, the government of kings, the frenzy for*

money that marked Western civilization and its first messenger to the Americas, Christopher Columbus.

In case you're wondering, the Arawaks used spears for fishing.

Civilized people have always found it bewildering to learn about the gentle kindness so-called "savages" express when they are first encountered. This is because we're not aware that these Original-People viewed the entire world as one organism. Even rocks, water, air, and plants are part of the oneness perspective—a perspective that is quite likely more accurate than the individualistic view of civilized people.

Certainly, it's difficult for individuals like ourselves to imagine what it would be like to view everything, even strangers, as part of one whole, and therefore as parts of ourselves. To overcome that difficulty, we can approximate the way all of reality might look to an Original-Person by considering how we view various parts of our own body. Earlier, the example of cutting one's finger with a saw revealed how illustratively helpful this can be.

When the perspective we have of our own body and its individual parts is overlaid onto the entire world, we can begin to imagine how reality looks to an Original-Person. By transferring how you view your own body out to the entire world, you can start to make sense out of how the Original-People lacked fear, had childlike openness, lacked blame, were willing to share everything they own, lacked hierarchy, and never discussed differing viewpoints. All of these characteristics fit the way we treat or view parts of our selves.

CHILDREN ARE LIKE ORIGINAL-PEOPLE

Many people have noticed how the Original-People's traits are similar to those of young children who have been nurtured by a dedicated mother. My Soul guided me to understand why young children are like Original-People:

Before a child is born, it resides in its mother's womb. The umbilical cord physically connects the fetus to the placenta that interfaces with the mother's blood delivering oxygen to the baby and taking away waste products. Even though they have separate minds and Souls, when the fetus is in the womb, mother and child are essentially one organism.

Then, when the baby is born, the umbilical cord remains connected to the placenta. In some cases, it's cut quickly, while in other cases, the midwife waits until the cord stops pulsing. Jean Liedloff's book, *Continuum Concept*, plus other changes reintroduced by midwives, have brought back older methods of "natural childbirth," making the birthing process gentler and slower—allowing the baby's physical separation from the mother to be more gradual and less traumatic.

When these methods are used, the baby is often placed on the mother's bare belly in a dimly lit room. When the cord stops pulsing, it is cut. Then, when the baby seems ready, the mother gently shifts the baby's position to offer the newborn her breast.

This process is so gradual that one could wonder: when does the baby come to see itself as a separate individual? Having become aware of the little-known fact that Original-People can live their entire lives with a perspective of oneness, the question arises:

When and how do civilized babies become individuals?

This would certainly depend on the particular child and the experiences they encounter. What type of treatment do they receive? Did a doctor hang the baby by its feet and whack it on its butt? How available is the mother? Does she hold the baby continuously until it chooses to push away of its own volition as Leidoff witnessed?

Interestingly, Original-People are childlike in many ways.

Although some people believe developing into a proper adult is an important step in human development, I find children with loving parents to have superior values when compared to typical adults. A common example of this is their honesty—in fact, some children can be so honest that they often embarrass their parents who have become accustomed to telling white lies.

I noticed that some words with negative connotations begin with "adult:" "adulterate," which is to corrupt or reduce in quality; "adultery," meaning cheating on one's spouse; "adulterous," one who cheats on their spouse; etc. Etymology doesn't seem to support a connection between "adult" and these words, still the coincidence seems both intriguing and fitting to me.

As I mentioned earlier, Romantic people are somewhat childlike, while Pragmatic people tend to be more "adult" in their demeanor. Personally, I believe it's healthy for grownups to retain some of the carefree, happy-go-lucky, open-hearted ways of being childlike. The stodgy, business-like attitude of "proper adults" feels cold and heartless to me. But, I'm a hopeful Romantic.

Anyhow, it appears that young children and Original-People do not behave like individuals. Also, even though Romantics are individuals, they retain some childlike characteristics.

By taking into account how remarkably different the oneness perspective is, in comparison to the individualistic perspective civilized adults have, it seems this difference in perspective is what separates Original-People and young children from everyone else.

INDIVIDUALITY AND OUR PERSONAL OPINIONS

In civilization, everyone has an opinion. Generally, there are many different opinions on the same subject. In fact, these days, it seems everyone's opinion is at least slightly different from everyone else's, indicating that our level of individuation is increasing.

A 2002 BBC documentary entitled, *Century of Self* reviews the 20th century from 1900 to 2000. It shows how the level of human individuation has been increasing beyond anything ever experienced before. It's very informative and unexpectedly interesting.

The process of dividing people into separate individuals has continued to proceed even further during the first eighteen years of the 21st century. Cell phones, video games, the internet, and social media have propelled the individuation process further than ever.

Although we originally expected that most of these technologies would connect people and bring us closer together, an unexpected boomerang effect has isolated people from each other more than ever before. More information is available to more people, but we each access it on an **individual** basis.

As individuals, a common pastime of civilized people is to discuss or debate our differing opinions. Despite that, some people choose to avoid debating certain subjects. Politics and religion are often avoided at social gatherings. This is because discussing these subjects often leads to arguments. Many civilized people have strongly held beliefs regarding politics and religion. Opposition to those beliefs can cause emotions to erupt, resulting in heated debates. In more extreme cases, physical fights have taken place.

In civilization, differences in our beliefs or opinions are the primary cause for nearly all human conflict. These conflicts range from a minor disagreement all the way up to a world war!

"People with opinions just go around bothering one another."

—Buddha

On the other hand, it's quite remarkable that all three anthropologists that I interviewed told me that the Original-People they lived with never discussed differing viewpoints. I doubt that it was because they chose to avoid discussing them. It's likely that their viewpoints were all so similar that any minute difference didn't warrant discussion. If all Original-People pay close attention to their Soul's guidance, and the wisdom of all Souls come from the One, their beliefs could be nearly identical. Over and above that, their oneness perspective would cause them to presume that everyone has the same beliefs.

It seems quite clear that today most Original-People have been transformed into civilized individuals who now have differences of opinion. Even though this evolutionary development of differing opinions has lots of negative effects, a very important positive effect is how our differences make us able to meet <u>mysterious</u> others.

Surely, our differences of opinion automatically make us mysterious to one another. Additionally, the fact that our differences of opinion provoke civilized people to engage in conflict uncovers a common misconception regarding Original-People. Many people still believe that Original-People were savages while this is nearly the opposite of what has been discovered to be true.

ORIGINAL-PEOPLE WERE PEACEFUL

In the last thirty-plus years, archeologists have discovered that early humans appear to have lived in more peaceful and harmonious ways than we do today. Pottery pieces dating from 10,000 years ago back to 30,000 years ago have no illustrations of war or fighting. There are scenes of men hunting animals, but scenes of men fighting men don't appear on pottery until 10,000 years ago. This timing coincides with the birth of the civilizations that have developed into what exists today.

Moreover, the pottery pieces depicting men fighting men appear in the very location where modern civilization was born: Mesopotamia. This makes a strong case for the theory that violence between humans didn't begin until the birth of civilization, about 10,000 years ago.

These archeological records, plus the reports from Columbus and other European explorers, show how the idea that primitive people were barbarians or savages is a myth. Beyond that, the anthropologists that I spoke to in person all agree that the Original-People they lived with were "absolutely not individuals," confirming that these gentle, childlike people's lives were based on a perspective of oneness.

With a oneness perspective, fighting and wars don't take place.

Today, some people are pushing for humanity to return to a perspective of oneness. If this was possible it would likely resolve most of humanity's ills. Selfishness, hoarding, starvation, arguments, fights, wars, mass shootings...essentially every challenge we have these days, except overpopulation, would disappear if we returned to a oneness perspective.

Even though that may be true, the divisive state of affairs that exists in our modern "civilized" society is individualizing our children. Additionally, any remaining Original-People are being gradually individualized by encounters with divisive civilized people.

The reverse process of returning to a oneness perspective is extraordinarily rare, but it does exist. For instance, in India, a few brave and dedicated individuals leave civilization by retreating up into the mountains to find solitude in a cave. Once far from civilization, they endeavor to regain the oneness perspective that was crushed by the divisive activities of civilized adults when growing up in civilization.

Reverting to a oneness perspective would likely make our reality peaceful, but we wouldn't be able to accomplish the goal of the universe—finding out how it feels to meet mysterious others—simply because no others would appear to exist from the oneness perspective.

INDIVIDUALITY IS NECESSARY

To accomplish the goal of the universe, the illusion of individuality had to be achieved. So, even though the Original way of life is closer to the truth, and it's much more peaceful than our civilized way of life, that original way of life failed to provide the individuals that are needed to find out how it feels to meet mysterious others.

The next chapter shares the Consciousness-Origin Cosmology's explanation of how the process of individualizing humans takes place.

Chapter 12
The Final Step of Individualizing Humans

To deal with the lack of individuality in Original-People, something needed to be done to individualize humans. The Consciousness-Origin Cosmology claims that a special type of human was introduced by the One-Who-Is-All. Dr. Katz explained that these special people exhibit divisive traits that push people apart, causing people to shift their perspective from viewing everything as one to viewing each person as a separate individual. These special people and their divisive influence is a defining feature of civilization. Even today, divisive people individualize children as they grow up in civilization.

Although the Triality of human consciousness was well designed, making humans gullible enough to be duped into believing the illusion of individuality, we initially perceive reality in alignment with the ultimate truth: all is One. Therefore, a divisive push was needed to jumpstart the illusion of individuality. This divisive push provokes each human to perceive themselves and all humans, as separate individuals. That viewpoint causes everything to appear to be separate.

Without the divisive activities of the special people, the Original-People would remain in oneness-consciousness forever. Beyond that, each child born also views the world from a oneness perspective. That being the case, each child needs divisive activities to provoke them into adopting an individualistic perspective.

Thus, the special people play very important roles that divide all humans into individuals by pushing us apart and making the illusion of individuality feel real to us all. Once individualized, we are then able to find out how it feels to meet mysterious others.

This aspect of reality answers two great questions:

> "If there's a God, why do bad things happen to good people?"
> "If there's a God, why is evil so prevalent in the world?"

The single answer is, to separate everyone into individuals.

SO, WHO ARE THE SPECIAL DIVISIVE PEOPLE?

To discover what's special about these people, let's consider the mysterious human trait called "conscience."

conscience: noun;
an inner feeling or voice viewed as acting as a guide to the rightness or wrongness of one's behavior.
ORIGIN Middle English (also in the sense 'inner thoughts or knowledge') [23]

According to the definition, **Conscience** is remarkably similar to **Soul-intuition**. Our conscience and intuition both come from inside. They both appear in the head as a thought, a voice, or a feeling.

When someone does something that indicates they don't have a conscience, it's common for people to exclaim, "he doesn't have a heart," or "he doesn't have a soul." Those sayings seem to come from people who intuitively know our conscience comes from our Souls in our hearts. Finally, if the Soul plays a parental role, part of that role would surely include being our conscience.

In support of this, I've found people who appear to lack Soul-intuition also seem to lack a conscience.

In Chapter 10: Humanity's Pivotal Divide, I shared a set of questions that I often use to determine if a person has intuition or not. By asking over a thousand people those questions, and in several cases following up to determine how honest or trustworthy the people are, I found that people with intuition appear to have a conscience, while those without intuition don't seem to have a conscience either. Therefore, it appears our conscience is part of our Soul-intuition.

This implies that people who turn away from their Soul and end up with a calcified pineal gland develop an additional unexpected side effect—their conscience disappears.

CONSCIENCE ALSO COMES FROM OUR SOUL

My Soul informed me that Soul-intuition, Romantic promptings, and conscience all come from the divine Soul as forms of intuitive guidance. All of these forms of esoteric knowledge reach our conscious-mind in our head through the pineal gland. So, once a person's pineal gland is calcified, that condition turns off all of their divine inner guidance—including their conscience.

Once Pragmatic people are cut off from their conscience, they no longer receive intuitive messages deterring them from unconscionable activities. Without being warned that an action they're contemplating is "a bad idea," they can more easily follow through and do it. Afterwards, without being notified from within that what they did was inappropriate, they're less likely to feel guilt or shame. This makes the Pragmatic people a special type of human that has greater freedom to play the divisive roles that are needed to individualize all of humanity.

To fulfill the purpose of the universe, finding out how it feels to meet mysterious others, it's essential that some people behave in ways that provoke all humans to buy into the illusion of individuality. Without a conscience, the Pragmatic people become especially well-suited to participate in divisive activities that deviate from the morality of human conscience, giving them the ability to fill the very important need for divisive activities.

WHAT DRIVES PEOPLE TOWARD DIVISIVE ACTIVITIES?

Once a person is disconnected from their Soul, their inner source of happiness, they're certainly going to look elsewhere to fill the hole in their heart. Since they have forsaken their Soul, their Soul formalizes the disconnection by calcifying the pineal gland. Once this has taken place, the Soul uses its control over the Pragmatic person's desires to cause that person to engage in extreme activities.

So, in a Pragmatic person who ignores their Soul, the Soul plays a very different role than it does in a Romantic person who listens to and follows their Soul's guidance. In a Pragmatic person, the Soul uses its control over the person's desires to cause them to strive for extremes. Regardless of what those desires propel the person to reach for, their struggle to quench extreme desires make the Pragmatic person into a taker. Takers impinge on other people, providing a divisive effect.

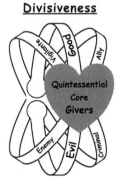

Divisiveness

Thus, divisive people venture out toward extremes that could be labeled good or evil. The divisiveness is not based on the side that is chosen. It's the extreme nature of the desire and the striving taker-approach to life that makes Pragmatics divisive. The illustration on the right depicts this idea by combining three Trialities, each with its own pair of opposite polarities, but all having "Givers" in the one Quintessential Core.

Even though a Romantic giver can venture out toward one of the polarities, their Soul will guide them back to the Quintessential Core by using intuitive messages and desires that draw Romantics toward the beneficent balance point. Some of that guidance may include warnings that fit into the conscience category of Soul guidance.

By offering appropriate intuition, conscience, and desires for balance, Souls guide Romantic people toward the straight and narrow. This Quintessential Core is labeled "Givers" because, giving what one is guided from within to give, is a behavior that people who follow their hearts tend to have in common.

On the other hand, Pragmatics are free to go as far out toward an extreme polarity as their desires press them to go. Their life becomes one of reaching to satisfy their extreme desires. By striving to satisfy their desires, the special divisive people tend to adopt a taker way of life that causes people they encounter to feel separate.

Pragmatic people are most likely not aware of what they're getting into when their heartache or hunger for power drives them to turn away from their Soul's divine guidance. Many Pragmatics simply want to stop the pain of heartache, others have an ego that chooses to reach for personal glory. Certainly, other reasons exist. In spite of the reason, a person's choice to deviate far enough from their Soul's guidance to incite calcification has unexpected side-effects. Without being aware of it, Pragmatics inadvertently choose to be transformed into divisive takers that individualize humanity.

For example, consider a friend of mine who had a lovely wife, a darling son, a healthy body, and a sharp mind. He and his family were living their dream. Their mutual pursuit was a very positive extreme—optimal living. Both parents actively contributed to the greater community in positive ways.

Together, the couple wrote songs about peace, love, and harmony. She sang like an angel. He had a beautiful voice and played his guitar masterfully. Amongst other talents, he was a skilled palm frond weaver, and a very capable builder. She had marvelous talents as well. Their lives appeared to be quite idyllic.

Whenever I asked this man how he was doing, he always smiled and said, "Better than ever!" The smile seemed a bit forced, and I did wonder why he never had an "off day," but I didn't think much about that until I heard the awful news that he had committed suicide.

His demise was a big surprise to everyone who knew him.

From what I could see, he had acquired and become everything he could possibly desire. The most divisive things about him were how he outshined everyone else, and the way he demanded more from his tenants than they believed to be a fair trade.

The way he appeared to be so perfect left me feeling inferior and consequently separate. The perception that he required more from his tenants than they felt fair must have felt divisive to them. So, even though this man lived according to extremely positive ideals his extreme positivity was divisive.

In his parting letter, he explained that his father treated him in a way that made him believe he wasn't good enough. Somehow, he dragged this pattern into his marriage and came to believe that he failed to be good enough for his wife. It seems that the deeper reality was that he wasn't good enough for himself. Ironically, his valiant attempts to be better than ever, every day of his life, left people around him feeling inferior or taken advantage of.

Clearly his claim that he was always, "better than ever!" was what he was striving for. Unfortunately, all extremes reach a practical limit. When there's nothing left to improve, and you still aren't good enough to satisfy your longings to be better, then what?

By standing as straight and tall as a pillar of light, never wavering until the end, this man made me feel inferior and separate. My commitment to humility enabled me to accept that, but I still felt it. He was so awesome, such a light worker, physically fit, handsome, and gifted in so many ways, that he left me in the dust. Little did I know that he was in agony, trying to be good enough to reach the unachievable optimal living ideal that his desires drove him to strive for.

I knew him for eighteen years and had shared with him the idea that one's source of happiness came from the heart, not out at an extreme polarity. He invited me to present my Way-of-the-Heart theories at his idyllic home where he also invited his tenants to my presentation.

I was surprised by his invitation. He seemed to have it all worked out, so why was he interested in my middle Way-of-the-Heart?

At that gathering, it seemed as if he was the only person unable to relate to my message. Being well aware of his extreme goals to find perfection in optimal living, I began to suspect that he had become disconnected from his Soul.

His parting letter revealed that he ended his life because he held the belief that he wasn't good enough for the most important people in his life. Despite his belief, I was close enough to him to know that he was better than anyone needs to be. So much better that most everyone fell short of the high standards he maintained. This man's life is a testament to the idea that striving for an extreme is divisive for oneself and others. In this case, the polarity he chose was on the side of good, revealing how the nature of divisiveness is not the side one chooses, but rather how far from the center one ventures.

Additionally, while on an extreme journey, does the adventure involve becoming a taker? When an extremist is reaching for the stars, how many people must they step on to grasp hold of those stars?

On top of that, by revealing how he was secretly suffering, I discovered that he was lying about being "better than ever." Instead, he was getting closer and closer to the end of his rope. He was a great actor, playing the role of a happy, fulfilled, and psychologically healthy man, even though he was tormented by his extreme desire to be better than ever.

His divisive, extremist role may have fooled everyone but himself. Despite that, this example reveals the sacrifice this man's Soul took to orchestrate his divisive role. Residing in the heart of a person who is suffering so much that he would take his own life, in spite of the numerous blessings he had, must be very difficult. His conscious-mind, his subconscious-mind, and his Superconscious-Soul must have all found his life very painful to be involved in.

Next let's take a look at the negative polarities of the dualistic spectrums, some Pragmatic people end up in an evil extreme of one duality or another. For example, I recently saw a documentary entitled *The Heart of Man* that was released in 2017. In that documentary, several real people tell their personal stories of living secret lives that are driven by their insatiable desire for some sort of deviant sexual activity. They further reveal how their insatiable desires destroy their relationships and, in some cases, break up their families. On top of that, these real people explain how their secret lives end up tormenting themselves.

Most explain that the cause of their plight came from sexual abuse that they suffered as children. These heartbreaking experiences caused them to turn away from their Souls earlier than most.

One of the men very eloquently explained how he was very skilled at presenting himself to the world as an exceptionally happy person with an especially wonderful life. He claimed that he was often the life of the party and admired by many at social gatherings. All the while, he admitted that he secretly hated himself and felt horrible about his deviant hidden life.

This sort of double-life scenario was referred to by most of the people who shared their personal stories in this eye-opening documentary. A few of the testimonials came from people who held prominent positions. They managed to share their stories in a careful way that didn't reveal their specific issues, but conveyed how difficult it was to live with a socially unacceptable deviant desire that persisted.

When their deviant activities were eventually found out by their spouses, the betrayal cut so deeply that it ruined their relationships and broke up their families. Reaching to take more than what is enough eventually destroyed their lives.

Extremes are divisive and cause hardship regardless of whether the extreme is good or evil. Additionally, although extremists may be quite skilled at covering up their suffering, these Pragmatic takers could be the ones who suffer the most.

In the following quote, the mean or middle is recommended:

"For both excessive and insufficient exercise destroy one's strength, and both eating and drinking too much or too little destroy health, whereas the right quantity produces, increases or preserves it. So, it is the same with temperance, courage and the other virtues... This much then, is clear: in all our conduct, it is the mean that is to be commended."

—Aristotle (384 BC–322 BC) philosopher and scientist

Conversely, the polarized trajectory of Pragmatics forms a sizable gap between extreme Pragmatics and humble Romantics. As a Pragmatic person travels further from the Quintessential Core, the gap grows larger, their need to take increases and their divisive effect grows stronger.

Despite all of those difficulties, the special divisive people are accomplishing an essential service that individualizes humans making us able to fulfill the goal of the universe. To accomplish this, some Souls guide their humans into agonizing Pragmatic roles.

Although it's popular for people to think in terms of good versus evil, the Triality model shows how the key is in the middle. When the Quintessential Core is overlooked, the remaining duality misleads people into thinking their choices are between one of two extremes.

Additionally, the dualistic illusions of good versus evil offer the false belief that peace will come when everyone chooses good. The deeper truth is that peace and happiness reside in the middle.

In the song presented below, Donovan poetically explains how war will never end as long as people continue to choose sides and play the extreme role that he calls the Universal Soldier.

Universal Soldier

He's five foot-two, and he's six feet-four,
He fights with missiles and with spears.
He's all of thirty-one, and he's only seventeen,
He's been a soldier for a thousand years.

He's a Catholic, a Hindu, an Atheist, a Jain,
A Buddhist and a Baptist and a Jew.
And he knows he shouldn't kill,
And he knows he always will,
Kill you for me my friend and me for you.

And he's fighting for Canada,
He's fighting for France,
He's fighting for the USA,
And he's fighting for the Russians,
And he's fighting for Japan,
And he thinks we'll put an end to war this way.

And he's fighting for Democracy,
He's fighting for the Reds,
He says it's for the peace of all.
He's the one who must decide,
Who's to live and who's to die,
And he never sees the writing on the wall.

But without him,
How would Hitler have condemned him at Labau?
Without him Caesar would have stood alone,
He's the one who gives his body
As a weapon of the war,
And without him all this killing can't go on.

154

He's the Universal Soldier and he really is to blame,
His orders come from far away no more,
They come from here and there and you and me,
And brothers can't you see,
This is not the way we put an end to war.

Soldiers are trained to march forward taking the lives of the enemy without being able to get to know the people on the other side. Fraternizing with the enemy is a violation of military law.

Then, propaganda labels the enemy "evil." The condemnation of an entire group of people makes genocide acceptable. The "good soldiers" on one side, are ordered to destroy the "evil enemy soldiers" on the opposing side.

Meanwhile, over on the opposing side, the labels of good and evil are reversed. Both sides provide propaganda that convinces everyone that they are good, while the enemy on the opposite side is evil.

In spite of all of this good versus evil conflict, and the pain it causes for survivors, the underlying consciousness remains indestructible. Once a physical body dies, the head and gut minds escape in their astral body to visit the astral afterlife realm where they prepare for their next incarnation. Meanwhile, the divisive activities that took place during the war accomplish the final step of individualizing the humans who remain alive in the physical realm.

So even though many people, myself included, pray for peace, divisive extremists who get involved in all sorts of battles are performing a necessary individuation service.

PRAGMATIC QUALITY OF LIFE

When considering the divisive people who are involved in individualizing all of humanity, it's important to consider how difficult those divisive roles are to play. The people who play divisive roles are often plagued with inner conflict that produces a tormented life.

Even though some are pillars of society, captains of industry, political leaders, famous actors, celebrated entertainers, or highly successful in their profession or chosen pursuit, divisive people are often suffering inner torment due to the insatiable nature of their desires and the taker mentality that develops from the striving that ensues. Some extremists may have attractive spouses, lovely children, and a beautiful home, but their endless reaching for more will rob them of happiness. Even if they're able to fool all of their friends and associates by putting on a happy face, are any of them able to fool themselves?

When it comes to happiness, the feeling of deep satisfaction and an inner sense of gratitude for the wonders of life emanates from a Romantic person's heart to provide lasting happiness.

Certainly, Pragmatic people experience happiness, but lasting joy and long-term happiness apparently elude them because their insatiable desires persist, causing Pragmatics to continue reaching for more. Even when divisive activities are positive in character, like with my friend who was an extreme proponent of light, love, and optimal living, striving for more makes life painful enough to commit suicide.

Unfortunately, these Pragmatic extremists will never find enough of what they yearn for to quench their insatiable thirst that arrives as a desire from the very Soul they had forsaken. Sadly, these people become takers who ironically suffer from wanting more.

BUDDHA'S COMPASSION FOR THOSE WHO SUFFER

Over 2,500 years ago, the Buddha discovered how reaching for extremes leads to suffering. To deal with this problem, the Buddha developed a practice that can be used by Pragmatic people to reduce their suffering by choosing a middle path with their conscious-mind.

The Buddhist middle path is defined to be halfway between unrestrained sensual indulgence and severe self-discipline that would include avoidance of all forms of indulgence. The Buddhist system encourages the practitioner to use their intellect to navigate toward the middle of these opposite polarities. To follow this middle path, the person must override or ignore their desires using their conscious-mind to push forward in defiance of their Soul.

Thus, it's quite fitting that Buddhism denies the existence of a Soul or Atman, as it's referred to in Hinduism, which was the Buddha's initial spiritual path.

Therefore, the Buddhist middle path is very different than the middle Way-of-the-Heart that's shared in this book. In the Way-of-the-Heart, the practitioner surrenders to the Soul in their Heart-Center. The Superconscious-Soul lies halfway between the head and the gut, therefore, following the Soul's guidance is a middle way that is nearly the opposite of the Buddhist middle path that defies the Soul.

156

To practice the Way-of-the-Heart, a person must be connected to their Soul. When they are, they receive intuition that guides them down the straight and narrow—the Way-of-the-Heart. Additionally, people who willingly follow their heart are blessed with inner happiness, childlike wonder, and an inherent love of life. Obviously, the Way-of-the-Heart doesn't work for Pragmatics.

Nonetheless, for Pragmatics who are disconnected from their Soul-intuition, the Buddhist middle path is a proven system to reduce the suffering that results from excessive desires. This alternate approach is perfect for Pragmatic people.

Additionally, the Buddha's denial of the Soul's existence fits the Pragmatic condition of being disconnected from the Soul. Once disconnected, a person doesn't seem to have a Soul—which fits the Buddhist theory that the Atman or Soul doesn't exist.

It's important to keep in mind that this isn't a black and white issue. Even though a Romantic person has intuition and a conscience, they may, at times, choose to ignore it. The Soul is a guardian that never violates the free will of the person it guards. The final choices are left up to the ego-mind, which can choose to ignore advice from the Superconscious-Soul. So, even if a person's Soul advises them to be honest and remain near the Quintessential Core rooted in giving from the heart, a Romantic person can still choose to explore extremes and reach for excess. Eventually this type of behavior may lead to becoming a Pragmatic. However, exploring extremes occasionally can be part of a Romantic person's life.

On the other hand, Pragmatic people who don't have a conscience can choose, of their own free will, to follow ethical guidelines that instruct them to be fair and honest.

For instance, the Buddha offers Five Moral Precepts which instruct practitioners to refrain from: harming living things; taking what is not given; sexual misconduct; lying or gossip; and taking intoxicating substances e.g. drugs or drink.

Additionally, some Pragmatics choose to live a humble, balanced life. Buddhist teachings prescribe this as well. There's much Buddhism has to offer Pragmatics who are interested in reducing their suffering. The Buddha held deep compassion for people who suffer and was dedicated to helping these people to alleviate the suffering that seems to be growing more common as time marches on.

Even though a Soul may be willing to incarnate into what it knows will be a difficult Pragmatic mission, the conscious- and subconscious-minds are created or selected after that decision has been made. Therefore, these smaller portions of consciousness seem to be taken for a ride. When a person is born, their ego-mind has no idea of what their destiny is. The head- and gut-minds that end up on a divisive mission could be innocent victims who are tricked by their Soul or other beings into living a divisive Pragmatic life.

There are claims that the astral realm, and at least some of the permanent residents of that realm, have the job of luring people away from their Soul. So, it seems that innocent conscious- and subconscious-minds are lured into divisive lives and deserve compassion.

If you believe your life has gone awry and you would like to come back into balance, then Buddhism may be quite helpful.

If you suspect that your pineal gland is calcified, a head x-ray can be used to evaluate its condition. If it is calcified, and you would like to decalcify it, I provide a method at the end of Chapter 19.

I personally hope that everyone who has challenges and issues that cause them to suffer, find remedies. The healing tools at the end of Chapter 19 may be helpful.

THE AGE OF INDIVIDUATION

The current *Age of Individuation* began about 6,000 to 10,000 years ago, after the Great Flood. There are multiple geographic locations where survivors of that catastrophic event regrouped and began to multiply. Before the Great Flood, experimental testing of individuation methods took place in pre-alluvion civilizations.

In the Atlantic Ocean, near the island of Bimini, large, flat, rectangular basalt slabs appear to form a road on the ocean floor, as shown on the left.

Close by, large carved stone columns lie on the ocean bed as shown on the right.

These are claimed by some to be the remains of a sunken civilization that Plato referred to as, "Atlantis."

On the other side of the Earth in the Pacific Ocean between Hawai'i and Japan, stone structures that appear to be man-made have been discovered. One is shown on the right in a picture taken by Dr. Masaaki Kimura, from Okinawa, Japan. Some claim this is the remains of the legendary continent of Mu.

These artifacts are evidence of two ancient human civilizations that sank. There are legends claiming that something went wrong in Mu and Atlantis, consequently they were destroyed or somehow self-destructed, ultimately sinking to be covered by the great oceans.

Fortunately, folklore has kept these legends alive and inspired people to keep looking for evidence of their existence.

My Soul informed me that these ancient civilizations were used to experiment with a variety of methods to accomplish the final step of individualizing humans. This individuation process has been a very challenging endeavor. The physical/astral universe, life, humans, and the Triality of consciousness came close to forming individuals out of the One, but a divisive push finally achieved individuality.

That divisive push included an especially sensitive issue: how might the divisive push be performed in ways that produce individuals who are opened to love?

Love and divisive separation are essentially opposites. Despite that, individuality is needed before loving another can be explored.

Therefore, a significant number of individuals who are interested in love must emerge from the divisive process to adequately explore the delightful sorts of relationships that involve love.

Atlantis and Mu were established to experiment with this sensitive final step of individuation. Once that experimentation was complete, a fresh start was needed to properly implement what was discovered at these experimental sites. So, to clear the slate and use the best divisive methods, these land masses were lowered into the Great oceans, sinking them during the Great Flood.

Even though many physical bodies perished, all the Souls and other portions of consciousness, being indestructible, still exist today. New physical bodies became available for additional lives via reincarnation.

Additionally, some people survived the Great Flood and repopulated the Earth. Some of their descendants built new civilizations that emerged in Asia, India, Africa, Mesopotamia, and the Americas. Any of these could have produced the predominant individuation system, but we now know that the Judeo-Christian-Muslim system that began in Mesopotamia spread around the entire world to become the predominant divisive individuation system for the entire world.

BOOMERANG INTO LOVE

Unexpectedly, this divisive system comprised of male domination, war, violence, power-hungry leaders, excessive wealth contrasted by extreme poverty, has produced a large number of loving open-hearted people. They may be a minority, however there are many people who champion the wonderful power of love.

My Soul has helped me to understand how a boomerang effect can turn negative divisive events around to achieve positive loving results. While a plethora of awful activities take place daily, this boomerang effect has caused love to emerge in many people's hearts. An explanation of how this paradoxical property of reality occurs is provided in the first chapter of **Part 3.**

Before that is presented, the next chapter shows how the *Book of Genesis* corroborates much of what has been presented so far.

Chapter 13
Support from Genesis

The oldest written records of humanity are the clay tablets found in the deserts of Mesopotamia. This is where Iran and Iraq are located today. Tens of thousands of these tablets contain epic stories that are summarized in the *Book of Genesis*, from the *Old Testament*. Although much has been lost in summarization and translation, the essence remains.

It's my understanding that Jews, Christians, and Muslims all see the *Book of Genesis* as their cosmology of the universe. That makes *Genesis* the most widely acknowledged cosmology available. Additionally, it comes from the civilization that emerged in Mesopotamia and spread around the world to individualize humanity.

When considering *Genesis*, a wide variety of interpretations have been proposed. This is especially true when it comes to Adam, Eve, the garden of Eden, the Tree of Life, the serpent, and the Tree of Knowledge of Good and Evil. The numerous interpretations offered have been used to support a wide range of philosophies and beliefs. In keeping with that tradition, this chapter examines *Genesis* showing how it fits the Consciousness-Origin Cosmology surprisingly well.

I've chosen to excerpt passages from the English Standard Version (ESV) of the Holy Bible for the following reasons:

The ESV is an "essentially literal" translation that seeks as far as possible to capture the precise wording of the original text and the personal style of each Bible writer. As such, its emphasis is on "word- for-word" correspondence, at the same time taking into account differences of grammar, syntax, and idiom between current literary English and the original languages. Thus, it seeks to be transparent to the original text, letting the reader see as directly as possible the structure and meaning of the original.

IN THE BEGINNING

{1:1} In the beginning, God created the heavens and the earth. {1:2} The earth was without form and void, and darkness was over the face of the deep. And the Spirit of God was hovering over the face of the waters.

Interestingly, the beginning describes a Triality. God is placed at the Quintessential Core of everything, with the Heavens and the Earth being the opposite polarities that make up a dual universe of life versus death.

In other words, the One-Who-Is-All extends out from Itself the polarities of Heaven (the astral realm) and Earth (the physical realm), and what's left of the One, hovers above the face of the waters in the darkness. This fits the Consciousness-Origin Cosmology's first step of creation perfectly.

Next, the creation of a light versus dark Triality is described:

{1:3} And God said, "Let there be light," and there was light. {1:4} And God saw that the light was good. And God separated the light from the darkness. {1:5} God called the light Day, and the darkness he called Night. And there was evening and there was morning, the first day.

Dark and light, or night and day, are a duality in which the evening and morning are the Quintessential Core midpoints. Sunrise and sunset are both halfway between midday and midnight. Thus, the first five sentences of *Genesis* describe two Trialities that make up reality.

This first day of creation is quite likely symbolic of a longer period of time that encompasses the process of creating the Grand Illusion. Calling that period of time a day could be a way of indicating how time doesn't exist in the foundational realm of consciousness.

The second day (or period of time) involves the formation of the Earth's primary physical features. The events are described in ways that appear to imply evermore Trialities. For example: "{1:6} And God said, let there be a firmament in the midst of the waters, and let it divide the waters from the waters."

These first two days are full of things that can be easily fit into the Triality model. Beginning *Genesis* with descriptions of Trialities indicates they are fundamental building blocks of the universe.

Then, the third day through the fifth day summarize the formation of life. Plants, fish, birds, and animals are all produced in

162

abundance during these three "days" of creation that roughly follow the evolutionary sequence, apart from the time factor.

One oddity is how the sun, moon, and stars aren't mentioned until day four. In the book *Egyptian Myths and Mysteries*, Rudolf Steiner explains the formation of the Earth, sun, and moon in a very interesting, unusual, and complex way that offers an explanation to this oddity. The length and detail of that explanation prohibit including it here. If you're interested in more details regarding the formative stages of the Earth's development, that book may be of interest to you.

THE CREATION OF HUMANS

On the sixth and last day of creation, God creates humans:

{1:27} So God created man in his own image, in the image of God he created him; male and female he created them. {1:28} And God blessed them. And God said to them, "Be fruitful and multiply and fill the earth and subdue it and have dominion over the fish of the sea and over the birds of the heavens and over every living thing that moves on the earth." {1:29} And God said, "Behold, I have given you every plant yielding seed that is on the face of all the earth, and every tree with seed in its fruit. You shall have them for food."

Making humans in God's image means that each human contains the essence of God. The Consciousness-Origin Cosmology proposes that each Soul contains the essence of the One-Who-Is-All's consciousness made into a small portion, a mini-One. Placing a Soul in the heart of each human makes each one of us a likeness of God.

My Soul notified me that our physical appearance is not what makes us like God who is formless. Rather, it's the Superconscious-Soul that is a likeness of God. Meister Eckhart agrees:

God created the soul so like himself that nothing in Heaven or on earth is so like God as the human Soul.

—Meister Eckhart (? -1328) theologian, philosopher and mystic

The end of the sixth day is also the end of the process of creating the universe and life. The last thing created are humans. This indicates that humans must be appropriate for God's purpose.

Curiously, no purpose is offered in *Genesis*. God's decision to undertake the colossal task of creating the universe is not linked to a purpose. Considering the massive effort involved, there must be sufficient reason for the tremendous undertaking, still no reason is offered.

The Consciousness-Origin Cosmology begins with a reason: discovering how it feels to meet mysterious others. In previous chapters I showed how that reason fits with reality and makes sense. Here, in interpreting *Genesis*, the absence of a reason leaves an opportunity to fill in the missing purpose. Therefore, I'm going to presume that the Consciousness-Origin Cosmology's purpose is accurate. Then, in what follows, I'll show how astonishingly well that purpose fits *Genesis*.

WHAT ABOUT ADAM AND EVE?

Chapter One of *Genesis* ends at the end of the sixth day of creation once humans are formed. Even though humans have been created, there hasn't been any mention of Adam or Eve.

Chapter Two begins by discussing the seventh day, a day of rest. This day is blessed and made a holy day.

> *{2:1} Thus the heavens and the earth were finished, and all the host of them. {2:2} And on the seventh day God finished his work that he had done, and he rested on the seventh day from all his work that he had done. {2:3} So God blessed the seventh day and made it holy, because on it God rested from all his work that he had done in creation.*

Next, the creation process is summarized in a strange way that ends with, "...there was no man to work the ground."

It's reasonable to presume that Original-People were created on the sixth day and these people don't work or till the ground. Civilized people work the ground. Original-People simply gather their food as it's provided to them. Chapter One confirmed this as follows:

> *{1:29} And God said, "Behold, I have given you every plant yielding seed that is on the face of all the earth, and every tree with seed in its fruit. You shall have them for food."*

Now that God has rested and reviewed the results of creation, it has become clear that there is no man to work the ground. Why is this important enough to expressly point it out?

Identifying a man by calling him "a man who works the ground," would fit a civilized man in two ways. First of all, civilized humans work or till the ground while Original-People don't. Secondly, civilized people are divisive, and working the ground is also divisive. When working the ground, soil is split apart and turned over to break it into separate little pieces. In a similar way, divisive people individualize people, making them believe they are separate from one another.

Next, God forms Adam from the ground.

{2:7} then the LORD God formed the man of dust from the ground

Presumably he is made to till the ground. However, since he is made of ground, he was allegorically, made to till men.

Apparently, when God rested on day seven, he must have become aware of the oneness perspective held by the Original-People (or pre-adamic people, meaning people created before Adam). Then, to make everyone into separate individuals, God makes Adam to be the first divisive human, a tiller of the ground and divider of people.

THE GARDEN OF EDEN

Even if this is Adam's destiny, God still needs to maneuver Adam into becoming a divisive person. To accomplish this, God places Adam in a special setting, the garden of Eden:

{2:8} And the LORD God planted a garden in Eden, in the east, and there he put the man whom he had formed.

Noting that this garden is located in the east indicates that something new is coming. The sun rises in the east and brings with it a new day; accordingly, the east is a symbol that indicates something new is arriving. In this case, the first divisive person is being forged.

{2:9} And out of the ground the LORD God made to spring up every tree that is pleasant to the sight and good for food. The Tree of Life was in the midst of the garden, and the Tree of the Knowledge of Good and Evil.

Two special trees are specifically identified, the Tree of Life and the Tree of Knowledge of Good and Evil. The Tree of Life is clearly located in the midst (or middle) of the garden. The other important tree is the Tree of Knowledge of Good and Evil.

My Soul informed me that the Tree of Life symbolizes the Soul that's located in each person's Heart Center. Making Adam out of ground allegorically links his body to the garden which is made of ground. Planting the Tree of Life in the middle of that garden links it to the heart and Soul that are located in the middle of the human body.

Another parallel is how the Soul's home, the physical heart, is critical to life, therefore naming the central tree—the Tree of Life—fits the necessity of the heart for life. On top of that, our heart reaches out to every cell of our body with veins and arteries that are like tree branches and roots. Thus, the Tree of Life symbolizes the Soul that resides in our heart and fills us with the fire of life: consciousness.

On the other hand, the Tree of Knowledge of Good and Evil would symbolize our head and gut polarities. These parts of our consciousness form a built-in duality. By associating our intellectual-head with good and our emotional-gut with evil, we get the long-standing association of rational intelligence with good and irrational emotions with evil. This association quite naturally links the duality of human consciousness, our conscious versus subconscious minds, with the Tree of Knowledge of Good and Evil.

Such a large number of allegories may seem overly complicated for such an ancient document, but it's actually well known by ancient language scholars that the people who wrote this stuff often layered metaphors, allegories, and even multiple stories within one text. Their ability to do this is claimed to go beyond what modern writers are able to accomplish today. Accordingly, what I'm sharing is in alignment with the literary practices of early civilization. John Allegro, the greatest Dead Sea scroll's ancient language scholar of the twentieth century, explains this literary practice in his recently republished book, *The Sacred Mushroom and the Cross*.

OTHER PLACES AND THINGS

Later in Chapter Two of *Genesis*, the rivers in the region are listed by name and the precious materials found in the nearby places located along those rivers are catalogued as follows:

> {2:10} A river flowed out of Eden to water the garden, and there it divided and became four rivers. {2:11} The name of the first is the Pishon. It is the one that flowed around the whole land of Havilah, where there is gold. {2:12} And the gold of that land is good; bdellium and onyx stone are there. {2:13} The name of the second river is the Gihon. It is the one that flowed around the whole land of Cush. {2:14} And the name of the third river is the Tigris, which flows east of Assyria. And the fourth river is the Euphrates.

Because the nearby regions have names they must be inhabited, presumably by pre-adamic Original-People. Additionally, gold and attractive stones have been found and named, further indicating humans exist in these locations. Bdellium is a tree resin used in perfumes by early humans. This passage provides extensive support for the idea that the pre-adamic people are plentiful and exist outside the garden of Eden along the four rivers that lead away from the garden.

THE FORBIDDEN FRUIT

> *{2:15} The LORD God took the man and put him in the garden of Eden to work it and keep it. {2:16} And the LORD God commanded the man, saying, "You may surely eat of every tree of the garden, {2:17} but of the tree of the knowledge of good and evil you shall not eat, for in the day that you eat of it you shall surely die."*

We all know how these sorts of warnings work with people. Forbidden things peak our curiosity. Still, time needs to pass for the interest to build, so the story continues.

CREATION AGAIN?

Next, even though everything has already been created in Chapter One and it appears that man has been around quite a while, the creation of plants, land animals, and birds is discussed again. This second time, the process is rehashed after Adam is created.

This raises the question: Why is the sequence of events so out of whack in Chapter Two of *Genesis*?

In Chapter One, when pre-adamic Original-People were created, the sequence of creation roughly followed what would be expected. The sun, moon, and stars were a bit late, but the rest makes sense.

Then, in Chapter Two, the sequence of creation is out of order which fits with the topsy-turvy nature of civilization. The disordered sequence symbolizes the numerous misconceptions held by civilized people. Several examples of our modern misconceptions were shared in previous chapters. For instance, the divisive nature of civilized people versus the kind, childlike nature of Original-People is commonly reversed by calling the hospitable Original-People "savages."

So, if the original six days in Chapter One describe pre-civilization, and Chapter Two, which introduces Adam the worker of the ground and divider of people represents the beginning of civilization, then *Genesis* shows how Original-People align with truth while Adam aligns with civilization's misunderstandings regarding reality. Soon it will become undeniable that Adam and Eve are the parents of civilization and could not have been the first people.

DEALING WITH ADAM BEING ALONE

Next, God points out how Adam is alone:

{2:18} Then the LORD God said, "It is not good that the man should be alone; I will make him a helper fit for him."

This indicates that being with others is important, which fits with the proposed purpose of the universe, meeting others. To deal with Adam's loneliness, God brings all the birds and beasts of the field to meet Adam:

{2:19} Now out of the ground the LORD God had formed every beast of the field and every bird of the heavens and brought them to the man to see what he would call them. And whatever the man called every living creature, that was its name. {2:20} The man gave names to all livestock and to the birds of the heavens and to every beast of the field. But for Adam there was not found a helper fit for him.

The process of Adam naming every animal further aligns him with civilization. Language is a very important part of civilization, so including this naming process associates Adam with civilization and distances him from the pre-adamic Original-People who hardly speak.

After the naming is finished, it is determined that none of these creatures are appropriate to be Adam's companion. Therefore, God makes Eve from Adam's rib, as follows:

{2:21} So the LORD God caused a deep sleep to fall upon the man, and while he slept took one of his ribs and closed up its place with flesh. {2:22} And the rib that the LORD God had taken from the man he made into a woman and brought her to the man.

Now God has taken action twice to resolve Adam's loneliness. Bringing this issue up twice indicates that God is extremely interested in having Adam be involved with others. This tightly links the *Genesis* cosmology with the Consciousness-Origin Cosmology's purpose of meeting others and having relationships.

MAKING EVE FROM ADAM

It's contrary to nature for God to extract one of Adam's ribs and fashion Eve out of this little part of Adam. Women naturally birth men, but in this particular instance, the man births a woman in a very strange way. Nonetheless, this topsy-turvy event fits the upside-down nature of civilization in the following way:

During the current Age of Individuation (civilization) men have ruled over women. In fact, until recently, most women were the "legal property" of their husbands who had the right to physically punish them. In some cases, men had the right to legally kill their wives.

Regardless of the fact that men have been in power throughout the history of civilization, the well-known truth is that every man first appears as a little infant popping out from between a woman's legs. This had obviously been working for the Original-People who were fruitful and multiplied, so why isn't this the case for Adam and Eve? Why is Adam fashioned first and then Eve is extracted out of Adam?

To answer these questions let's review some recently discovered history. The pottery and other artifacts discovered over the last thirty or more years, plus the anthropological information that has been gathered over an even longer period of time, indicate that Original-People were mostly matrilineal with the women involved in leadership roles. Also, based on the prevalence of goddess images found on the pottery and sculpted into the pottery, nearly Original-People, those who began to form villages, focused mostly on goddess worship.

Ancient Greek cosmology originated amongst nearly Original-People. That cosmology proposes that Chaos, a goddess, came first. She birthed Nyx, the goddess of night who finally birthed a god, Eros. So, Greek mythology doesn't include gods until the third generation of deities.

As we all know, civilization has been led mostly by men until very recently. Most Judea-Christian-Muslim people imagine a male creator. Also, in Shivaism, a popular branch of Hinduism, the male deity Shiva is viewed as the Supreme Being. On top of that, the religious clergy of developed civilizations have been almost exclusively men.

Thus, Original-People had mostly female leadership while civilized people have traditionally been led by mostly male leadership.

Soon, we'll discover that this Garden of Eden story leads to the birth of civilization when Adam's son Cain builds the first city. So, when introducing Adam, the man who breaks away from the original way of life to found civilization, it would be disgraceful to have him pop out from between a pre-adamic woman's legs.

Instead, to portray this event diplomatically, emphasize how Adam is different, and align with civilization's male dominance, God fashions Adam by hand. Then, later, Eve is extracted out of Adam.

169

{2:23} Then the man said, "This at last is bone of my bones and flesh of my flesh; she shall be called Woman, because she was taken out of Man."

This appears to be the first public relations stunt. Moreover, it fits civilization's obsession with diplomatic deceptions that are used to influence public opinion, in this case endorsing male leadership.

Additionally, this upside-down birthing event fits the founding of civilization—an upside-down way of life characterized by loads of misconceptions that come from external sources.

LEAVING THE FAMILY TO FIND ANOTHER

After Eve arrives, she and Adam unite in an intimate way:

{2:24} *Therefore a man shall leave his father and his mother and hold fast to his wife, and they shall become one flesh.*

This fits the purpose of the universe: meeting mysterious others. In this case, sexual reproduction is identified as an important arrangement that causes a man to leave his parents in order to bond with a mysterious other, a suitable mate from another clan. It is also in alignment with the way Original-People formed the family around the mother while the men moved out to find their mate in another clan.

ADAM AND EVE ARE STILL ORIGINAL-PEOPLE

The concluding line of *Genesis'* Chapter Two is:

{2:25} *And the man and his wife were both naked and were not ashamed.*

Pointing out that they were naked and not ashamed indicates that Adam and Eve are not yet civilized. They're still much like the pre-adamic Original-People, who are not ashamed to be naked.

According to the multivolume *History of the Indies*, by Bartolome de las Casas who participated in the conquest of Cuba beginning in 1508, "Indian men and women look upon total nakedness with as much casualness as we look upon a man's head or at his hands."

Based on that lack of shame regarding nakedness, Adam and Eve are still Original-People at the end of Chapter Two.

THE SERPENT AND EXOTERIC ADVICE

In the beginning of Chapter Three the serpent shows up:

{3:1} Now the serpent was more crafty than any other beast of the field that the LORD God had made. He said to the woman, "Did God actually say, 'You shall not eat of any tree in the garden'?" {3:2} And the woman said to the serpent, "We may eat of the fruit of the trees in the garden, {3:3} but God said, 'You shall not eat of the fruit of the tree that is in the midst of the garden, neither shall you touch it, lest you die.'" {3:4} But the serpent said to the woman, "You will not surely die. {3:5} For God knows that when you eat of it your eyes will be opened, and you will be like God, knowing good and evil."

In this passage, the crafty serpent claims that God lied. Despite what God said, they will not die if they eat the fruit of the Tree of Knowledge of Good and Evil. Instead, their eyes will be opened and they will be as gods, knowing good and evil. By offering Eve a way to become godlike, the serpent lures Eve to eat by hooking her ego's interest in being godlike.

The serpent's advice marks the second time an external advisor has spoken. The first advice came from God when he told Adam to refrain from eating the fruit of the Tree of Knowledge of Good and Evil. This second time, the serpent advises Eve to eat this very fruit, making the second bit of external advice the opposite of the first.

These two exoteric messages come from God and God's creation that, "... was more crafty than any other beast of the field that the LORD God had made." Interestingly, these exoteric messages contradict each other showing how exoteric knowledge flips around depending on the source.

EATING THE FORBIDDEN FRUIT

Next, based on alluring exoteric advice, Eve samples the fruit:

{3:6} So when the woman saw that the tree was good for food, and that it was a delight to the eyes, and that the tree was to be desired to make one wise, she took of its fruit and ate, and she also gave some to her husband who was with her, and he ate.

Without a single word drawing attention to it, Eve ignores the Tree of Life, a symbol of her Soul. This passage even mentions how the dualistic Tree of Knowledge of Good and Evil is a delight to the eyes. This is consistent with how the polar extremes of a Triality overshadow the Quintessential Core, drawing attention away from the more magnificent central component. In this case, the Tree of Life

171

symbolizing the Soul is ignored and the Tree of Knowledge of Good and Evil symbolizing the head and gut is a delight to the eyes.

Another point of interest is how the serpent addressed Eve, not Adam, even though he was clearly present. This fits with the notion that female leadership was prevalent in Original-People prior to civilization. The way Eve took the lead and ate the fruit, then offered "some to her husband who was with her, and he ate," strongly indicates that Adam was her follower at that point in this symbolic story.

An additional indication that Adam is the follower is how he isn't even referred to by name, but as "her husband," as if she owns him.

BECOMING CIVILIZED PRAGMATIC PEOPLE

{3:7} Then the eyes of both were opened, and they knew that they were naked. And they sewed fig leaves together and made themselves loincloths.

All of a sudden, the two of them notice that they're naked, and they become ashamed. Shame is a common characteristic of civilized people. The quote from Las Casas, offered earlier, points out how Original-People are comfortable being naked, while we all know that most civilized people are ashamed of being naked. Thus, Adam and Eve covering themselves indicates that they have become civilized.

The process that converted Adam and Eve from Original-People into civilized individuals included:

- ♥ Ignoring the Tree of Life—their Souls in their hearts.
- ♥ Following exoteric advice from outside of themselves.
- ♥ Violating God's command in order to become godlike.
- ♥ Focusing on their head and gut minds.

All of this is perfectly in alignment with the development of Pragmatic civilized people, who use their ego-mind to ignore their Soul—an inner god. Pragmatics choose to follow exoteric sources of guidance and focus on their head and gut-minds, which are allegorically represented by the Tree of Knowledge of Good and Evil. Additionally, Pragmatic people endeavor to be godlike, wanting power and prestige.

Conversely, Romantics humbly surrender to their Soul to follow its infallible esoteric guidance represented by the Tree of Life.

ADAM TAKES CHARGE AND THEY HIDE

Next, Adam and Eve hide from God, knowing they have fallen from grace by disobeying his single command, to refrain from eating of the Tree of Knowledge of Good and Evil.

{3:8} And they heard the sound of the LORD God walking in the garden in the cool of the day, and the man and his wife hid themselves from the presence of the LORD God among the trees of the garden.

Now, the two are described as, "the man and his wife" rather than "her husband who was with her," indicating the leadership reversed.

Also, before the fruit eating incident, the serpent addressed Eve and ignored Adam, but in the following passage God calls out to Adam and ignores Eve. This further indicates the leadership has reversed.

{3:9} But the LORD God called to the man and said to him, "Where are you?" {3:10} And he said, "I heard the sound of you in the garden, and I was afraid, because I was naked, and I hid myself." {3:11} He said, "Who told you that you were naked? Have you eaten of the tree of which I commanded you not to eat?" {3:12} The man said, "The woman whom you gave to be with me, she gave me fruit of the tree, and I ate." {3:13} Then the LORD God said to the woman, "What is this that you have done?" The woman said, "The serpent deceived me, and I ate."

In the beginning of this exchange between Adam and God, the two speak as if Eve isn't present even though she's right there next to Adam. Specifically, Adam says, "The woman whom you gave to be with me, she gave me fruit of the tree, and I ate." This is how highly dominant men arrogantly talk about their wives, even while the wife is present. This indicates that they've both become civilized.

Beyond the way Adam spoke, it's common for civilized men to blame women for their mistakes. While Eve did offer the fruit to Adam, he could have refused to eat it. Yet, in this passage, he blames Eve. Historically, civilized men have been known to blame women or the feminine emotions that come from one's own gut-mind even though we all have a conscious-mind to make our final choices.

When asked about what she had done, Eve blames the serpent. Blaming others is part of civilization which is fraught with lawsuits and arguments regarding blame. Conversely, Original-People don't blame. Earlier, I presented an example of an Original-boy accidentally shooting an arrow into another boy's chest. His Original-mother is surprised, but she doesn't blame, reprimand or condemn her son.

173

WHAT DID THEY EAT?

On the left is a photograph of a fresco painting found in Plaincourault chapel, France, dated 1291. It depicts a giant amanita muscaria mushroom as the Tree of Knowledge of Good and Evil. Adam and Eve are standing on either side with a serpent wrapped around the "trunk" offering Eve a sample. The amanita is a well-known entheogen that grows in the location identified by the aforementioned rivers. Being the only red-capped mushroom with white spots, its identity is unmistakable. The actual fresco depicts a red cap with white spots.

Many other color amanita images have been found in stained glass windows of old churches and in a well preserved 12th century bible. Some of these old images depict Jesus and the amanita together.

Now, let's reconsider God's original warning:

"... {2:17} but of the tree of the knowledge of good and evil you shall not eat, for in the day that you eat of it you shall surely die."

This riddle-like warning can be decoded to mean: if you eat an amanita, the entheogenic journey will take you to the astral afterlife side of the veil, as if you had died. On top of that, entheogenic journeys often feature serpents, making that curious element of the story fit perfectly with the use of entheogens. Resolving this confounding mystery in this way, supports the idea that nearly all religions began with entheogenic substance use or some sort of astral travel method.

Moving on, after cursing the serpent, God curses Eve:

"I will surely multiply your pain in childbearing; in pain, you shall bring forth children. Your desire shall be for your husband, and he shall rule over you."

Referring to Las Casas' *History of the Indies*, and his direct experience of Original-People:

"Marriage laws are non-existent: men and women alike choose their mates and leave them as they please, without offense, jealousy or anger. They multiply in great abundance; pregnant women work to the last minute and give birth almost painlessly; up the next day, they bathe in the river and are as clean and healthy as before giving birth."

174

Based on that excerpt and God's curse, it's clear that Eve is being pushed further toward being a civilized woman who obeys her husband and experiences pain in childbirth.

Finally, God curses Adam:

"Because you have listened to the voice of your wife and have eaten of the tree of which I commanded you, 'You shall not eat of it,' cursed is the ground because of you; in pain, you shall eat of it all the days of your life; {3:18} thorns and thistles it shall bring forth for you; and you shall eat the plants of the field. {3:19} By the sweat of your face you shall eat bread, till you return to the ground, for out of it you were taken; for you are dust, and to dust you shall return."

By listening to his wife instead of God, Adam provided sufficient grounds to be cursed. This verifies how the leadership has been taken away from Eve and bestowed onto Adam.

The final part of the curse, "By the sweat of your face you shall eat bread, till you return to the ground," further supports the transformation from the way Original-People live without cultivation, toward a civilized way of life that includes bread which is made from grain, a cultivated crop that requires tilling the land.

BANISHED FROM THE GARDEN

{3:21} And the LORD God made for Adam and for his wife garments of skins and clothed them. {3:22} Then the LORD God said, "Behold, the man has become like one of us in knowing good and evil. Now, lest he reach out his hand and take also of the Tree of Life and eat, and live forever—" {3:23} therefore the LORD God sent him out from the garden of Eden to work the ground from which he was taken.

After God clothes these guilt-ridden victims with animal skins, He explains that they must be driven out of the garden of Eden so they will not eat of the Tree of Life and live forever. This curious reference to living forever by eating of the Tree of Life will be decoded in **Part 2,** which begins at the end of this chapter, in just seven pages.

What's obvious at this point is how sending Adam and Eve out of the Garden of Eden symbolizes taking them out of the Original-Peoples' way of life. This makes Adam and Eve the first people who leave paradise and the abundant food it provides.

Additionally, {3:23} "God sent him out from the garden of Eden to work the ground from which he was taken" undeniably links back to the beginning of Chapter Two where it states, "there was no man to work the ground." Now Adam has been molded by God and lured by the serpent, a symbol of the astral realm, into being a worker of the ground. As such, the Garden of Eden story doesn't appear to be an accidental fall of man, rather it appears that Adam was intentionally lured away from the original way of life, and away from his Soul symbolized by the Tree of Life, toward a Pragmatic civilized lifestyle.

Adam and Eve were not the first people, but they were the first Pragmatic civilized people. Their important purpose will be to individualize the pre-adamic Original-People created in Chapter One.

To maneuver this innocent couple into this situation, an external serpent lured the couple away from their Souls' inner guidance, symbolized by the Tree of Life. This separation from the Soul takes place during out-of-body entheogenic mushroom trips when the Soul remains in the physical body while the head and gut minds explore the astral realm in their astral body.

KEEPING ADAM AND EVE AWAY FROM THE TREE OF LIFE

{3:24} He drove out the man, and at the east of the garden of Eden he placed the cherubim and a flaming sword that turned every way to guard the way to the Tree of Life.

The easterly direction is mentioned again, indicating that something new has begun. In this case, it's the Age of Individuation which has begun. Then, to keep these new Pragmatic people from the Tree of Life—a symbol of their divine Souls—God places cherubim and a flaming sword that turned every way to block their way back.

Since God is keeping Adam and Eve disconnected from their Souls, he clearly wants them to be Pragmatic people. So, how do the cherubim and the flaming sword fit with keeping them Pragmatic?

Cherubim is plural for cherub, a second-order angel that is often depicted as a baby with wings. These are the angels who shoot arrows into peoples' hearts. Cupid is commonly considered to be a cherub.

Historical records state that Cupid sharpened his arrows on a grindstone whetted with the blood from an infant! This clearly indicates that cherubim arrows are not meant to inspire love, but heartache. The heartache symbolically caused by cherubim arrows turn people away from their Souls, making them Pragmatic people. Then without a conscience, they're able to be divisive and divide humans, thereby accomplishing the difficult task of individualizing humanity.

The youthful appearance of these cherubim is clearly symbolic of prepubescent children. As mentioned earlier, nearly all children have normal pineal glands that offer them access to their Soul's intuitive guidance that's symbolized in the *Genesis* story by the Tree of Life.

The symbolic meaning of these cherubim can then be interpreted to represent the heartache that causes people to turn away from their Soul, develop a hardened heart, and become Pragmatic after puberty. If their heart was not hardened, they would remain Romantics, maintaining their childlike state—a condition that a cherub's baby appearance plainly symbolizes.

However, once one's heart is hardened (or, more accurately, their pineal gland is calcified), a person becomes a Pragmatic adult—a special type of civilized person who lacks esoteric Soul-intuition.

Accordingly, these angelic cherubim are meant to keep Adam and Eve from returning to the Tree of Life, their Souls in their hearts.

THE FLAMING SWORD

The second guard that God set in place to keep Adam and Eve from returning to the Tree of Life was a flaming sword that turns in every direction. Regarding the flaming aspect of this symbol, the following comes from the Building Beautiful Souls website:

> *The Element of Fire has great power for forging will and determination. It is our inner light as well as a living symbol of the Divine fire that burns in every soul.* [24]

So, fire or flames are symbolically linked to consciousness. At this point in *Genesis*, humans are already physically separate. The flaming aspect of this sword indicates that the final step of the individuation process is psychological. People need to mentally view themselves as separate individuals to become true individuals.

The way the sword turns in every direction ties in with the divisive activities that individualize all of humanity. The illustration on the right was shown earlier, when the divisive idea was introduced. You may be able to imagine how that image resembles a sword turning in many directions to divide people in many different ways.

Divisiveness

177

The divisive activities that Pragmatic people get involved in and their taker mentality help to keep people from returning to the Garden of Eden. For instance, civilized life is made difficult by the takers who get others to work for them. Additionally, a common misconception claims that life is even more difficult for Original-People, making the idea of going back to a natural way of life seem foolish.

Despite that misconception, studies have found that Original-People who live in the tropics work just nine hours per week!

Even though natural living is actually much easier, property taxes levied by civilized governments force everyone to make enough money to pay their property taxes. Otherwise one's property is taken away by the sheriff via the foreclosure process that leaves the occupants homeless and, more importantly, landless. Today sheriffs carry a gun, but in the past, they brandished a sword.

Over the last several centuries, property taxes have forced countless Original-People out of their "Gardens of Eden." Once removed, the sheriff's sword makes returning to the garden impossible.

On top of all that, a turning sword is quite like a farmer's plow that is used to till the ground, breaking it up into little pieces symbolizing the process that the Pragmatic people carry out using their divisive activities to individualize people. This ties into Adam's purpose, which was brought about because there was no man to till the ground.

Finally, in the case of a beheading, swords have been used to literally divide people in two.

All of this symbolism fits the Consciousness-Origin Cosmology's claim that special Pragmatic people were introduced to individualize humans. Additionally, this story symbolizes the process of creating Pragmatic people during adolescence and throughout people's lives.

ACCOMPLISHING THE INDIVIDUALIZATION IMPERATIVE

The divisive activities of the Pragmatic people who have been disconnected from their Tree of Life—their Soul in their heart—behave in divisive ways that ensure civilized people will not find their way back to the Garden of Eden. Instead, the divisive process symbolized by a sword turning in every direction has been set into motion. Over time, this process is expected to individualize all of humanity, forging everyone into civilized individuals. According to the Consciousness-

Origin Cosmology, individuality is an imperative. We must be individuals and remain individuals to experience meeting mysterious others.

Thus, Adam and Eve symbolize the special divisive people who are needed to individualize humanity.

GOD PROVOKES CAIN TO KILL ABEL

Soon after leaving the Garden of Eden, Adam and Eve begat Cain and Abel. These brothers make offerings to God:

> Now Abel was a keeper of sheep, and Cain a worker of the ground. {4:3} In the course of time Cain brought to the LORD an offering of the fruit of the ground, {4:4} and Abel also brought of the firstborn of his flock and of their fat portions. And the LORD had regard for Abel and his offering, {4:5} but for Cain and his offering he had no regard. So, Cain was very angry, and his face fell.

Then, apparently out of the jealousy incited by God's disregard for Cain's offering, Cain kills Abel. The first murder takes place, and the process of individualizing humanity advances to include murder!

> And the LORD said, "What have you done? The voice of your brother's blood is crying to me from the ground. {4:11} And now you are cursed from the ground, which has opened its mouth to receive your brother's blood from your hand. {4:12} When you work the ground, it shall no longer yield to you its strength. You shall be a fugitive and a wanderer on the earth." {4:13} Cain said to the LORD, "My punishment is greater than I can bear. {4:14} Behold, you have driven me today away from the ground, and from your face I shall be hidden. I shall be a fugitive and a wanderer on the earth, and whoever finds me will kill me." {4:15} Then the LORD said to him, "Not so! If anyone kills Cain, vengeance shall be taken on him sevenfold." And the LORD put a mark on Cain, lest any who found him should attack him. {4:16} Then Cain went away from the presence of the LORD and settled in the land of Nod, east of Eden. {4:17} Cain knew his wife, and she conceived and bore Enoch. When he built a city, he called the name of the city after the name of his son, Enoch.

In spite of the fact that Cain killed Abel, this passage claims that God chose to protect Cain from being executed for the crime of murdering his brother. Then, with God's blessing of protection, Cain settles in the land of Nod. There he finds a woman to marry—proving that *Genesis* includes pre-adamic people. Cain has a son with his pre-adamic bride and builds a city. The city is built east of Eden, which indicates that this is a new development, presumably the first city. To

179

erect a city, there must have been plenty of pre-adamic Original-People in the land of Nod. This construction of a city confirms the theory that people were created on the sixth day of the *Genesis* story, well before Adam was formed, giving them time to be fruitful and multiply.

More importantly, the first murderer was protected by the Lord who sent him eastward to become the founder of the first city! Considering the corruption that's a common feature of cities, this fits reality quite well. It also supports the theory that the One-Who-Is-All encouraged divisiveness to take root and flourish on Earth. This is because divisiveness is needed to individualize all human beings.

The first four chapters of *Genesis* that have been analyzed so far indicate that civilization can be traced back to an astral serpent tempting Adam and Eve to eat amanita muscaria mushrooms.

Similarly, ayahuasca—the vine of the dead—is the sacramental basis for recently established churches in South America. For example, the Santo Daime is an ayahuasca church that was founded in the 1930s and has legal presence in the USA. That church has been described as a Catholic-style ayahuasca church. This church links the ayahuasca shamans to the beginning of organized religion and early civilization as these Original people move out of their idyllic way of life. For example, those shamans report that their astral spirit brothers (the grays) have told them that the big God is in Heaven. On the other hand, those same spirit beings don't mention the divine presence residing within human hearts. This is a subtle way of leading people away from following their Souls within their hearts.

The civilized parishioners of the Santo Daime are legally allowed to consume ayahuasca as a sacrament in several counties. That entheogenic concoction enables the parishioners to exit their physical bodies and visit the astral realm in their astral bodies. On their adventures, modern explorers encounter visions much like those shared in ancient scriptures regarding Heaven and Hell where spirit beings who reside on the other side of the veil are encountered. Common examples include the serpent, the grays, and angles.

In ancient Mesoamerica, entheogenic mushrooms of the genus psilocybe are depicted in numerous artifacts of the Mayan Civilization. Today, those mushrooms can still be found growing in that region. So, it appears that entheogens and astral beings have been involved in founding civilizations.

Additionally, most religions began with the ritual use of some type of entheogenic substance or an astral projection method like meditation, shamanic drumming, etc. Over millennia, astral spirit beings have lured humans away from the original way of life and toward civilization in order to individualize everyone.

Getting back to *Genesis*, Chapter Five lists the descendants from Adam to Noah. I'll skip over that and continue with Chapter Six.

THE FLOOD

Over time, generations unfold and things get so corrupt that God decides to flood the Earth, but before instigating the flood, God advises the most righteous man, Noah, to build an ark:

{6:9} These are the generations of Noah. Noah was a righteous man, blameless in his generation. Noah walked with God. {6:10} And Noah had three sons, Shem, Ham, and Japheth. {6:11} Now the earth was corrupt in God's sight, and the earth was filled with violence. {6:12} And God saw the earth, and behold, it was corrupt, for all flesh had corrupted their way on the earth. {6:13} And God said to Noah, "I have determined to make an end of all flesh, for the earth is filled with violence through them. Behold, I will destroy them with the earth. {6:14} Make yourself an ark of gopher wood.

God also instructs Noah to use the ark to save his wife, his three sons, their three wives, and two of each animal on Earth.

This flood corresponds to the sinking of Atlantis and Mu where individuation experiments had taken place. The flood cleared the entire Earth of any inappropriate results that had developed while testing various divisive methods. By flooding the Earth, the physical stage was cleared to make way for the individuation methods that had been found to work best. Then, after the water reached a new equilibrium, God had a meeting with Noah and his three sons.

{9:1} And God blessed Noah and his sons and said to them, "Be fruitful and multiply and fill the earth. {9:2} The fear of you and the dread of you shall be upon every beast of the earth and upon every bird of the heavens, upon everything that creeps on the ground and all the fish of the sea. Into your hand they are delivered. {9:3} Every moving thing that lives shall be food for you. And as I gave you the green plants, I give you everything. {9:4} But you shall not eat flesh with its life, that is, its blood. {9:5} And for your lifeblood I will require a reckoning: from every beast I will require it and from man. From his fellow man I will require a reckoning for the life of man. {9:6} Whoever sheds the blood

of man, by man shall his blood be shed, for God made man in his own image. {9:7} And you, be fruitful and multiply, teem on the earth and multiply in it."

Based on that passage, the new individuation system includes kosher animal consumption (flesh with the blood drained). Additionally, retribution for killing men was upgraded to execution. Given this proclamation, it's clear that the divisive process was modified. Before the flood, when Cain killed Abel, the murderer was merely banished. In this new arrangement, the punishment for murder is execution.

In the rest of the chapters of *Genesis* numerous examples of divisiveness are chronicled. In fact, most of what is shared is rather disturbing for people who are opened to love. The portion of *Genesis* analyzed so far supports the Consciousness-Origin Cosmology in enough ways to show how these cosmologies parallel one another.

A key parallel is how God or the One-Who-Is-All supports the divisive process indicating that divisiveness is in alignment with the divine plan. Being aware of the necessity of divisiveness and the support it receives from the One offers a way to stop blaming individual people who play divisive roles in the play we call life. Going even further, forgiveness can emerge and gratitude can be given to the people who play the painful divisive roles that need to be played in order to individualize humanity. Later, in **Part 3: Tools and Techniques,** the chapter, entitled Forgiveness and Gratitude, address this issue thoroughly.

This is the end of **Part 1: A New Model of Reality.**

Part 2 is just two chapters long. In it, I share the Consciousness-Origin Cosmology's future predictions. Those prophecies explain how the divisive reality that is growing evermore chaotic is predicted to miraculously transform into a new *Age of Love.* I explain how such a dramatic change could occur quite easily.

Support for the prophecies is provided based on scriptures from Judaism, Christianity, Islam, and Hinduism. I also explain how Buddhism is in alignment with some of the prophecies.

In spite of the general support found in the scriptures of world religions, the predictions presented in the next two chapters are quite different from the popular idea of punishment versus reward. Instead, the transition presented rewards everyone in personally appropriate ways for playing their role. Hence, you'll most likely find what is offered in **Part 2** to be very encouraging.

Part 2: Future Predictions

Chapter 14
Global Transition

CONSIDERING THE LIMITATIONS OF PREDICTIONS

I was able to present scientific research and real-life examples to support the theories presented in **Part 1** concerning reality. Unfortunately, predictions about the future can't be supported that way. Predictions aren't based on facts, and predictions may not come true, especially predictions about the weather. Therefore, many people are reluctant to consider predictions, prophecies, or weather forecasts.

People with scientific backgrounds, like myself, often find prophecies difficult to take seriously. Due to my technical education, I was so resistant to considering future predictions that it took me 17 years and several transformational experiences to seriously consider the prophecy presented here in **Part 2**. Therefore, I don't expect you to embrace this prophecy readily.

In spite of that, if reality is actually founded on consciousness, and you're willing to consider a consciousness-based reality, then the One-Who-Is-All's plan for the universe will most likely take place.

To shift away from the mythical materialistic model that has been scientifically proven to be false, and instead consider the consciousness-based theory presented in **Part 1**, one must let go of random chance and replace it with a consciousness-driven course of events. This dramatic shift in perspective views reality as a process that's controlled by the underlying consciousness that formed the Grand Illusion. Since an overall plan could actually exist, it's worth considering what's offered here in **Part 2: Future Predictions**.

Although this middle part of the book is not necessary for you to accept or even be aware of, my Soul has guided me to present the full Consciousness-Origin Cosmology from the beginning of time all the way to the end of time. Besides, it only takes 26 pages to share this very positive future possibility.

Additionally, the positive outlook that's offered for everyone's future can provide hope for all of humanity in a time when our future appears quite dismal. A glimmer of hope for a glorious future, may help you let go of worries about the future and enjoy the present moment with an open heart, following your Soul's guidance.

THE TRANSITION

The prophecy shared in this chapter predicts that the current divisive Age of Individuation will end and a final *Age of Love* will follow. According to the Consciousness-Origin Cosmology, the transition from one age to the next will take place in a way that will result in an ideal experience for every human being.

Given the current state of affairs, that's hard to imagine.

HUMANITY'S PREDICAMENT

To set the stage for presenting the details of the transition, I'll begin by briefly reviewing our current state of affairs:

Human population continues to grow faster than ever before. Our technology has enabled us to accelerate our population growth by commandeering more and more of the finite amount of land and resources available on Earth. As our population expands, we seize more land, and in turn, cause other life forms to perish at faster and faster rates. When our population overruns the limited land and resources available on Earth, what then?

Many envision a gruesome Armageddon battle for survival which has been portrayed in popular books and movies.

A UNIVERSALLY BENEFICIAL RESOLUTION IS PREDICTED

The Consciousness-Origin Cosmology's predictions that Dr. Katz shared with me are quite different in comparison to the popular versions that I'm aware of. The biggest difference is how the scenario presented here resolves the global chaos in a way that **benefits every human being simultaneously!**

So, with hopes for a positive future, I'll begin by discussing when the global transition is predicted to take place.

According to Dr. Katz a big event will take place when every human on Earth has been individualized.

Today, there are still Original-People who maintain a oneness perspective. The fact that so few of these Original-People remain, indicates that the individuation process is nearly complete.

In the meantime, the Age of Individuation is predicted to grow evermore divisive, increasing the chaos right up to the big transitional event. Then, when every human being on Earth has been individualized, the Age of Individuation will end, and the Age of Love will begin.

Even though we haven't reached the end of the current Age, a transitional overlap period is taking place as I write. The new Age of Love has germinated in the hearts of the Romantic people who are transforming from within via our Soul's guidance. We're learning to open our hearts further, follow our hearts more attentively, become more grateful, and find ways to forgive ourselves and others. All of this is helping us open to love more than ever before.

In short, the Romantic people are being transformed by our Souls into a new type of human. We're becoming individuals who live with our hearts open, following our hearts as we open to love. This gradual process is preparing the Romantic portion of humanity to be part of the new Age of Love that appears to be close at hand.

As we draw nearer to the transitional event, the Romantic heart-oriented people are splitting away from the mainstream culture that is primarily Pragmatic. From the Romantic point of view, the Pragmatics appear to be stuck in the divisive battle of good versus evil that has become a defining feature of the current Age of Individuation.

In spite of all the human conflict taking place, the most challenging problem we all face is human population growth. Some experts claim that the Earth can't sustain the 7 billion that already exist.

Forced population reduction is considered by most to be morally wrong and doesn't need to be discussed here.

Other alternatives being considered include: people colonizing other planets or relocating into some sort of huge spacecraft, or several spacecrafts, to live up in space. For example, Mars is being seriously considered for human habitation.

Although these and other options are being explored, none of them are likely to be operational in time to prevent humans from exhausting our precious home's limited resources.

Given this state of affairs, it seems impossible to resolve all of this in a way that **benefits everyone simultaneously.** So, let's see how this seemingly impossible feat is predicted to take place.

THE PIVOTAL DIVIDE

In the last few chapters, I discussed the pivotal divide between the Romantic and Pragmatic portions of humanity. Taking that split further, Dr. Katz told me that Steiner predicted that this pivotal divide will grow wider as the end of the current age draws closer. The two groups will become unable to relate to one another. The existence of this divide and it's widening gap that is already huge, indicates that the shift from the current age to the next may be very close at hand.

When Original-People have all been individualized, the Consciousness-Origin Cosmology predicts that the Pragmatic and Romantic people will follow the diverging paths that began with the humanities pivotal divide. Specifically, Katz told me:

- ➢ The people who are <u>unable</u> to open and follow their hearts and open to love will ascend up and away from the Earth.
- ➢ Meanwhile, the people who have learned to open their hearts, follow their hearts, and open to love inherit the Earth.

These two groups are what I've labeled the Pragmatic and Romantic people. Therefore, the Pragmatic people are predicted to ascend, while the Romantic people inherit the Earth.

ASCENSION OF THE PRAGMATICS

An obvious question that comes up here is: What exactly is ascension? Where do the Pragmatics actually go?

Although most people spend their lives in the physical realm and some don't believe that Heaven, Hell or what I collectively labeled the astral realm, countless people have been exploring the astral realm for thousands of years. Additionally, a majority of people are being drawn to the astral realm by astral spirit guides and the world's religions that lure people away from their Souls to follow external guidance that encourages followers to ascend up to astral Heaven. Many different tactics have been used to hook most of humanity. Even many Romantic people accept the idea that heaven is a better place.

Thus, ascension has been growing in popularity and is expected to draw everyone who is not dedicated to following their Soul in their heart, away from the physical Earth and up to astral Heaven (or astral Hell if that's what a sadistic or masochistic person prefers).

To synchronize the ascension event, on one fateful night, all the Pragmatics' Souls could cause each one of those folks to dream that they're involved in a dramatic escape from a dying Earth. Each person's dream could align with that individual's ideas regarding Armageddon. Then, while involved in these personalized Armageddon dreams, the astral bodies of the Pragmatic people will be hovering up above their physical bodies giving their Souls an opportunity to stop those people's hearts from beating and sever the silver cords without those folks knowing that their physical bodies have died. This is because the conscious- and subconscious-minds will be located up in the astral bodies dreaming about a fantastic Armageddon escape scenario. To support the transition, their "dreams" could include a sheading of their physical bodies to become astral light beings. Finally, those dreams would continue in ways that seamlessly become each Pragmatics' new reality, an astral realm reality.

Meanwhile, everyone who remains alive in their physical bodies inherits a new Earth with only Romantic people. Simple as that!

EXPERIENCING ONE'S GREATEST PASSIONS

According to Dr. Katz, the Consciousness-Origin Cosmology predicts that each person who ascends away from the Earth will experience their greatest passion to its endgame.

Conveniently, the upper and lower layers of the astral realm automatically accommodate the desires of whomever enters those outer layers. Accordingly, the upper heavenly and lower hellish layers of the vast astral realm are perfectly designed to satisfy the polarized desires that Pragmatic people are seeking to quench.

Spirit entities from the astral realm have been luring people away from their Souls and over to the astral realm where astral travelers obtain powers to manifest whatever they most deeply desire.

The final step is ascension, the permanent transfer of the Pragmatic people to the enticing and glamorous astral realm where they can fulfill all of their greatest passions. Passing over to the "other side," takes place when the physical body dies. This is when the silver cord is cut and the astral body is released from physical life on Earth.

Meanwhile the Romantic peoples' dedication to their Souls make them well-suited for the full blossoming of love that will take place on Earth in physical human bodies. So, once the Pragmatics have ascended, the Romantics inherit the Earth—a New Earth without any divisive people!

RETURNING TO THE ONE

Triality of Paths

Heavenly

Earthly

Hellish

Finally, Katz explained that after each Pragmatic person fulfills all of their desires, they return to the One-Who-Is-All. The illustration on the left shows how the Heavenly and Hellish paths all lead to the same final destination.

Katz also explained that their union with the One marks the end of that person's experience of individuality. This final reunion completely resolves any suffering a Pragmatic may have been experiencing on Earth.

This scenario is in perfect alignment with the Buddhist goal of reaching Nirvana to be released from the suffering that plagues divisive Pragmatic people. Jews, Christians, Muslims, and Hindus have similar endgame scenarios. In all cases, the release from suffering takes place on the other side of the veil, in the afterlife spirit inhabited astral realm.

The next chapter discusses the complementary inheritance.

At the end of that chapter, I offer support for the ascension/inheritance transition from the scriptures of popular religions.

Chapter 15
The Age of Love

INHERITANCE OF A NEW EARTH

An after-effect of the Pragmatic people ascending beyond the veil to the astral realm, is how the humble and generous Romantic people are left behind to inherit the Earth. This accomplishes the well-recognized and famously bewildering prophecy:

"Blessed are the meek, for they shall inherit the Earth."

In that biblical excerpt, the English word meek was used to translate the ancient Greek word "praus" that appeared in the original scriptures. Praus literally means "strength under control," indicating that these people are strong, but self-restrained.

One way that Romantics restrain their strength is by resisting the lure of power that awaits in astral Heaven. Even though anyone can ascend and fulfill their desires in astral Heaven, Romantics heed their Soul's guidance to resist the allure and remain on Earth instead.

Additionally, the heartfelt inclination to "live and let live," is common amongst Romantics. They're strong people who have the courage to live and let live. They might discuss differences of opinion, and even participate in heated debates however, Romantics heed their Soul's conscience to resist physically forcing others.

Because Romantic people are generous, self-restrained, and satisfied with the power they already have, peace will naturally commence as soon as they inherit the Earth.

With the human population dramatically reduced, the mother Earth will emerge from the stress of too many greedy humans to become a thriving "New Earth" populated with generous lovers.

With the Pragmatic taker/hoarder portion of humanity exploring their passions in the afterlife astral realm, an abundance of material goods and natural resources will be inherited by the much smaller population of Romantics that live on.

Thus, abundant prosperity will accrue to the Romantic givers who have humbly embraced the magic of life and love.

In this way, the final Age of Love will emerge from the ashes of conflict and greed that has ascended like a flame leaving behind a New Earth that, in the twinkling of an eye, transforms to offer abundant peace and prosperity to the open-hearted Romantic lovers.

THE COSMOLOGY'S PREDICTIONS FOR THE ROMANTICS

Dr. Katz provided some details regarding what the people who inherit the Earth are predicted to experience.

For instance, on the New Earth, the inheritors will rejuvenate to youthful vigor and live without aging until the end of time. This may be hard to believe. However, if reality is founded on consciousness, our Souls' Supreme-Power-of-Wholeness can theoretically rejuvenate us and maintain our youth till the end of time.

Along with the end of death, no more births will occur. The people who will have learned to open and follow their hearts, and open to love will be the only humans appropriate for the Age of Love. New people can't be added after the global transition takes place. One reason for this is that there won't be any divisive people available to individualize new children. More importantly, a new child could turn out to be Pragmatic. Finally, without death, population growth would be more of a problem than ever before. For all these reasons, those who inherit the New Earth will be the only people who live during the Age of Love.

LIKE-MINDED COMMUNITIES

Even though Romantic people have important similarities, they're also individuals with a variety of viewpoints regarding how they would like to live and the type of people they would most like to live with. To accommodate the variety of individual tastes, the Cosmology predicts that the inheritors of the Earth will be guided by their Souls to numerous specific gathering places. Each location will be a collection point for a particular type of like-minded people.

Once the Romantic people have coalesced into like-minded groups by following their hearts, each group will form a community based on the group's shared preferences. This process provides idyllic communities that are home to land mates with compatible interests.

As each community lives in their ideal way, they will abide by the "live and let live" principle that affords other communities the right to live in their preferred ways. This mutual acceptance of differences in lifestyle choices is a key to maintaining peace on the New Earth.

SOUL MATES AND SOUL GROUPS

All community residents will meet their *Soul Mate* by following their Soul's guidance and inspiring feelings of love. The Souls' will work in a coordinated way that insures the success of these unions.

For the Age of Love to be inclusive of the wide variety of relationships that are being explored these days (polyamorous, gay, etc.), each group of alternatively-minded Romantics will form communities that accommodate their specific interests. The myriad of communities will provide all types of Romantic people with the opportunity to experience the full blossoming of love in ways that fit with their lifestyle.

For instance, polyamorous Romantics can form *Soul Groups*. A Soul Group could include three or more people who all share loving connections with everyone in the group.

EMPATHY, TELEPATHY, AND THE BLOSSOMING OF LOVE

During the Age of Love, Dr. Katz also explained that the open-hearted people will, over time, develop some empathetic and telepathic abilities. Souls can provide these abilities by sharing some of their empathetic and telepathic capabilities with people's subconscious- and conscious-minds.

Then, with everyone aware of some of what everyone else is feeling and thinking, the Romantic people are predicted to discover that everyone who remained on Earth is endowed with desires for everyone to be happy. As people discover how universal this desire for mutual happiness is, that knowledge builds a solid foundation for lasting peace and prosperity on Earth.

Additionally, the empathetic and telepathic abilities help everyone interact with more grace, harmony and consideration for one another which also promotes peace on Earth.

The peace and harmony offer fertile ground for love to grow. As hearts open wider than ever before, the full blossoming of love is predicted to unfold in this new world of abundant peace and prosperity.

THE WAY-OF-THE-HEART IS ESOTERIC

The people who inherit the Earth to explore the full blossoming of love must listen to their Soul and follow its guidance to be directed to their community of like-minded people. Soul guidance also enables these open-hearted people to find their Soul Mate or Soul Group. Then, as love blossoms these people's Souls will be guiding everyone to interact with one another in ways that mesh with and support one another in mutually beneficial ways.

All of this requires the people who have inherited the Earth to have learned to open their hearts, follow their hearts, and open to love making the pivotal divide in humanity perfectly designed to facilitate the success of the final Age of Love here on Earth.

Thus, esoteric Romantics who are dedicated to their Souls will inherit the Earth to live till the end of time.

Conversely, the exoteric people who search outside of themselves for guidance via spirit guides, technology, angels, ascended masters, sacred texts, demigods, etc., are guided over to the afterlife astral realm. Once relocated to Heaven (or Hell), the exoteric people can explore their greatest passions and return to the One.

Thus, this global transition is beneficial for everyone!

WHAT IS LOVE?

Although the word love is tossed around quite a bit these days, a clear and realistic definition of love is hard to find. Luckily, one that captured what I had personally experienced to be the essence of love was offered to me. It begins with a description of lust.

Lust occurs when a person sees something that they believe has the ability to bring them sensual enjoyment and, hopefully, happiness. A person can lust after food, objects, power, money, or people.

For instance, when I see a chocolate cake, my mouth waters, and I imagine that eating that cake will be enjoyable. Hopefully the experience will make me happier than I was before I ate the cake. Eating the cake may be enjoyable, but that feeling doesn't last very long. Once the flavor has disappeared, the joy fades. There are some mood-modifying chemicals in chocolate that prolong the positive effects beyond the initial taste sensation, but those wear off soon enough.

Lust for a sexually attractive person involves the belief that a sexual encounter with that person will be enjoyable, and the sensual pleasure will bring some happiness with it. Just as in chocolate, there are chemicals produced during sexual activities that prolong the joyful feelings after the encounter ends. Still, that chemistry also dissipates.

In the case of sexual lust, people who are used as sexual objects to fulfill someone else's lustful desires often feel degraded and misused. At its core, lust is essentially taking what one desires without regard for how others are affected—making lust divisive.

Now let's see how love is nearly the opposite of lust. With love, a person feels a willingness to sacrifice themselves in order to please the one they love. In a boomerang way, doing something or making sacrifices to please one's beloved, brings joy and happiness to the giver as well as the beloved. This makes love a win-win arrangement that brings people closer together. When love is mutual, the reciprocal willingness to please each other is wondrously beneficial for all.

On one occasion, I loved someone so much that I thought to myself, "I would be willing to sacrifice my life to provide this woman with more joy." I had no particular idea of how giving my life might bring her more joy, I simply noticed how I felt willing to make the ultimate sacrifice if some unexpected situation provided an opportunity for me to help my beloved by sacrificing my life.

Later, when my heart wasn't so wide open, it seemed absurd for me to sacrifice my life in order to increase my beloved's happiness.

Despite my skepticism, several years later I read the transcripts of a series of lectures that Osho presented in 1972, therein he described love to be a "willingness to sacrifice oneself for their beloved."

While reading that, I recalled the time when I had the thought that I would be willing to give my life to provide my beloved with more joy. I further remembered how that took place when I felt the most love that I have ever felt. Finally, it made sense. I realized that the idea of sacrificing my life indicated how unreservedly willing I was to sacrifice myself in order to benefit my beloved. Being ready to make the ultimate sacrifice indicated the depth and sincerity of my love for that woman at that moment. A moment I will never forget.

There are many romantic love stories in which one or both of the lovers sacrifice their life for their beloved.

For instance, in the classic movie *Casablanca*, two men love the same woman so much that they're both willing to take the bullet to give the woman and the other man an opportunity to escape together.

Having experienced the willingness to sacrifice my life for my beloved, I got a glimpse of how surprisingly powerful love is. What's more, it became perfectly clear that love is about giving, which aligns it with the Romantic givers.

With intuitive guidance from our Souls that prepare things behind the scenes, what one person is guided to offer their beloved can be precisely what their beloved desired at that very moment. Certainly, the full blossoming of love will be filled with synergy that is serendipitously synchronistic.

In summary, lust is selfish, while love is a generous desire to please one's beloved. When love is mutual it has unbridled potential for abundant prosperity for everyone involved. So, even though "the full blossoming of love" might come across as self-indulgent, it's really about people giving to one another with open-hearted generosity.

MANY TYPES OF LOVE

The many types of love include: the love of a child by their parent, and the love of a parent by their child. I've experienced being in love with life. Some people love their work.

Self-love is a type of love that many seek. It has been said that "until you love yourself, you can't truly love another."

In a unique form of self-love, I fell in love with my Soul. I don't know why it took me so long to discover this form of self-love. Now that I've delved into it, I've found that loving my Soul is the most consistent and beneficial form of love that I've ever experienced. Later, in Chapter 20: Soul Love, I'll share more about this inner relationship of loving one's self by loving the Soul in one's heart.

Some people develop a loving relationship with their external god and/or goddess. Of course, each person has their own idea of what their god or goddess is, and their own approach to loving their deity. In this book, I encourage Romantics to connect with the divine consciousness in their heart, the Soul—a personal mother/father God. Still, if you feel drawn to an external deity do what feels right for you.

There's also the love of a pet, one's personal companion. Or love of a friend who can be trusted and depended upon.

There are many ways to open one's heart and open to love.

Opening the heart and opening to love are intertwined such that one can lead to the other, and synergistically, they each support the other. If you're a Romantic person who's interested in love and living your life in an open-hearted way, then it's up to you to find the forms of love that open your heart.

A HISTORICAL OVERVIEW OF LOVE

The ancient Greeks had five separate words for five different types of love: eros is sexual passion, philia is deep friendship, ludus is playful love, agape is love for everyone, and philautia is love of oneself. Then in the 1970s, John Allen Lee added pragma, a practical form of love. The ancient Greek plays included comedy, satire, and tragedy, but romance is curiously missing from ancient Greek history.

Courtly love, a form of love between a knight and a noble woman, emerged during the late 11th century in medieval Europe. Initially practiced in France courtly love spread to English courts where it was practiced from the 14th to the 16th centuries. Historians believe that courtly love developed into romantic love around 1600AD.

This means that romantic love is only 400-years-old. Some historians go further to show that the modern view of romantic love emerged during the late 1800s and early 1900s.

Fictional books and movies that are set in ancient times often insert romantic love into the story misleading us to believe that romantic love always existed. Despite those fictitious stories, historians claim that romantic love emerged only 400 years ago.

Accurate historical accounts find Original-People practicing serial monogamy, casually changing partners without heartache or offense. As noted earlier, in the 1500s Bartolome de las Casas described the Indians of the Caribbean as follows:

"Marriage laws are non-existent: men and women alike choose their mates and leave them as they please, without offense, jealousy or anger."

When it comes to lust, Las Casas reports:

"Indian men and women look upon total nakedness with as much casualness as we look upon a man's head or at his hands."

Those first-hand accounts indicate that the Original-People didn't experience love nor lust. This fits their oneness perspective.

My Soul guided me to see how the advent of individuality provided a context for love to appear. Love and lust both take place across a gap of separation. Love of one's self exists, but the first account of it comes from the story of Narcissus. He fell in love with his image that was reflected back to him by a pool of still water. That reflection created the separation needed for narcissistic self-love to emerge.

All relationships take place across a gap of separation, a gap that individuality provides. Considering all the relationships available, the ones that include some type of love are exceptionally wonderful to experience. Certainly, there's still much to learn about this very complex and powerful relationship dynamic we call love.

Regardless of where love came from or when it first appeared, love is certainly the most wonderful way to connect with another, making love the most important relationship dynamic of all.

To experience the full blossoming of love people must open their hearts wide. To be able to do that we need a peaceful environment that feels safe enough to unbridle our hearts completely.

Currently, the world is filled with all sorts of dangers. For instance, con artists fake being in love to take advantage of their patsy. Divisive activities that take advantage of open-hearted people make it difficult to explore love much further than we already have.

Thus, we need a global transformation that removes the con artists and other divisive activities from the Earth to bring about world peace, and abundant prosperity. In that setting, the Romantic people who inherit the Earth will be able to explore the love to its fullness.

UNCONDITIONAL LOVE

Certainly, some parents unconditionally love their children. One of my personal friend's ex-wife went berserk, destroyed his life and left him to start over. In spite of all the damaging lies and physical violence that she committed, he told me that he still loves her.

There are many people who I have loved and will always love regardless of what they do or have done. This is because love isn't based on external conditions that are tabulated and graded by the ego-mind. On the contrary, love is an intuitive feeling that emerges from the Soul in association with whomever or whatever one loves.

Unlike lust, infatuation, affinity, codependency, hatred, disgust, and other condition-based feelings, love isn't based on conditions. It's naturally unconditional, making the phrase "unconditional love" redundant. Even so, adding unconditional to love emphasizes that important feature of this precious treasure we call love.

THE THEORY THAT EVERYTHING IS LOVE

I've heard some people claim that everything is love.

If love was ever-present and the basis of everything, then why don't we have a world of abundant peace and prosperity today? Could a world made of love result in widespread competition and wars that grow evermore challenging as time marches on? In making an honest review of reality one finds most people lusting for power and prestige, a sure sign that love is sorely missing from most people's lives.

The history of love presented earlier clearly supports the idea that love emerged once individuality appeared. While love may not be the foundation of reality, my Soul and the experiences it has guided me through have convinced me that love is the most precious treasure that has been discovered since the beginning of time. To explore love to its fullness, the Age of Love will emerge in a loving way that honors everyone.

THE NATURE OF LOVE

Gratefully, love dissolves the self-serving lust for power that can accompany individuality. It draws people together with desires to support one another in spite of the convincing illusion of separation and the individuality that divisive activities conjure up.

If you're a Romantic who is opening to love and learning about it presently, as I am, you may have noticed how the power of love dissolves desires for power over others and replaces them with desires to give generously. Additionally, you may have discovered how the power of love seems inexhaustible and wonderfully beneficial for all of life as it encourages synergy amongst everything and everyone.

Eventually, at the end of the Age of Love, when love has blossomed to its fullest, the One-Who-Is-All will have discovered much more about love. Those revelations will quite likely inspire the next adventure, the one that will commence after the end of time.

THE END OF TIME

The experiences of rejuvenation; meeting one's Soul Mate (or Soul Group); living in a world of abundant peace and prosperity; and above all, experiencing the full blossoming of love will be truly extraordinary and unquestionably magnificent for everyone involved in the Age of Love that takes place here on Earth. Even so, over a long enough period of time, even the glorious Age of Love will become normalized and, consequently, it will eventually feel ordinary.

This notion has been named hedonic adaptation, or the hedonic treadmill concept. Observation has discovered that humans return to a relatively stable level of happiness despite major positive or negative events or life changes.

So, once the experience of the full blossoming of love becomes normalized, Steiner's cosmology predicts that new ideas for a new adventure begin popping up in the minds of the Romantic people who inherited the Earth. The process of sharing these ideas is purported to grow into a global discussion. Eventually, everyone on Earth is expected to be guided by their Souls to choose one of these new adventure ideas as the best idea of all.

Let's not forget that everything and everyone are parts of the One. Thus, this great idea is actually the One's idea. Even so, Dr. Katz explained that all the people who experience the full blossoming of love will be involved in a process that eventually reaches a worldwide consensus regarding what the next adventure ought to be.

Then, with everyone who has remained alive on Earth interested in the same new adventure, they will all develop desires to set the new adventure into motion. To move forward, toward that new adventure, their Souls will simultaneously guide everyone to close their eyes and focus their intellect and emotions on the new endeavor.

To collectively empower it, everyone's Souls will further guide everyone to use their telepathic and empathetic abilities to synchronize their thoughts and feelings so that everyone on Earth is thinking and feeling the same new idea simultaneously. Once global synchronization is achieved, the existing universe will dissolve.

As the Grand Illusion collapses back into the pure consciousness from which it emerged, time will come to an end.

That's when the new adventure will begin.

Of course, no one will know what that new adventure will be until the end of time. I hope to be on earth—along with you—then.

CONSIDERATIONS REGARDING THIS PROPHECY

Few consider "the meek shall inherit the earth" prophecy to be of any consequence. Since most people are Pragmatic, their path will follow the famously popular ascension process that leads to the astral realm. Its seven layers will fulfill the wide variety of polarized interests that fascinate Pragmatic people.

Meanwhile, the Romantics who have opened their hearts, followed their hearts and opened to love, inherit the Earth to explore meetings between Soul Mates. Those meetings will kick off the full blossoming of love in a world of abundant peace and prosperity.

If the purpose of the universe is discovering how it feels to meet mysterious others, then this fairytale ending is perfectly fitting.

Additionally, transforming the painful split in humanity into a blessing for everyone is divinely brilliant. The resulting inheritance produces an appropriate setting for the Romantic people to explore love further than has been possible in the divisive circumstances that were required to individualize us all.

It's quite clear that civilization has been expanding its divisive conflicts ever since it began about 10,000 years ago. This means that no individualized human has lived in a world of abundant peace and prosperity simply because divisive conflicts have continued to take place ever since the first individuals appeared.

If the ascension event actually takes place and countless proponents predict it will, then the Romantic people may finally inherit a world of peace and prosperity, one where they can explore uncharted depths of mutual love in a globally cooperative setting.

Beyond what takes place on Earth, all who ascend experience their version of a glorious climax in the astral realm.

Miraculously, this elegant solution to all the world's problems provides an ideal experience for every human being.

If everything is actually founded on consciousness, and you're willing to consider a consciousness-based reality, then this remarkably clever global resolution could take place over night, as described in the previous chapter on page 189.

With the astral realm available for the ascension process to take place, the horrific Armageddon predictions being proposed these days can unfold in the astral "dreams" of the Pragmatic people who ascend up to the astral realm. Meanwhile, on Earth, peace quietly emerges.

Since we can't be sure what's actually going to happen in the future, in makes sense to contemplate a positive future. The catastrophic scenarios being offered these days can be replaced with this miraculously positive alternative. Then, with a positive outlook, you can focus on contributing to the world in a healthy way that makes your life, and the lives that you touch, evermore full of joy today.

SUPPORT FROM POPULAR RELIGIONS

After investigating popular world religions, I've discovered that all except Buddhism, have scriptural passages that predict a global transition in which many people leave the Earth while others inherit the Earth and live until the end of time.

SUPPORT FROM JUDAISM

In Psalm 37 of the Old Testament, King David predicts that the Pragmatic people (referred to as the wicked) will leave the Earth while the Romantics (referred to as the meek or righteous) inherit the Earth:

> *{37:10} In just a little while, the wicked will be no more; though you look carefully at his place, he will not be there. {37:11} But the meek shall inherit the land and delight themselves in abundant peace. {37:12} The wicked plots against the righteous and gnashes his teeth at him, {37:13} but the Lord laughs at the wicked, for he sees that his day is coming. {37:14} The wicked draw the sword and bend their bows to bring down the poor and needy, to slay those whose way is upright; {37:15} their sword shall enter their own heart, and their bows shall be broken. {37:16} Better is the little that the righteous has than the abundance of many wicked. {37:17} For the arms of the wicked shall be broken, but the LORD upholds the righteous. {37:18} The LORD knows the days of the blameless, and their heritage will remain forever; {37:19} they are not put to shame in evil times; in the days of famine, they have abundance. {37:20} But the wicked will perish; the enemies of the LORD are like the glory of the pastures; they vanish—like smoke they vanish away. {37:21} The wicked borrows but does not pay back, but the righteous is generous and gives; {37:22} for those blessed by the LORD shall inherit the land, but those cursed by him shall be cut off. {37:23} The steps of a man are established by the LORD, when he delights in his way; {37:24} though he falls, he shall not be cast headlong, for the*

LORD upholds his hand. {37:25} I have been young, and now am old, yet I have not seen the righteous forsaken or his children begging for bread. {37:26} He is ever lending generously, and his children become a blessing. {37:27} Turn away from evil and do good; so shall you dwell forever. {37:28} For the LORD loves justice; he will not forsake his saints. They are preserved forever, but the children of the wicked shall be cut off. {37:29} The righteous shall inherit the land and dwell upon it forever. {37:30} The mouth of the righteous utters wisdom, and his tongue speaks justice. {37:31} The law of his God is in his heart; his steps do not slip.

This excerpt ends with King David clarifying that the righteous follow their hearts by writing, "The Law of his God is in his heart; his steps do not slip." Additionally, the meek and the righteous are used interchangeably—both inherit the Earth and live in it forever.

An important point that is repeated four times in this excerpt is that the Romantic people, labeled the meek/righteous, inherit the land and live in it forever. This fulfills the prediction made in *Genesis* about eating from the Tree of Life to live forever. By seeing the Tree of Life as a symbol of the Soul in one's heart center, following the Soul's guidance leads to everlasting life.

Conversely, the Pragmatics, who are labeled the wicked, will be no more—foreshadowing their shift from the physical Earth plane, where life takes place, to the afterlife astral realm that is not visible to people who remain alive. Thus, those who pass over will be no more.

By turning away from their inner gods in their living beating hearts, they unwittingly choose the afterlife astral realm with its catch all Heaven and Hell layers that readily fulfill their desires.

DEMONIZATION IS ANTIQUATED

My Soul has guided me to understand that these old biblical scriptures demonized the Pragmatic people by calling them wicked to encourage people to remain in alignment with their Soul-intuition. The harsh and dualistic message offered by David may have been appropriate for those times. In any case, the type of behavior that's preferred comes through clearly—follow the law written in your heart, be generous and live simply.

Having said that, my Soul has guided me to point out that the wording, blame, and condemnation contained in these scriptures is antiquated. It's time for forgiveness, love, and gratitude to grow. Rather than being angry and frustrated with what we're unable to change, it's time for us to have compassion for the people who play divisive roles and consequently live tormented lives. This issue will be discussed thoroughly in Chapter 22: Forgiveness and Gratitude.

SUPPORT FROM CHRISTIANITY

In the *Book of Matthew* from Christianity's *New Testament*, Jesus predicts the split between the open-hearted and closed-hearted portions of humanity in his Sermon on the Mount:

{5:2} And he [Jesus] opened his mouth and taught them, saying:
{5:3} "Blessed are the poor in spirit, for theirs is the kingdom of Heaven.
{5:4} Blessed are those who mourn, for they shall be comforted.
{5:5} Blessed are the meek, for they shall inherit the earth.
{5:6} Blessed are those who hunger and thirst for righteousness, for they shall be satisfied.
{5:7} Blessed are the merciful, for they shall receive mercy.
{5:8} Blessed are the pure in heart, for they shall see God.
{5:9} Blessed are the peacemakers, for they shall be called sons of God.
{5:10} Blessed are those who are persecuted for righteousness' sake, for theirs is the kingdom of Heaven.
{5:11} Blessed are you when others revile you and persecute you and utter all kinds of evil against you falsely on my account. {5:12} Rejoice and be glad, for your reward is great in Heaven, for so they persecuted the prophets who were before you."

The five beatitudes in the middle are highlighted with bold type. These five fit the Romantic people who are: meek, hunger and thirst for righteousness, are merciful and pure in heart, and live and let live, which makes them peacemakers.

The fact that these particular beatitudes are located in the middle of the list fits with the Quintessential Core Triality concept, which places the Romantics in the central giver portion of humanity.

Considering the endings of the five middle Beatitudes, we have:

- ♥ Inherit the Earth.
- ♥ Be satisfied (with the righteousness they thirst for).
- ♥ Receive mercy (for being merciful).
- ♥ See God (which the open-hearted see in everything).
- ♥ Be called sons of God.

This last one is confirmed in the final book of the Bible when describing the people who inhabit the New Earth: Revelation {21:7} "The one who conquers [has his name in the Book of Life] will have this heritage, and I will be his God and he will be my son." By remaining true to their hearts, their Trees of Life, the Romantics are the people named in the Book of Life and consequently live till the end of time.

All of these middle beatitudes fit the Romantic people and tie into their inheritance of the Earth.

The other four beatitudes fit the Pragmatic people, who explore many different extremes. The first one is extraordinarily fitting. Pragmatics who have turned away from their Soul, the divine spirit within, are "poor in spirit." Thus, theirs is the kingdom of Heaven.

In the second one "mourning" fits in two ways. First, Pragmatics suffer, and mourning is a form of suffering. Secondly, the physical bodies of the Pragmatics must die so they can ascend to the astral realm, and mourning is how people respond to physical death.

Then, skipping over the middle Romantic group, the eighth beatitude identifies people who are persecuted for righteousness' sake. This fits the Pragmatics who seek an extremely good polarity like my friend who committed suicide. Although they choose "good," they don't follow their hearts to chart their path of goodness. Instead, they outdo others making their righteousness excessive and divisive.

The final beatitude refers to another type of "good Pragmatic," people who are persecuted due to their extreme views regarding Jesus. These last two appear to refer to overbearing proselytizers.

They may also include other extreme religious fanatics or martyrs who go overboard by engaging their ego rather than their heart.

The first two beatitudes are based on a negative polarity that lacks spirit, while the last two are based on extreme positive positions that may over-emphasize God, likely in an evangelical way that may demonize people who don't worship the "correct" god. Three of these get their reward in Heaven, while the mourners get comforted.

If the mourners suffer so much that they're identified as mourners, then being comforted would fulfill an important desire which could easily take place in astral Heaven.

Putting all of this together, we find a fitting confirmation for the Consciousness-Origin Cosmology's prophecy of a transition from the

Age of Individuation to the Age of Love, in which the extremists of either polarity, good or evil, go to astral Heaven, while the meek in the middle inherit the Earth to find peace.

At the end of the New Testament in the Christian "Book of Revelation," John further supports the Earth inheritance:

> *{21:3} And I heard a loud voice from the throne saying, "Behold, the dwelling place of God is with man. He will dwell with them, and they will be his people, and God himself will be with them as their God. {21:4} He will wipe away every tear from their eyes, and death shall be no more, neither shall there be mourning, nor crying, nor pain anymore, for the former things have passed away."*

In this excerpt God dwells with man, likely in everyones' hearts. In this New Earth, there will be no more tears, death, mourning, or pain, for these "things have passed away," ...into the astral realm. All of this aligns with the Age of Love in which the open-hearted Romantics live in peace till the end of time.

SUPPORT FROM ISLAM

More support is found in *The Quran*:

> *{2:2} This is the Book in which there is no doubt, a guide for the righteous. {2:3} Those who believe in the unseen, and perform the prayers, and give from what We have provided for them. {2:4} And those who believe in what was revealed to you, and in what was revealed before you, and are certain of the Hereafter. {2:5} These are upon guidance from their Lord. These are the successful. {2:6} As for those who disbelieve—it is the same for them, whether you have warned them, or have not warned them—they do not believe. {2:7} God has set a seal on their hearts and on their hearing, and over their vision is a veil. They will have a severe torment.*
> [Source: **The Quran**, Translated to English by Talal Itani]

This excerpt identifies two groups:

1. The righteous, who believe, give, and follow the guidance from their Lord (Romantics follow their inner God)
2. Those who disbelieve, have a seal on their hearts, and have a severe torment (Pragmatics with calcified pineal glands)

In examining *The Quran*, I found fifteen passages claiming that God placed either a seal, a veil, or a screen over the hearts of people who had strayed from the straight and narrow. In many of those passages, *The Quran* mentions that the person whose heart was sealed by God had lost their ability to know, see, hear, etc. All of those passages support the calcified pineal gland theory and the Pragmatic versus Romantic concept.

The following excerpt from *The Quran* tells the story of God creating Adam and supporting Satan's interest in taking an active role in helping to divide humanity into two groups.

{15:28} Your Lord said to the angels, "I am creating a human being, from clay, from molded mud." {15:29} "When I have formed him, and breathed into him of My spirit, fall down prostrating before him." {15:30} So the angels prostrated themselves, all together.

{15:31} Except for Satan. He refused to be among those who prostrated themselves. {15:32} He said, "O Satan, what kept you from being among those who prostrated themselves?" {15:33} He said, "I am not about to prostrate myself before a human being, whom You created from clay, from molded mud."

{15:34} He said, "Then get out of here, for you are an outcast." {15:35} "And the curse will be upon you until the Day of Judgment."

{15:36} He said, "My Lord, reprieve me until the Day they are resurrected."

{15:37} He said, "You are of those reprieved." {15:38} "Until the Day of the time appointed."

{15:39} He said, "My Lord, since You have lured me away, I will glamorize for them on earth, and I will lure them all away." {15:40} "Except for Your sincere servants among them."

{15:41} He said, "This is a right way with Me." {15:42} "Over My servants you have no authority, except for the sinners who follow you." {15:43} And hell is the meeting-place for them all. {15:44} "It has seven doors; for each door is an assigned class."

{15:45} But the righteous will be in gardens with springs. {15:46} "Enter it in peace and security." {15:47} And We will remove all ill-feelings from their hearts—brothers and sisters, on couches facing one another. {15:48} No fatigue will ever touch them therein, nor will they be asked to leave it.

In passage 15:41 of this excerpt, the Lord states his approval of Satan's proposal to lure away those who are not sincere followers. This is an example of an external astral angel working to lure people away from their inner guidance. In this passage, the Lord approves saying, "This is a right way with Me."

Because this Lord is the one who placed the seal on their hearts, it seems unfair for Him to declare that these people will meet in Hell. Even so, *The Quran*, was revealed to Muhammad in the early 600s. At that time, many people believed it was appropriate for those who didn't believe in, nor serve the Lord, to be punished in Hell. My Soul informed me that this threat of severe punishment was intended to encourage people to follow the guidance they receive from their hearts.

As I pointed out on the previous page, the idea of a seal being placed over the heart is presented fifteen times in *The Quran*. Also, the first excerpt begins, "This is...a guide for the righteous. {2:3} Those who believe in the unseen, and...who believe in what was revealed to you." Therefore, it appears that *The Quran* is a guide for people with open hearts who follow their esoteric Soul-intuition (what was revealed to you). It appears that part of *The Quran's* strategy is to threaten those who turn away from their divine guidance with a final meeting in Hell. The *Quran's* description of Hell states, {15:44} "It has seven doors; for each door is an assigned class." Those seven doors correspond to the seven layers that are found in the astral realm linking the Quran's Hell with the entire astral realm where the Pragmatic people's desires are fulfilled.

On the other hand, the righteous who follow their hearts are rewarded with gardens, springs, peace, and security. All ill feelings will be removed from their hearts, and the males and females will face one another on couches. That last part about facing one another on couches could be meant to suggest the pairing up of Soul Mates.

Finally, the righteous will not be fatigued nor will they be asked to leave, indicating that this arrangement will continue forever.

Here again, we have the predicted fork in the road; people who are cut off from their hearts go to a place with seven doors, while those who remain sincere servants, the open-hearted, live with gardens and springs which is clearly an earthly physical setting.

Fourteen hundred years have passed since these scriptures were written. As we approach the transition, a more honorable and compassionate way of viewing the two paths is offered in these pages. According to that perspective, everyone is respected for playing their role; good, bad, or middle.

The Pragmatics have suffered for an entire age. It's time for forgiveness and gratitude to fill our hearts as we let go of resentment and open more completely to love. Tools are offered in **Part 3**.

SUPPORT FROM HINDUISM

In Hinduism, there are numerous scriptures, and I admit that I have not researched all of them. Despite that, in the 1987 book, *Incarnation in Hinduism and Christianity: The Myth of the God-Man*, Daniel E. Bassuk explains:

> *"According to traditional Hindu mythology, toward the end of the Kali yuga, wealth and power will be the standards for ruling, hypocrisy will dominate business dealings, and carnal pleasures will rule the relationships between men and women. Virtue and religion will have disappeared, as rulers, outwardly arrayed in the apparel of justice, but inwardly evil, will harass the people. The people will begin to leave the wicked cities and greedy rulers and take refuge in the valleys where they will overpopulate the earth, endure harsh weather, and many will die young.*
>
> *At the conclusion of the Kali yuga, Vishnu will appear as Kalki. He will be born into the family of the Vishnuyashas, the chief Brahmin of the village of Shamballa. He will be revealed in the sky seated on a winged white horse with a drawn sword blazing like a comet. He will be endowed with eight supernatural faculties. He will destroy the wicked and barbarian and save the righteous."*
> [From pages 43 and 44.]

This excerpt from Bassuk's book clearly aligns with the Consciousness-Origin Cosmology's prophecies. The presentation is very dramatic, still the split between the "wicked" and the "righteous" is quite clear.

SUPPORT FROM BUDDHISM (A PHILOSOPHY)

Buddhism is dedicated to helping the divisive people who suffer. The Buddhist goal is to work one's way up to Nirvana. Although some Buddhists may claim that Nirvana is a state of mind, Nirvana can also be linked to the highest astral layer.

Because Buddhism is an intellectual philosophy that denies the existence of the Soul, it ignores the Romantic people who inherit the Earth. In spite of that omission, the ascension path for the Pragmatics is self-evident.

CUTE SPELLING COINCIDENCE

"Earth" is "heart" with the "h" moved to the end of the word possibly indicating that there is a linkage between the Earth and the heart. Somewhat silly, but true.

SUMMARY FOR PART 2

All the major <u>religions</u> have scriptures that support the Consciousness-Origin Cosmology's prophecy of a global transition that separates the wheat from the chaff. An ascension/inheritance process that ushers in the final Age of Love on Earth.

Although the scriptures don't offer details about the rarely mentioned inheritance of the Earth, **Part 2** of this book has provided numerous details. When considering this prophecy, it's important to remember that most people are divisive Pragmatics. Accordingly, popular religions and the horrific future predictions that are also popular these days are appropriate for the Pragmatic majority. Typically, those predictions claim that the surface of the Earth will be uninhabitable, making ascension or descending underground the only viable options. Those types of predictions obviously push people toward astral Heaven or Hell. So, even though following the heart is linked to righteousness and inheritance of the Earth, the Way-of-the-Heart path is not what the scriptures, churches, and other popular sources focus on. Instead, they encourage the divisive people to escape via the astral realm.

This book is unusual because it concentrates on the divine Soul within. Because Romantics are guided from within, they don't need external support, like this book, to find their way. Despite that, my Soul has guided me to present the Way-of-the-Heart alternative to encourage Romantic people to follow their Soul's guidance evermore wholeheartedly.

In his famous poem, Robert Frost wrote, "Some say the world will end in fire. Others say Ice." Hopefully, for Romantics, it's going to end in love. The full blossoming of love!

The final part of this book, **Part 3: Tools and Techniques**, will focus on the art of living in that world with an open-heart, following your Soul-intuition as you open to love more than ever before.

Part 3: Tools and Techniques

Chapter 16
Open–Hearted versus Closed–Hearted Living

"Sometimes the heart sees what is invisible to the eye."
—H. Jackson Brown, Jr., (born 1940) author

WHAT DOES "OPENING THE HEART" MEAN?

When a person's heart opens, the Superconscious-Soul expands to embrace the head- and
gut-minds as illustrated on the right.

States-of-Mind

Closed-Hearted   Open-Hearted

The heart symbol is enlarged and stretched
out transforming it back into the older Mandorla
symbol. These particular symbols are used for
convenience and because they're fitting. What's
important is how the Soul grows in size to embrace the head- and gut-minds.

Head   Head

Heart   Heart

Gut   Gut

This expansion would not be possible based
on the materialistic model of reality commonly
assumed to be true; however, with consciousness placed at the foundation of reality, the Soul can change its size, shrinking or expanding
without being restricted by the physical human body.

For example, the Superconscious-Soul can shrink down small
enough to locate itself completely inside the heart. Conversely, the
Soul can expand enough to embrace the head- and gut-minds, as illustrated in the diagram. My Soul has informed me that this type of
expansion is what happens when the heart opens.

For instance, when a person falls in love, their heart opens,
meaning that their Soul expands to encompass their head- and gut-
minds. When this condition develops, the Soul upgrades the normally
feeble minds to make them more like the divine Superconscious-Soul.

THE EFFECT OF AN OPEN HEART

When a person's heart opens they begin to behave and feel more like their True-Self. They align more tightly with their intuition as it comes through more clearly. They also begin to perceive the world around them from a more balanced, holistic perspective; one that's similar to the perspective their Superconscious-Soul sees with its Supreme Power of Wholeness.

The shift that takes place in the person's viewpoint results in important changes. The world appears to be more delightful. Problems seem to disappear. Colors become more vibrant. A knowing that all is well is felt deep in one's heart. A feeling of joy emerges from within. All of this is accompanied by a smile that emerges from inside and forms on the person's face.

The combination of all these changes cause the world to appear to be perfect. Issues still exist, however there's an inner knowing that, in spite of their negative appearance, these problems have a purpose that somehow makes them perfect.

EVIL'S SILVER LINING

After becoming aware that everything, even "evil," is included in perfection, I became interested in understanding how awful things could be perfect. My inquiries regarding this mystery persuaded my Soul to share an explanation of how "evil" produces perfect results. Here's what I learned:

On the surface, an evil activity appears awful. Nevertheless, the activity triggers a chain of events that take place like dominos falling, one onto the other. This chain of events occurs out of sight, in the darkness, eventually turning the initial negative momentum around like a boomerang to result in a "perfect" or very positive outcome.

I was guided to name the way that negative events produce perfect results, *Evil's Silver Lining*.

Even though the initial event appears deplorable, the result that eventually emerges is perfect. It's possible for the domino effect to span moments, years, lifetimes, centuries, and even millennia.

For example, I once had a tantric experience that was the most wonderful experience of my life. It all began with a terrible accident. I was using a powerful and very dangerous 12-inch diameter compound miter saw. This woodworking tool could have easily cut off my entire hand. Luckily, I pulled away quickly to find that the saw had only cut halfway through my middle finger, slightly damaging the tendon.

The doctor, who stitched me up and put a splint on the finger, told me that I needed to take two weeks off work to properly heal the tendon. Later that day, I explained to my beloved that I needed to take an unexpected two-week vacation.

She asked me if I could still make love. I told her I could as long as I didn't use my fingers. She proposed that we could use this opportunity to go on a tantric lovemaking adventure in the spectacular wilderness of Maui. At the end of that seven-day tantric journey, I dropped into the deepest transcendental experience of my life and, as I explained earlier in Chapter 5, I recalled why the One had chosen to make many out of itself. That experience was the most amazing adventure of my life. It even included becoming an infinite orgasm.

If the terrible finger-cutting accident hadn't occurred, I wouldn't have had the unexpected two-week vacation that provided the time needed for my beloved and I to go on this adventure. This real-life experience shows how an awful, or "evil" accident can turn out to be a glorious blessing.

You may recall something like this happening in your life. An initially nasty event occurs; then later, unexpectedly positive results emerge. With hindsight, you can see how the awful event led to a positive outcome; yet, in the beginning, the initial incident appeared to be terrible.

Let's consider an even bigger example of Evil's Silver Lining. Several years ago, there was a forest fire up in the Polipoli Spring State Recreation Area. This beautiful land is located up on the western slope of the 10,024-foot-tall Haleakala volcano on Maui, Hawai'i. The fire blazed through a large area, devastating many trees and countless other plants.

A few months after the fire, I went hiking up in Polipoli and was surprised to find more fertility than I had ever seen there before. There were so many new trees growing that they looked like blades of grass in a wild field. Even though the fire was devastating for many of the trees, some survived, and millions of new ones emerged. On that hike, I discovered that a phoenix actually does emerge from the ashes.

A final example of Evil's Silver Lining was presented earlier in Chapter 3 when I shared my black widow spider incident. To refresh your memory, I put my head into a wooden box that contained a black widow spider. Once the spider came into focus, just inches from my nose, I was terrified. Subsequently, my Soul convinced me that this seemingly awful experience affected me in a way that caused me to follow my heart more than most people. Over the years that followed, my Soul in my heart taught me most of what I've shared in this book.

These examples show how "evil" events can, over time, achieve positive results in accordance with the Evil's Silver Lining principle.

In terms of the Consciousness-Origin Cosmology and the process of individualizing humans, divisive activities are used in a diabolical way that accomplishes the desired result; we become individual humans who can meet one another and experience love.

Although the popular concept is that good (which is right) must overcome evil (which is wrong), a deeper understanding reveals that all extremes have divisive effects. Extreme good and extreme evil both create individuals. Moreover, despite how some events appear to be diabolically evil, the boomerang effect of the Evil's Silver Lining principle claims that those awful events can produce individuals who are loving, open-hearted people.

EVERYTHING IS PERFECT

In an extraordinarily open-hearted state-of-mind, one's Soul can enable them to become aware of the universal perfection that exists. This perfection includes the entire good versus evil Triality. On the right, an illustration depicts how this occurs.

Viewing Reality
Closed-Hearted | Open-Hearted
Good | Good
Perfection | **Perfection**
Evil | Evil

In the closed-hearted state-of-mind, some things appear to be good, others evil and those in the middle are perfect.

When a person "opens their heart," their Soul expands and shifts the person's perspective making them able to see perfection embracing all things, even the extreme good and evil polarities.

Over the years, I've experienced this type of exceptionally open-hearted state-of-mind several times. In discussing this with other people, some have confirmed that they also discovered this open-hearted perspective in which they became able to see perfection in all things.

"It was easy to love God in all that was beautiful. The lessons of deeper knowledge, though, instructed me to embrace God in all things."

—Francis of Assisi (1181–1226) saint, founder of Franciscan family

Here we find the most venerated of all western saints explaining that God is in all things. "All things" includes "evil" things.

Having experienced this ability to see perfection in all things repeatedly, I investigated this phenomenon further.

During that investigation, my Soul guided me to coin the phrase "Supreme Power of Wholeness" in order to capture the idea that a whole portion of consciousness, one that has nearly equal portions of intellect and emotions integrated together, possesses divine powers. One of those powers is the ability to see that everything is unfolding perfectly. So, when a person opens their heart wide enough, a Holy state-of-mind ensues. Their Soul shares some of its power to see beneath the superficial illusion of good versus evil, enabling them to know that the awful activities they witness will, sometime in the future, achieve perfect results.

Maybe you can recall a time when your heart was wide open, and at that time you could see that everything appeared to be perfect.

In the *Book of Matthew* from Christianity's *New Testament*, Jesus advises his followers, "Do not resist evil."

{5:38} "You have heard that it was said, 'An eye for an eye and a tooth for a tooth.' {5:39} But I say to you, Do not resist evil. ..."

This only makes sense if evil is somehow appropriate.

LONGEST NIGHT OF THE YEAR

Although many people link darkness to evil and both terms have been demonized for the entire Age of Individuation, darkness is the mother of Everything.

For example, the egg and sperm join together in the darkness of a mother's womb where a human baby is formed. In a similar way, a seed is planted in the dark soil of the Mother Earth to germinate and grow into a plant. There, in the darkness, the seed wakes from its dormant condition coming alive to extend its roots and grow into a magnificent plant that provides oxygen and food for the animal kingdom. The darkness gets it started, then later, the sunlight adds more energy so it can grow into a healthy mature plant.

217

In a similar way, evil acts through the darkness to individualize us so we can come together and love one another. By considering this perspective, one begins to realize that everything is perfect; good and evil, light and dark. They work together to achieve perfect results.

Curiously, this little section about darkness came to me on the night of the winter solstice—the longest night of the year. I woke up in the middle of that rainy night and turned on a lamp to jot this down.

Most people don't notice that their longest night of the year is simultaneously the longest day of the year on the other side of the equator. On top of that, in the very middle of that long night it's the middle of the longest day on the opposite side of the Earth!

In spite of the appearance of imbalance, balance is forever present. It's all perfect. To see this clearly one must open their heart wide.

FALLING IN LOVE

When a person falls in love, their heart opens. Their Superconscious-Soul expands and engulfs the head and gut in a way that blesses the conscious-mind in the head, and the subconscious-mind in the gut, with a toned-down version of the Soul's balanced, holistic, divine point-of-view, one feature of the Supreme Power of Wholeness. This shift in consciousness introduces a perspective that is more accurate than the normal closed-hearted viewpoint.

Conversely, people have been led to believe that the opposite is true based on the common misconception: "love is blind." Love is not blind; when in love, a person actually sees a deeper truth.

In terms of romantic love, the person who has opened their heart by falling in love becomes able to see beyond outer appearances and into their beloved's Soul. This deeper perception enables the lover to appreciate who their beloved truly is, inside and out. Additionally, from the open-hearted point of view, one is able to see more than who the person is today. This divine perspective sees beyond the present moment to reveal the potential of who their beloved has the potential to become—their True-Self.

My Soul helped me understand that Souls can connect with other Souls through the continuum of consciousness to ascertain the potential each person has hidden in their hearts.

The dormant qualities hidden within one's beloved's Soul are revealed to an open-hearted person as they are given some of their

218

Soul's ability to peer into their beloved's heart and connect with their beloved's True-Self.

The full capabilities of the Soul are <u>not</u> provided to the conscious and sub-conscious minds. Only a toned-down version is made available to enable the open-hearted person to see in a powerful way that is superior to normal perception. The full abilities of the Superconscious-Soul can't be shared because full-disclosure would destroy the illusion of individuality that is critical to accomplishing the purpose of the universe—finding out how it feels to meet mysterious others.

The Superconscious-Soul is aware of much more than the physical outer appearance of other people. In the realm of pure consciousness our Souls are in contact with each other. They're coordinating human encounters to facilitate the goal of the universe.

The Soul is the True-Self, it's the Quintessential Core of the human Triality of consciousness. The Soul contains the full potential of who a person can become. This potential is hidden inside one's treasure chest, out of sight from the conscious- and subconscious-minds. Even so, with the heart wide open, the conscious- and subconscious-minds have some ability to perceive other people's potential.

This viewpoint is more accurate than a person's normal point of view. The normal perspective is shallow, and limited to the visible surface, a facade that can be very misleading, as you have probably discovered in your life.

In a completely different way, the open-hearted perspective is also deceptive. By seeing who one's beloved could become, the open-hearted person is not seeing the reality of who that person is today.

Parts of a person's True-Self may be hidden deep in their heart. Only when their heart is open wide do some of these wonderful potentials come out to express themselves in a person's actions. When their heart is closed or only partially open, this person may behave quite differently.

By healing personal wounds a person can release more of their hidden treasures from within their heart. Fears and resentments keep some of these precious jewels locked up. Letting go of guilt, shame, fears, and resentments can allow more of a person's inner beauty to emerge.

Methods to let go of these debilitating issues will be presented in the remaining chapters.

AFTER THE HONEYMOON

As it is, when the honeymoon is over, and the lovers' hearts close, their Souls contract back into their Heart-Centers and leave the lovers to revert back to their closed-hearted ways and shallow views of one another.

In a closed-hearted state-of-mind, a person views the world from the polarity they're most accustomed to. Some people are more comfortable operating from the upper head polarity, while others tend to operate more from the lower gut polarity.

When operating from the head polarity, one's masculine, intellectual, focused viewpoint is confounded by the irrational, emotional aspects of reality. That's why trying to think one's way through life intellectually can be very frustrating.

Conversely, from the gut polarity, one's feminine, emotional, diffuse viewpoint is uncomfortable with the cold, logical aspects of reality. Thus, attempting to feel one's way through life can be emotionally exhausting.

All humans possess both polarities, and even though the actual portions of consciousness responsible are segregated into the head and gut, both polarities are represented in the head, through the extensive neurological pathway along our spine. This linkage was explained earlier, in Chapter 8: It All Comes Together in the Head.

The reason I mention this is that while some people tend to operate more from their feminine gut polarity, they're still using their conscious-mind in their head, where both polarities convene.

This clever design enables some people to view reality from an emotional, gut perspective, while others adopt a more intellectual, head perspective, even though everyone is using their conscious-mind to some degree.

Of course, there are also people who toggle back and forth between the two polarities.

The most important point here is that both the intellectual and emotional polarities have partial, one-sided perspectives. Both are biased, incomplete viewpoints that succumb to the Feebleness of Incompleteness principle.

The feeble head and gut minds normally see the outer surface which is a façade that covers the consciousness contained deep inside. These feeble portions of consciousness are not able to peer into other people's Souls to divine the potential that's hidden inside their beloved's heart. So, regardless of which polarity a person views the world from, the superficial and feeble nature of either of the polarized perspectives leaves the person somewhat confused and uncomfortable with the world at large, and their beloved in particular.

In the case of Romantic love, when the heart closes, a lover loses the ability to see how truly wonderful their beloved is or, more precisely, the potential their beloved has. Once they've reverted back to their normal state-of-mind, they often wonder, "What caused me to believe that this person was so wonderful?" Sadly, they don't realize that their beloved is still wonderful, or that their beloved has the potential to be wonderful.

With their heart closed, they've lost their ability to see with the deeper and fuller perspective that's available when a person is in love. They've lost the ability to sense the potential of their beloved to become their True-Self, the embodiment of their divine Soul.

Additionally, closed-hearted people revert back to their old ways of being. Parts of their True-Self that came out to play while their heart was open are returned to the treasure chest in their heart. The chest's lid is closed and the lock is clasped shut by the guilt, shame, fears, and resentments they're still burdened with.

In this closed-hearted state-of-mind, people move through life in an out-of-balance, agitated way. Interpersonal connections become highly dependent on which polarity people are operating from. To illustrate this, let's consider two people interacting with each other:

If both people tend to operate from their emotional polarity, their communication and interaction may be reasonably productive and harmonious, because they're both emotionally inclined.

If they both tend to operate from their intellectual polarity, their communication and interaction could also be productive and harmonious, because they're both intellectually inclined.

However, if one person tends to operate from their emotional polarity and the other tends to operate from their intellectual polarity, their communication can seem like they're speaking different languages. They'll be frustrated and unable to relate to each other. This is because they're coming from opposite poles of consciousness: the focused-intellectual head versus the diffuse-emotional gut.

In Romantic relationships, opposites are often attracted to one another. Of course, there are no hard and fast rules. Similarities can be very important in making a connection, as well as in making a relationship last.

The reason I mention this is because the tendency for opposites to be attracted to one another brings together people who often tend to operate from opposite polarities. This can lead to the typical challenges that couples often run into when their Romantic relationship goes beyond the honeymoon stage and their hearts close.

When they fell in love, their hearts opened to enable them to connect in the expanded open-hearted state-of-mind. Then, when the honeymoon ends, their hearts close, and they discover the challenges that develop when their minds return to the polarized feebleness they're accustomed to.

A PERPETUAL HONEYMOON VIA OPEN-HEARTED LIVING

It's important to be aware that one's heart doesn't need to close. You can live with your heart open even when you aren't in the honeymoon stage of a romantic relationship. It's possible to live with your heart open all the time. The remaining chapters provide tools and techniques.

Before all of that is shared, let's consider what happens when two people who have their hearts open, but are not in love with each other, interact with one another.

When two people who both have their hearts open come together, they can interact in a harmonious, loving, cooperative, and productive way, because they're both communicating from the balanced perspective of their Superconscious-Soul. They're talking the same language: the holistic language of the Soul. They're both infused with the natural qualities of the heart: joy, honor, sincerity, love, respect, and kindness. Additionally, when their hearts are open, both are behaving more in alignment with their True-Selves. Finally, they're seeing each other in a deeper way that uncovers wonderful potentials.

All of these factors make interactions between open-hearted people delightful experiences. Even if the people aren't in love with each other, their open-hearted state-of-mind enhances their interactions to make their encounters more enjoyable.

Accordingly, to make any relationship as harmonious as possible, it's best for both parties to keep their hearts open as much as possible. The benefits of an open heart are numerous.

You'll:

- ♥ know all is well,
- ♥ feel joy fill you from within your heart,
- ♥ rekindle your childlike wonder,
- ♥ find yourself smiling most of the time,
- ♥ be more connected to your Soul,
- ♥ be more in alignment with your True-Self,
- ♥ connect more easily with other people, and
- ♥ have an extraordinarily enjoyable life!

All of these qualities are attractive, infectious, and beneficial.

THE RED ROAD OF BEAUTY

Regardless of how a person opens their heart, open-hearted living is quite different from closed-hearted living. Some Native Americans call open-hearted living the Beauty Way, or the Red Road of Beauty.

Many years ago, a Native American elder explained to me:

"The Red Road of Beauty is in the middle of everything. When one is walking on it, one's life is beautiful. This road is very narrow and one can easily fall off of it. When one falls off, the world is no longer so wonderful. Once separated from this narrow Red Road, it can be very difficult to find one's way back to this narrow road."

Back in the late 1980s, when I was offered her wisdom, I didn't grasp the symbolism and depth of this woman's message. Later, when I discovered the middle path of love, I realized that the Red Road of Beauty is living with an open heart, following the Soul's intuition to experience a more beautiful life.

Each person's "middle of everything" is their Soul. That's where the Red Road of Beauty patiently waits.

Still, when a person is living with their heart open, the chaos of the world can trigger challenging emotions that may cause their heart to close. This is how a person falls off the narrow Red Road of Beauty. Herein lies the greatest challenge, how does one re-open their heart to find their way back to the Red Road of Beauty?

Her guidance was realistic. As we all know, withdrawal and bitterness can make it difficult to re-open one's heart.

Fortunately, I was gifted a powerful tool, the *Heart-Opening Breath*, that can open a heart in as little as one breath. That tool is presented in detail in the next chapter. The Heart-Opening Breath has helped me live in a balanced, open-hearted way, walking the Red Road of Beauty to live a more wonderful life.

With this tool, I open my heart and experience a toned-down version of the Supreme-Power-of-Wholeness that's always available. The Soul always resides in one's heart, where it's willing and ready to upgrade one's life.

Overcoming guilt, shame, and fear, and releasing resentment enables a person to live with their heart open more consistently. A method to assist you in vanquishing fear will be shared later. Also, even later, I'll share how to use the powers of forgiveness and gratitude, to release resentment, guilt, and shame.

Love is the most powerful way to keep your heart open so you can access the Red Road of Beauty. By opening to love in one or multiple ways at the same time, you will be blessed with a truly glorious experience of life.

Following the Way-of-the-Heart provides the energy and abilities for you to give from your heart. By giving what you are guided to give, you help to make our shared home, the Earth, more wonderful for everyone.

In this chapter, another viewpoint has been turned right-side-up. Love is not blind; love provides a more beautiful way to view the world, be in the world, and give the blessings that you have to give!

Chapter 17
The Heart–Opening Breath

The original form of what evolved into the Heart-Opening Breath was taught to me by a woman named Indigo Ocean. She had developed a system she called "Bliss Therapy." Her system enabled her to commune with her client's Soul, and share with them what their Soul had been unable to guide them to do.

At the beginning of our session, she explained to me that she was going to go into a trance to connect with my Soul, and then tell me what my Soul wanted me to understand or do that I hadn't been able to understand yet. After she closed her eyes, she told me that she was being guided to lead me in a breathing meditation.

She told me to close my eyes and imagine that I was sending a root down from the tail-end of my spine, deep into Mother Earth, all the way down into her red lava core. She asked me to inhale through my nose while I imagined that I was drawing the red Mother Earth essence up through this root into my heart. She then told me to hold this essence in my Heart-Center while I held my breath, then to exhale through my mouth, releasing the red essence, and to repeat that breathing process two more times.

Next, she guided me to let go of this lower process and focus up above my head. Focusing there, she asked me to imagine that a white light was coming down from Father Sky, forming a funnel shape with the small circular end resting on the top of my head. She told me to inhale through my nose while imagining white Father Sky essence coming down through the funnel, into my head and all the way down to my heart. Again, she guided me to hold this essence in my heart while I held my breath, then to let it out while I exhaled through my mouth. Then to repeat this upper process two more times.

Having practiced the lower and upper parts, she guided me to perform them both simultaneously as I inhaled through my nose.

Then, while holding my breath, she told me to imagine the red and white essences mixing together to become "pink loving wholeness."

Next, when I was ready to exhale out of my mouth, she instructed me to imagine that I was blowing up a pink balloon around my heart, filling it with the pink loving wholeness.

She told me to repeat this breathing process until the balloon grew to be bigger than me, such that I was completely inside it.

States-of-Mind
Closed-Hearted   Open-Hearted

Head   Head
Heart   Heart
Gut   Gut

The illustration on the left (and on this book's cover) shows the Soul expanding in a way that's similar to how the balloon expands to encompass the person.

Finally, she told me to sit calmly in the pink love balloon for as long as I felt appropriate, and tell her when I was done.

After I was done, she shared information about the heart and its role our lives. That information was consistent with the wisdom that had come to me from my Soul giving me confidence that she was successfully tapping into my Soul.

At the end of the session, she mentioned that my Soul wanted me to adopt a daily practice. Instantly, I knew that I wanted to practice the breathing technique daily.

After a few weeks of practice, I noticed that each time I bathed in the pink loving wholeness, a smile would emerge from within and appear on my face. I also noticed that my perception of the world shifted. Bothersome feelings would disappear by the time the smile emerged.

Remarkably, Chinese medicine asserts that the heart is connected to the face and tongue. This explains why a smile emerges when the heart is open. Hence, genuine smiles indicate that a person's heart is open.

This technique amplifies your Soul and shifts your perspective to place you on the Red Road of Beauty.

A SIMPLIFIED VERSION

Eventually, I developed a simplified version that I could do out in public, throughout the day. By using it, I'm better able to move through life in a balanced, calm way, feeling joy throughout my entire being all day long. I named the simpler revised version the "Heart-Opening Breath."

I've found that it's easy to get distracted by the drama in the world, and when I get drawn into those distractions, my heart can close. This tool enables me to quickly reopen my heart, putting me back on the Red Road of Beauty. By having a simple technique to return to an open-hearted state-of-being, the quality of my life has dramatically improved.

If I do the practice often, I find myself smiling all day long! Even when I'm doing something difficult or a task I consider unpleasant, I notice that I'm still smiling, and still happy. When walking the Red Road of Beauty, life is remarkably enjoyable.

The details of the simplified Heart-Opening Breath follow:

THE HEART-OPENING BREATH TECHNIQUE

In the simplified method, the Pubococcygeus (PC) muscle is tightened during the inhale. This muscle is located between your legs, in the space between the genitals and the anus. It's the muscle that you tighten when you want to hold back urine.

To locate the PC muscle, imagine that you need to urinate, then tighten the muscle that you would tighten to hold the urine in. Take a little time to determine which muscle this is, and practice tightening it a few times right now.

Once you've found and flexed the PC muscle, you're ready to begin.

Begin by sitting up straight or standing with your feet placed in a wide, sturdy stance, with your knees bent a little and turned slightly outward. The technique can be done in any position; however, it feels more natural when the body is vertical.

Step 1: As you inhale through your nose and expand your chest, imagine that you're drawing feminine essence up from the Mother Earth into your heart. At the same time, imagine that you're drawing masculine essence down from the Father Sky into your heart. During the inhale, tighten the PC muscle at the bottom of your body and raise your eyebrows slightly so you can feel a little tightness at the top of your head.

This muscle tightening mimics the way you pull liquid through a drinking straw. In this case, imagine you are drawing essence up from the Mother Earth and into your heart through your PC muscle, between your legs. Also, at the top of your head, pretend you're drawing essence down from Father Sky, through your scalp that tightens when you raise your eyebrows.

This first step draws essence from below and above, together, into your heart. You don't need to feel anything special happening. Just tighten the upper and lower ends and inhale strongly. Then, as your chest expands, imagine the essences are being drawn from below and above into your heart inside your chest.

Note: This first step can be a bit difficult initially. To ease yourself into it, do the bottom part a few times by itself. Each time, hold your breath for a moment, then simply exhale out of your mouth. Then, do the top part a few times by itself in the same way. Finally, try drawing inward from both polarities at the same time.

Once you master this first step, continue to Step 2.

Step 2: Once you've fully inhaled into your heart, hold your breath and relax your PC muscle and your eyebrows. Then, as you hold your breath, imagine that the masculine and feminine essences are mixing together in your heart, forming loving wholeness. Give this step adequate time while you focus your conscious awareness on your Heart-Center and imagine the two essences mixing together.

Step 3: Slowly exhale out of your mouth as you imagine that you are blowing up your Soul like a balloon filling it with the loving wholeness you formed in your heart. Each time you repeat the breath, imagine your Soul becoming larger until it is larger than you.

Finally: Repeat the three steps until a smile emerges from within and forms on your face. Be sure to allow the smile to emerge on its own. If you force the smile, you may trick yourself into thinking you're done when you really need to take more breaths.

TIPS

The most difficult part of this technique is to draw the feminine essence upward and the masculine essence downward at the same time. Once you've practiced that a few times, you'll get the hang of it.

I find that holding my hand over my heart makes it all easier.

Check out my animated Heart-Opening Breath instructional video at my website: https://www.SoulCovenant.org/videos

The Heart-Opening Breath can be practiced anytime, with the eyes either open or closed. I've done it while I'm driving my car, waiting in line, having a conversation, or playing percussion with other musicians. With a little practice, I became able to do it in front of other people without them noticing.

Practicing the Heart-Opening Breath expands the Soul and places you in the wonderful open-hearted state-of-mind.

This tool can help you to live your life with your heart open more consistently and wider than you may have thought possible.

For example, one morning I practiced the Heart-Opening Breath every time I noticed that I had stopped smiling. By noon I was in such an open-hearted state that I was able to see the perfection of everything that was discussed in the last chapter. Experiment to discover the joy and love that emerges from your Soul.

SUMMARY OF STEPS

For your convenience, the steps are summarized here:

Step 1: Inhale

- Tighten PC and raise eyebrows

- Inhale through nose and expand chest

- Draw from above and below simultaneously

Step 2: Hold Your Breath

- Relax your PC and eyebrows

- Imagine essences mixing together

Step 3: Slowly Exhale

- Breathe out of your mouth

- Imagine your Soul is expanding around your heart

Repeat until smile emerges from within.

TONING

As an additional consideration, if you like to tone, sing, or use sound with your personal practices, you can combine sounds with this breathing practice. I've found that toning makes the Heart-Opening Breath even more effective.

I've also discovered that it's very important to use a low frequency tone that can be felt vibrating in the Heart-Center; not one that is so low that it vibrates or resonates down in the gut, but one that is low enough that it can be felt vibrating in the chest area.

To find the right tone, just make a low frequency sound and pay attention to discover the part of your body that is slightly vibrating or resonating with that sound. As you raise the pitch, the position of resonance will move up. Conversely, a lower pitch will lower the position where the vibration is felt. Adjust the pitch to position the vibration in your Heart-Center.

Try a low "ha" sound during the exhale part of the technique.

In the Hawaiian language, "ha" means breath.

ELEVATING CHANTING PRACTICES USE HIGHER TONES

The popular chanting that I've encountered out in the world is performed with tones that vibrate above my chest, up in my throat and head. This includes Hindu kirtans and bhajans. These practices use tones that stimulate the upper chakras in the throat and head.

Personally, I've found these high frequencies to be ego-expanding. By stimulating the ego-mind in the head, these practices expand the ego increasing the practitioner's sense of personal grandeur. Going upward and heading to the stars is commonly considered a positive direction that's associated with ascension. The upward path is promoted by popular teachings that focus on ascension toward the heavenly god, but ignore the inheritance of the Earth alternative.

Chanting and repeating mantras distract a person from listening to the whisper of their divine Soul. They draw people up and away from the humble Way-of-the-Heart path. I choose to remain attentive to the subtle guidance from my divine Soul. To do so I avoid chanting and mantras which fit well with the ascension path.

INWARD IS BEST FOR ROMANTICS

If you're a Romantic, the Heart-Opening Breath can help you let go of the idea that "higher is better," by reinforcing the reality that **the most precious part of you is the Holy portion of the One that resides in your heart.** Thus, the closest you can get to holiness is to connect with your divine Soul in the midst of yourself.

Certainly, the One is everywhere and in everything. Still, your Soul is a portion of the One that is your personal representative of the entire One-Who-Is-All and this mini-One is located in your heart.

Looking outward, there are countless external entities ready and willing to lead you: humans, ascended masters, angels, demigods, etc. Unless they advise you to follow the divine within yourself, they're taking you away from your Soul, luring you to become Pragmatic.

Your Soul in your heart will give you the strength and guidance to discover your precious gift so you can give it to the world. Additionally, looking within brings happiness, joy and love into your life.

The Heart-Opening Breath brings your focus inward, toward your Heart-Center. Up, down, right, left, forward and backward are exoteric directions that lead to the astral afterlife realm. Trust your Soul to be your personal ambassador who deals with all the spirits that exist outside yourself.

If the prophecies presented in **Part 2** are correct, practices involving external entities are likely to lure a person away from the physical realm of life. They draw followers to the afterlife astral realm where selfish desires are fulfilled. Conversely, the full blossoming of love will take place here on Earth amongst Romantic givers.

SIGNS THAT THE HEART IS OPEN

When my heart is open, I feel happier, more joyful, and notice a clear sense of peacefulness. I also find myself experiencing more serendipitous synchronicities taking place. In addition, whenever my heart is open I discover myself smiling. I also feel more gratitude for everything and find myself better able to forgive myself and others. Finally, I've noticed an amplified willingness to help people in need and give to the world.

All of these are signs of being open-hearted.

THINGS THAT ENCOURAGE THE HEART TO OPEN

First and foremost, love opens the heart.

Having innocent fun also opens the heart.

Being in nature—breathing in the delicious air while witnessing the glorious beauty of life that abounds, surely opens one's heart.

Helping someone in need has a powerful heart-opening effect.

By practicing the Heart-Opening Breath, you'll notice what touches your Soul, puts a smile on your face and causes tears of joy to run down your cheek. Make those things a bigger part of your life.

STILLNESS VERSUS OPENING THE HEART

It's possible to seclude yourself from the chaos of the world and meditate to quiet your mind. In a state of stillness, you can connect with the divine Soul within. This approach works as long as you can remain still and quiet. But when you're participating in life, the ruckus of the chaotic world can drown out the heart's whisper.

Fortunately, the Heart-Opening Breath amplifies the divine guidance from your heart helping you remain connected to your inner guidance. Additionally, with a wide-open heart, your state-of-mind shifts, revealing a perfect world. When a terribly challenging incident closes your heart, you can quickly reopen it by performing the Heart-Opening Breath until your smile reemerges from within.

REMEMBERING TO BREATH

I've found that it's very difficult for me to remember to do the Heart-Opening Breath throughout the day. To help myself remember to do it I use a **vibrating countdown timer wristwatch with a repeat function**. I set the timer to 17 minutes. Of course, you can choose a different length of time between reminders.

Each morning I put on the watch and start the countdown timer (which is already setup) by pressing two buttons. Then I do the Heart-Opening Breath to begin my day.

In 17 minutes the watch vibrates and I press one button to stop the vibration alert. Then I do the Heart-Opening Breath again. Meanwhile the watch is repeating the countdown. This helps me keep my heart open throughout the entire day.

When I go to bed I take off the watch and pause the timer leaving it ready for the following morning.

BEING FILLED WITH THE HOLY SPIRIT

Open-hearted living corresponds to the Christian condition of "being filled by the Holy Spirit." That divine state is an extraordinarily blessed condition that can be your way of life!

Chapter 18
Following Your Heart

"Nothing is less in our power than the heart, and far from commanding we are forced to obey it."
—Jean Jacques Rousseau (1712–1778) philosopher

WHAT DOES FOLLOWING YOUR HEART MEAN?

Before I share the tools that I've used to "follow my heart," I'll begin by clarifying exactly what that phrase means to me.

The Soul in my heart introduces ideas, pictures, or feelings into my ego-mind via the pineal gland. This esoteric knowledge appears as a voice, an image, a feeling, or a compelling sense of knowing that arrives without my conscious-mind's reasoning conjuring it up.

Given one of those messages, "following my heart," means I follow through and do what the intuitive message guided me to do, or I heed the warning of my conscience advising me not to do something.

THE HUMBLE WATER WAY OF TAOISM

In following my heart, I've found it helpful to be humble and flexible while remaining true to my conscience and intuition.

The Water Way of Taoism is a Chinese philosophy that advocates a humble middle path, one in which a person surrenders to the natural unfolding of reality by becoming part of that natural flow themselves.

As Gravity draws the inner mass of water downhill the fluidity of the water enables it to gracefully flow around the rocks and through the passages that are open and available for it to pass through.

In a similar way, a person with Soul-intuition can gracefully navigate through their landscape of life by heeding inner warnings and following intuitive encouragements.

This water way is the Way-of-the-Heart that my Soul has helped me to understand and surrender to. Each step involves maintaining a flexible and resilient ego, one that is willing to live in alignment with the Soul's guidance which includes honoring the conscience and intuition. The further I walk this path, the stronger my relationship with my Soul becomes, the deeper I surrender and the more my True-Self emerges. Still, I'm just a feeble human who stumbles. When that occurs, I laugh at myself, pick myself up, breath into my heart and continue following the Way-of-the-Heart as well as I'm able to.

WHERE IS THE IDEA COMING FROM?

A particularly tricky part of following one's heart is how it can be difficult to tell whether an idea to do something came from one's Soul as intuition, or if the idea came from the ego-mind.

The next two sections offer methods for sorting this out.

SIMPLE THINGS

First of all, if I have an idea to do a simple thing, I just do it. If it's easy to do, I don't bother figuring out whether the idea came from my ego, my gut, or my Soul. If it's simple, the easiest course of action is to simply do it.

This approach handles most of the guidance you'll receive from your heart. As you may already know, most of the Soul's guidance is about little things. Of course, lots of little things eventually add up to produce a huge difference in your life.

One way to gauge how well you're doing is to pay attention to how often you find yourself thinking something like, "Darn, I knew I should have done that," or "Oops, I knew I shouldn't have done that." These types of thoughts arise when you fail to follow your heart.

So, when you find yourself thinking, "I knew I should or shouldn't have," you know that you failed to follow your Soul's infallible guidance. A more accurate way to describe what happened is, "I should have followed my heart. My Soul is always right! I need to do those simple things and stop putting them off!"

Thus, if you have an idea to do a simple thing, just do it.

For example, doing a little thing like checking the oil in your car can avoid completely destroying the engine. If the simple idea of "Check the oil," pops up in your head, do it! That way, you won't destroy your car's engine and find yourself thinking, "I knew I should have checked the oil!" You also won't need to purchase a new engine.

BIG THINGS

If I get an idea to do something big, then I'll take some time to check in with my Soul and clarify what my Soul's position is on the big endeavor. This big idea could have come from my feeble ego-mind. It could be a foolish idea that may waste my time or cause problems. To avoid adventures down blind alleys, I've developed a way to use the Heart-Opening Breath to help me connect with my Soul and check in.

First, I do the Heart-Opening Breath to deepen my heart connection. If you have another technique that you prefer, then by all means, use that method to open your heart.

Next, I literally ask my Soul: "Dear Soul in my heart, would it be good for me to (insert big endeavor)?" This question can be asked with your inner dialogue voice in your head by thinking the question. If you're alone, you might prefer to state it out loud.

Then, I focus on my chest. If my chest feels expansive or open and comfortable, I consider that to be a **yes** from my Soul. If my chest feels contracted and tight or drawn in, I view that to be a **no**.

Next, I ask my Soul the opposite question: "Would it be better to (insert an opposite or alternative to the big endeavor)?" Then, I focus on my chest again. This time, I can compare the way my chest felt after the first question to how it feels after the second question. By asking both questions and comparing the feelings, I usually notice a clear enough difference to be reasonably confident of my Soul's position. Obviously, more than two questions can be asked in order to choose between multiple alternatives.

Regardless of the number of options, the difference in how my chest feels can be very subtle or essentially the same. In those cases, I presume my Soul is leaving this decision to my ego-mind.

If I feel a noticeable difference in my chest, and the result indicated that the big endeavor would be good for me to do, then I do it. Often, my ego-mind may have other ideas and reasons to do something else, still I believe it's always best to follow my Soul's guidance.

This method of sorting out how my Soul feels about an idea is based on knowing that the Soul resides in the heart. By knowing the Soul's location, I'm able to focus on the sensations in my chest. Using this technique has helped me to live more closely in alignment with my Soul's guidance.

QUESTIONS FOR THE SOUL

There are all kinds of questions you can ask your Soul to receive its divinely wise council. To enlist your Soul's assistance, all you need to do is contemplate a question in your mind. There are a few different types of questions that are discussed below.

It's important to be aware that the Soul only provides advice for the present moment. Questions about the future don't seem to provoke a response from the Soul. This feature of the Soul helps the follower live in the present moment. Questions about the future only come up when a person is trying to plan their life out. Obviously, a plan has nothing to do with surrendering to your Soul nor living in the present moment. Thus, it's appropriate for the Soul to refrain from answering questions about the future.

YES OR NO QUESTIONS

The method for yes-or-no questions was discussed in the "BIG THINGS" section on the previous page.

Some people do this type of yes-or-no inquiry using a coin flip, tarot cards, muscle testing, or a pendulum. If you have Soul-intuition, then you can use the infallible wisdom of your Soul.

As you practice working with your Soul, you'll be developing a relationship with your Soul. This relationship is the most important relationship you can develop! Your Soul is your god within. It's your divine guardian, the True You. The more intimate your relationship becomes, the more you'll bring out your True-Self.

This process of interacting with your Soul is valuable, in and of itself. Accordingly, you can consider each session an opportunity to deepen your relationship with your divine Superconscious-Soul.

OTHER TYPES OF QUESTIONS

Next, let's take a look at other types of questions. While working as an inventor, designer, and builder, my Soul has guided me to solve problems that others believed to be unsolvable. Our Souls can assist us in all kinds of endeavors. In the following, I'll explain how I tap into my Soul's wisdom to help me with three types of issues that are common in any person's life:

1. The creative process, in which someone wants to explore new ideas or inventions.

2. Practical questions about reality, like, "What's causing this machine to malfunction?"

3. Personal issues that involve choices between options.

THE CREATIVE PROCESS

The creative process is the most difficult, so let's tackle it first.

Always begin with a big Heart-Opening Breath.

The creative process begins with a reasonably simple practical step: Regardless of whether you are creating a sculpture, an invention, a novel, or anything else, you must begin by asking the genius within for help. The quality of the request for help will greatly affect the creative guidance that emerges. To form a high-quality request, take some time to determine what is needed, but missing.

Having said that, you don't want to overthink it. When you keep thinking, and fail to settle on a clear request, you prevent the Soul from doing its magic. Successful creative people know when they have formulated a sufficiently clear request. To move forward they make the request for inner guidance and wait for the answer to come as an intuitive epiphany from within. The request primes the pump of creativity, but the Soul provides the creative epiphany.

"The soul creates, the mind reacts. The soul understands what the mind cannot conceive."
—Neale Donald Walsch (born 1943) author

Rather than burning the midnight oil trying to figure it out in your mind, it's best to settle on a clear request, make the request by stating it in your mind and then let go, knowing your Superconscious-Soul will do its creative magic. Later, when your mind is quiet enough to receive the message, the innovation will pop up in your mind.

The creative process is a form of conception that requires both feminine and masculine components. In terms of consciousness, the feminine aspect is diffused, emotional, and irrational. The masculine part is focused, intellectual and rational. The union of both forms a creative genius that has the ability to conceive of innovative solutions.

According to my Soul, here's how these opposites work together.

The diffuse irrational aspect offers a wide variety of emotionally driven suggestions. These are analyzed by the focused intellect to sort out which ideas are practical. With both features in one mind, the wild emotionally-driven sparks from the irrational portion offer the intellect fuel for thought, and eventually a brilliant idea emerges.

Neither our gut-mind nor our ego-mind have both of these important components of consciousness. The ego-mind is mostly masculine, while the gut-mind is mostly feminine. The only part of our consciousness that possesses both polarities in a balanced and whole combination is our Superconscious-Soul in our heart.

The head can think forever without conceiving. The gut can jump around, in vain. Without being integrated together, these divided portions of human consciousness suffer from the Feebleness of Incompleteness principle, making them incapable of creative conception.

The Superconscious-Soul, being whole, has the ability to conceive, devise, and conjure up new ideas, to produce fruitful results in the creative realm.

"If I create from the heart, nearly everything works; if from the head, almost nothing."

—Marc Chagall (1887–1985) artist

When embarking on a creative endeavor, the ego-mind must initiate the process by requesting help; then it must step aside and quietly wait for the Soul to come back with a response.

If you're working on an innovative invention or an avant-garde work of art, the unprecedented nature of the request may require some time before your Soul is able to offer guidance. Accessing knowledge from the One is instantaneous, but creativity takes time.

I've found it best to simply stop thinking about the issue and wait for the guidance to come. Often, it arrives the next morning after a good night's rest. I don't use an alarm clock so I can wake up in a gradual quiet way that provides an opportunity for the guidance to appear. When working on this book, I woke up with new ideas nearly every day. When I'm working on physical things and run into a difficulty, the next day I often wake up with an image of the solution in my mind's eye. I've found that naps can be a very effective way to provide additional opportunities for the creative ideas to be delivered.

Albert Einstein was famous for his daily 20-minute naps.

The challenging part of this process is that it takes time for the creative epiphany to arrive. These novel or creative issues don't have ready-made answers. Instead, the creative Superconscious-Soul must work out the solution before it can deliver guidance to your ego-mind.

If nothing comes by morning, try to formulate the request again. Be as clear and concise as you can.

Once your Soul provides inspiring guidance and you incorporate the "Soul-ution" into your project, new challenges may arise. Go back to the beginning of the process and repeat it with the new issue. Eventually, a complete result will emerge.

Later, new ideas for improvements or interesting variations on the theme may pop up. The same process can be used to refine and improve whatever you're working on. The creative process is usually repetitive in nature. On some occasions, the ideal "Soul-ution" arrives in the first attempt. More often, it takes a few tries.

The key to making huge leaps into wildly new realms is to let go of as many existing assumptions as possible. Give your Soul the most open request you can formulate. This gives your Soul the opportunity to leapfrog over what exists and break into entirely new territory.

The most important thing is to enjoy the creative process, have fun with your Soul and take time to thank it for the precious assistance it provides. Always remember that the creative genius is in your heart. Gratitude and humility keep the process flowing.

As soon as your ego-mind begins to think it has the power to create, that arrogance will block the flow.

Conversely, when you realize that your Soul is the divine grand master and you approach that precious part of yourself with humility, respect, and love, your life will be filled with blessings beyond your wildest dreams. At least that's what I've found in my life.

THE DOUBLE-EDGED SWORD OF INNOVATION

Innovation is a double-edged sword. Even though your Soul may be willing to help you invent something new, it's up to you to consider the legacy that your invention may leave behind. Before you take on a project, consider the ramifications of what you're hoping to develop.

Who is going to use it? What will they use it for? How do you feel about those people and the activities involved?

I put years of my life into inventing a computer tool for mechanical engineers. Then I realized it would be used to develop military weapons and I shelved the project. Years of my life were wasted. Take some time to be sure that you will be proud of what you're working on before you put a lot of time into a creative endeavor.

SOUL'S GUIDANCE WITH PRACTICAL ISSUES

The second type of issue is a practical problem that you would like to fix. This method is actually quite easy and can be used in countless different ways.

Start out with a big Heart-Opening Breath.

Then, clarify your goal or intention.

Next, ask an appropriate question to get started. Some examples include, "What's the problem with this _____?," or "What should I do to fix this _____?," or simply, "Where should I start in working to fix this _____?"

Then, grab ahold of whatever answer pops up first.

My ego-mind will often have one or more competing ideas; but I've found that the first answer is the Soul's infallible answer that ought to be followed. Don't let your ego-mind convince you to try something else instead. This will only lead you astray.

If it's a one-step solution, you're done. If there are multiple steps to solving the problem, simply go back to the beginning and ask what needs to be done next. Keep repeating this process until the problem is resolved.

You'll usually know when you've found the problem. Often, you'll find a broken part that you may need to repair or replace.

When you think it's fixed, test it. If it works, you're done. If not, go back to the beginning and repeat the process.

A key ingredient is to have the courage to do what you're guided to do. Don't be afraid to get a screwdriver or a wrench and take the cover plate off. Don't be put off by your ego-mind's concerns that you don't know what you're doing. I've repaired countless things that I had never dealt with before.

I simply follow my inner guidance each step of the way.

Once you've found and fixed the problem, reverse the process and put it back together. To help yourself remember how it was assembled, you can take pictures as you take it apart.

These days, the internet has lots of advice so you may want to check that out. I've found the internet advice to be very helpful in some cases, but quite often that advice has wasted my time by leading me astray or wasted my money by replacing the wrong part. It doesn't appear that the divine Soul's infallibility will be bested by the internet.

Another consideration is that many modern consumer items have become throw-away products. Even so, some can be repaired. If you're going to throw it away and purchase a new one anyway, then it can be a valuable learning experience to try your hand at repairing it. You might surprise yourself.

When dealing with a complicated device that could be properly repaired by a person who is trained to repair it, there's the consideration that you might cause more damage by trying to fix it yourself. You must decide how far you're willing to go with repairing things on your own. Even though I've had lots of successes in a wide range of products, I still choose to employ a trained repair person in some cases.

Personally, I've found the experience of working with my Soul to solve problems very rewarding. There's something deeply satisfying about fixing something that was broken and giving it a longer life.

SOUL GUIDANCE WITH PERSONAL ISSUES

Finally, let's consider personal issues, life choices, and other private matters. Personal issues can be complicated by strong feelings that may include irrational fears.

Your irrational fears can hide some of your most wonderful gifts. When a traumatic experience occurs, valuable aspects of your True-Self can get locked away in the treasure chest of your heart. Those traumas can create irrational fears that keep those valuable parts of your True-Self locked away. In addition to valuable talents being hidden, it's common for people to forget the trauma because it's too disturbing to remember.

To help you uncover these hidden gifts, your Soul may encourage you to do things that push you to face the irrational fears that keep your hidden ability locked away. When this happens, you're being given an opportunity to vanquish one of your irrational fears and free parts of your True-Self from the treasure chest in your heart.

An elder once explained to me how to deal with these fears:

"When an irrational fear comes up, go into it, and keep going deeper and deeper until you come out the other side where you'll find that the fear was in your mind. It wasn't real."

So, when you feel guided to do something that brings up an irrational fear, the best thing to do is go into it and explore it. Don't retreat! Instead, find the courage to continue all the way through to the other side. Face the fear, confront it, and explore it, and as you do, you'll eventually discover it was an imaginary fear that has vanished.

Every time you're able to vanquish one of your irrational fears, you'll develop more courage, and the process will become easier, because you'll have greater confidence in obtaining a positive outcome.

By stepping out of your comfort zone and mustering the courage to face your irrational fears, more of your True-Self will come out to play. Additionally, if physical and emotional ailments were associated with the fear, they may heal, making your life more enjoyable.

The important point here is: When you're guided to do something that brings up an irrational fear, rather than interpreting that fear as a warning to be heeded, take it as an upside-down signal that actually means, "You really need to do this!"

The cave you fear to enter holds the treasure you seek.

—Joseph Campbell (1904–1987) mythologist and author

There are, of course, real fears that ought to be taken seriously, so only apply the above suggestion to irrational fears. To avoid any confusion, an irrational fear is a fear of something that's not considered dangerous by most people.

FIRST INSTINCTS: LISTEN!

Anytime you contemplate a question in your mind, your Soul **may** toss in an answer via intuition. If your Soul does toss in an infallible answer, it will always be the first answer.

Afterwards, your ego-mind may throw in alternatives. The alternatives often squelch or negate the Soul's infallible first answer. These inferior alternatives give the ego-mind a bad reputation. The truth is, the ego-mind is doing its best, it just doesn't have the Supreme Power of Wholeness that the Soul is blessed with. Instead, the ego-mind is designed to be gullible and feeble so it can enable us to be individuals and meet mysterious others. Being divinely wise isn't part of that role.

A tricky issue that can crop up is when you contemplate a question in your mind and your Soul doesn't provide any answer at all. If the Soul did provide an answer, it would be the first answer and the best answer. However, when your Soul doesn't provide any answer at all, you might think your ego-mind's first answer was an infallible Soul answer. Then later, when you find out this first answer was false or misleading, you might blame your Soul. Moreover, this misunderstanding may cause you to lose faith in your Soul's wisdom.

To make sure that the first answer came from your Soul, you can always use the Heart-Opening Breath and check in with simple yes-or-no questions to sort out the situation. Take time to play around with the yes-and-no process until you feel confident with the results.

If you're intuitive, don't let your intellectual head or your emotional gut drag you out of balance. Use the Heart-Opening Breath to shift your state-of-mind into the open-hearted perspective. With an open heart, you'll be better able to listen to your Superconscious-Soul and follow its divine guidance. Additionally, you'll be happier, healthier, and more skillful in everything you do.

SURRENDERING TO THE FLOW

Most of the time, all you need to do is feel your way down the path of least resistance. **Go with the flow.** Don't overthink it. Keep your heart open, and do what feels right in your heart.

I feel a grace and ease in my life most of the time. I suppose it could be likened to a plant growing—it's effortless and unstoppable. A plant can't decide to do something else. The plant just grows and blossoms. It effortlessly grows into what it's guided to become. The guidance comes from a consciousness that resides inside the plant, a consciousness that propels it to express the form that comes from within the seed out of which it emerged.

You're a human being, and in the grand play of life, you're an actor on a stage we call Earth. Your Soul is the director. By surrendering to your Soul and accepting its guidance, your life will unfold in a way that helps to fulfill the grand plan. Just as a plant grows effortlessly you can live effortlessly. In doing so, your life will become more glorious than anything you could imagine with your feeble ego-mind.

We must let go of the life we have planned, so as to accept the one that is waiting for us.

—Joseph Campbell (1904–1987) mythologist and author

Planning with your ego-mind and following that plan can cause your path to diverge from the natural flow of life. By charting your course with your feeble head- and gut-minds, you'll most likely discover difficulties cropping up. Your life can become disfigured. Your health may suffer, and life can turn sour.

Conversely, with a humble and willing ego-mind, life can be quite effortless and magical. On occasion, you might accidentally screw up by following a half-baked ego-mind idea. When that happens, it's time to laugh at yourself, remember how feeble your ego-mind is, take a Heart-Opening Breath, and get back to effortless magic.

This effortless Way-of-the-Heart is unexpectedly very productive. I accomplish quite a bit. Helping others is a big part of my life. Still, it doesn't seem to take much effort to get lots of things done. I simply take one step, then another, following my inner guidance.

Thinking in moderation is a normal part of heart-centered living. However, with too much thinking and obsessing on thoughts, very little gets accomplished. Calm, casual thinking works well.

Taking time to simply be is very beneficial. With a quiet mind the Soul can provide deeper and clearer guidance.

Finally, as you go about your life roadblocks can appear. Situations may develop in which you notice that something in your life is blocked, or that you're encountering resistance as you endeavor to do something. When life becomes a struggle, check in to see if there's a better direction, or if there's a feeling in your heart that you ought to scrap the whole idea. Check in by asking your Soul questions, using the tools above.

DOWNTIME

When you feel tired, stop and rest. It's important to get sufficient rest. **Relaxing downtime is very important.**

For example, I avoid schedules and alarm clocks. I sleep until I feel rested. Waking up slowly provides opportunities for my Soul to share inspirational ideas. If nothing comes and I feel ready to rise, I just get up and start my day.

I take little naps. Giving my mind and body a rest will often bring forth new inspirations, and off I go, eager to follow the motivation.

I don't plan my day, I prefer to let it unfold. Schedules seem to interfere with following my heart. When coordinating with other people I'm willing to make plans and be on time, but whenever possible I prefer to play it by ear, checking in and working things out on the fly.

BAREFOOT LIVING HELPS

Several years ago, I switched to barefoot living to be more intimately connected with the Mother Earth.

I've found that barefoot living helps me remain in balance allowing me to tune in to my inner guidance better. When on barefoot adventures I've found that my inner guidance arrives much clearer and more often than it did when I wore shoes.

There are also numerous health benefits.

If you're interested, check out www.barefooters.org

There are also many books on barefoot living.

LIBERATING YOUR GENIUS

Going beyond following the Soul's guidance, one can make way for genius abilities to emerge from their Soul.

Thus, this method is named: *Liberating Your Genius.*

Souls, being pure consciousness, are indestructible. Over many lifetimes, Souls have developed numerous talents. A person can discover these talents if and when they attempt to use them. Earlier, I referred to a treasure chest that contains these abilities. This aspect of the Soul is like a treasure chest in the following ways:

- ♥ These treasures are hidden in your chest.
- ♥ It's a bit tricky to find these precious gems.
- ♥ You don't know what treasures are in there or how many will be found.

To access one of my Soul's genius abilities, I focus on the task at hand, in the present moment, without planning ahead or thinking with my mind. I approach the task with an open heart while relinquishing all extraneous thoughts especially those of credit, rank, or outcome, to be fully engaged with the task at hand, in the present moment. This unlatches my treasure chest, allowing the genius to emerge from my heart boosting my ability, beyond normal human potential, to launch my skill level into the realm of mastery.

Thus, an open heart and humble focus on the task at hand, without thinking, is the elusive key to accessing your genius.

Most people believe that masterful abilities require hard work, years of practice, intellectual focus, and lots of detailed planning. But none of that is true when it comes to one of your Soul's hidden talents.

On the other hand, if your Soul hasn't developed masterful skills in the particular pursuit that you're interested in taking on, then you will need to go through the rigorous process of developing that ability. If you do work on developing a new skill, then hard work can enable you to become very good or even extremely skilled in that endeavor. Still, you'll never express genius level mastery unless you step aside and allow your Soul to boost your ability beyond what your conscious- and subconscious-minds can achieve.

Engaging the Soul's superconsciousness involves letting go of striving, fears, knowing, thinking, plans, and time. It requires being in the moment, with the heart wide open, allowing the divine consciousness in your heart to take the wheel and propel your body, or in other cases, your thoughts. When the Soul is engaged, the conscious-mind watches and often wonders how such masterful talent has emerged.

Rather than trying harder, one must surrender to swing open the lid of the treasure chest allowing the Superconscious-Soul's genius to emerge from within. By shamelessly surrendering, an open-hearted person brings forth the Supreme Power of Wholeness to enhance their life and share their Soul's masterful abilities.

Still, as soon as a person's ego wavers and they place some of their attention on how others, or they themselves, judge their skill, or on the results that may arrive in the future, those thoughts push the genius back into the treasure chest leaving the person to continue with normal human abilities.

Genius is only available to people who don't try to be masters, but simply focus on doing their best in the present moment without thinking while their heart is wide open. Paradoxically, humble surrender brings forth the greatest skills a human can express.

It's important to take into account the fear factor. Are you afraid to be better than others? Are you afraid to surrender in a way that allows the Soul's mastery to emerge? Are you afraid to take the leap of faith and trust that your Soul will ensure a safe landing? Are you afraid that you might fail and look foolish? Contemplating any of these fears will put the genius back in the treasure chest.

Take small steps at first. Build your confidence and develop your trust. As you gain confidence in your Soul, you'll be able to surrender more and more, allowing the inner genius to fully emerge.

I've heard some people call this process "fake it till you make it." For instance, when I play drums, I raise my hands up in the air and bring them down toward the drum without knowing what's going to happen. Somehow, without any effort, a beautiful rhythm is played. I can look around, and the beat will continue on its own. If the moment calls for you to be a drummer or a dancer, or for you to play any role that you may not think that you are able play, take a chance. Fake it, and you just might make it.

Your Soul has talents you will only discover if you give them an opportunity to emerge from your treasure chest. As you let go of fears, shame, guilt, and resentments, your Soul's awesome powers will more easily emerge. Still, you need to open the door by stepping up to bat and then engaging the task with a still mind.

As you live your life, opportunities to try new things appear. If you shy away from those opportunities, nothing will happen. However, if you take a chance, open your heart, and fake it till you make it, genius abilities may emerge and surprise you. This is how you'll discover that some of your greatest abilities have been hidden in your treasure chest.

Of course, the Heart-Opening Breath can help.

My experience with the *Liberating Your Genius* method is that it doesn't work all the time. The Soul may have many talents; however, it also has a limited set of skills. It may be like a god in comparison to the little ego-mind in your head, but it isn't the entire One-Who-Is-

All. Therefore, it's wise to test the waters to see if your Soul has a particular ability. Give it a shot, quiet your mind, and see if your Soul can take over. If it does, what unfolds will amaze you as much as it amazes others.

In some cases, you may need to learn the basics before you can engage your Soul's masterful abilities. For example, to play an instrument you may need to learn how to hold it, where to place your fingers. A little practice may be needed to get started. Then with the basics in hand, see what can emerge from within.

What is being referred to here as masterful genius is quite similar to what the New Testament refers to as being "filled with the Holy Spirit." Masterfully expressing your inner genius is an enhanced way of being. The inner divine spirit, the Soul, takes over and propels the person in ways that are beyond normal human abilities.

In some cases, the person may make profound or prophetic statements. In other cases, they may make beautiful music. Still, in most cases humble, generous people simply perform their task or job with masterful skill without anyone noticing. An open-hearted person may be a janitor, an office worker, or a high-level leader. Regardless of their position, they're simply doing their job in an open-hearted way. Quite often their genius goes unnoticed.

Hopefully what was shared in this chapter will help you follow your heart even better than you have been.

The next chapter offers a variety of ideas, suggestions, techniques, and considerations related to open-hearted living.

Chapter 19
Soul–Magic, Miracles, and More

"None of us will ever accomplish anything excellent or commanding except when he listens to this whisper which is heard by him alone."

—Thomas Carlyle (1795–1881) philosopher

SERENDIPITOUS SYNCHRONICITIES

Serendipitous synchronicities are events that appear coincidentally fortuitous on the surface, but are actually examples of the Soul guiding a Romantic person into extraordinary experiences.

By way of illustration, I recall a time when I made six wreaths out of a huge pile of vines. The vines had been dumped at a dilapidated horse ranch where I was living. The manager of the property told me that I was welcome to use the vines for anything at all, as he was simply leaving them to compost on their own.

Christmas was on its way, and an idea to make the vines into wreaths for Christmas gifts intuitively popped up in my mind. I preferred to make gifts, rather than purchase them, so I went to work and fashioned some of the vines into six wreaths.

Then, I took a moment to step back and look at the wreaths. They looked okay, but they were too bland for Christmas gifts. They needed to be decorated to make them more gift-like. The idea of using dried flowers to decorate them occurred to me, but the thought of buying dried flowers from a store didn't feel right.

At that time, I was connecting with nature and wanted to make the gifts out of natural found objects, not store-bought items. As I wondered where or how I might find natural dried flowers to decorate the wreaths, the phone rang.

It was Ruby, a friend that I hadn't seen or talked to in over a year. She told me that she was hoping to visit a good friend of hers—a lady who grows flowers organically and dries them. She further explained that her car was broken so she didn't have a way to get to her friend's place, which was a long drive out into the country. As she was wondering how to get there, the idea had come to her to call me and ask if I might be interested in going out to visit the flower farm and possibly make some dried flower arrangements.

The fact that I hadn't made a dried flower arrangement in my entire life made this call very unexpected. I'm not really into decorating. I'm more into function and simplicity. The idea of making the wreaths was a practical use of material destined to simply decompose. The idea of decorating them came when they didn't look gift-like.

In spite of that, Ruby had called at the perfect moment with the ideal solution to decorate the wreaths.

When we arrived at the flower farm, the flower lady took us into her barn. As we entered, we saw an outrageous array of dried flowers. They hung from the rafters by strings. Bundles of all different kinds of flowers at various different heights were suspended throughout the large, open space, making a spectacularly beautiful and truly unusual scene. The wide variety of colors, shapes, and textures dangling in midair was breathtaking.

The flower lady explained that we could pick any flowers we liked. Afterward, she would come up with a price. She also told us that we could use the wood-fired sauna out by the pond and go for a dip in the pond if we wanted to take a break at some point.

My friend and I had a great time. We fired up the sauna, did most of the flower decorating, sweat together for a while in the sauna, dove into the pond for a cold dip, and wrapped up the decorating. We expressed our sincere gratitude to the flower lady, paid a very reasonable fee, and left as the sun was setting.

Serendipitous synchronicities that turn out so marvelously fortuitous can cause a person to wonder how this magic works.

There are various theories that exist to explain it, one theory that has become quite popular is the manifestation theory.

THE POPULAR MANIFESTATION THEORY

Shakti Gawain was one of the early pioneers of the now-skyrocketing field of manifestation. Certainly, its roots go back much further into the past, however Gawain's landmark book, *Creative Visualization* that came out in 1978, seemed to popularize the theory.

Other names for this theory include "creating your own reality," "the law of attraction," and "creative visualization."

The manifestation theory claims that our thoughts influence reality to align with those thoughts. In the example provided above, my desire to find a way to decorate the wreaths with dried flowers would be responsible for causing Ruby to invite me to the flower farm.

This theory proposes that thoughts and desires trigger a chain of events that take place in the subconscious realm, where any adjustments to physical reality or any arrangements that need to be made to accommodate the thought are worked out. Claiming that human thoughts are the root cause, implies that our thoughts have the power to alter our physical reality!

With that theory presented, let's consider a very different theory, one that my Soul intuitively revealed to me.

THE SOUL-MAGIC THEORY

The *Soul-Magic* theory claims that our Souls arrange these fortuitous events using their knowledge of the future; Soul-to-Soul communication for coordination; the intuition that Souls provide; and their control over human desires.

In the case of the Christmas wreaths, this theory proposes that my Soul and Ruby's Soul had a meeting before the incident took place. In the realm of pure consciousness, our Souls decided that Ruby and I ought to get together. Then, knowing that Ruby was planning to visit the flower lady, and also knowing that a pile of vines had been dumped on the property where I was living, our Souls concocted a plan for me to make wreaths out of the vines and go to the flower farm with Ruby to decorate them.

To put this plan into motion, my Soul gave me the intuitive idea to make wreaths out of the available vines. This fit with my interests in making gifts, so I easily followed this intuitive guidance. Once I completed the wreaths and took a look at them, my Soul used its ability to control the emotional chemistry in my head to make me feel unimpressed with the results. In addition to making me feel blasé about the wreaths, my Soul sent me the intuitive thought that the wreaths needed to be dressed up with some decorations.

Next, the idea that natural dried flowers would be the ideal decorations was intuitively delivered to my ego-mind. Then, to pull it all together, my Soul added the intuitive question, "Where and how might I find natural dried flowers to decorate the wreaths?"

On the other end of the arrangement, Ruby's Soul sent her the intuitive idea to call me and see if I was up for a trip out to the flower farm. She needed a ride, and we hadn't seen each other in quite a while, so this idea made sense to her. Then, to follow her heart and do what her Soul had guided her to do, Ruby called me. I gladly accepted the invitation, and the synchronic magic was felt by both of us.

Even though the Soul-Magic theory is completely different than the manifestation theory, it provides a very plausible explanation.

WHAT IS REALLY GOING ON?

Beyond these two theories, there are numerous other theories. Examples include good karma and simple coincidence.

So, what's really going on?

I'm going to limit the following discussion to just two possibilities: the popular manifestation theory, and the Soul-Magic theory which were both presented above.

The manifestation theory presumes our conscious-minds have the power to manifest events. Proponents of this theory go further by proposing our thoughts can manifest physical objects, physical healing, and even a person's entire reality! In fact, that theory claims that our thoughts create our reality whether we know it or not, therefore, the theory goes on to recommend that people ought to carefully control what they think in order to obtain what they really want.

Conversely, my Soul has guided me to believe that our conscious- and subconscious-minds are intentionally designed to be feeble and gullible so we can be tricked into believing we're separate individuals. As explained earlier, our feebleness is based on our conscious- and subconscious-minds having been divided into two portions. The conscious-mind in the head is nearly all intellectual, while the subconscious-mind in the gut is nearly all emotional. When separated in this way, the Feebleness of Incompleteness principle predicts that these minds will be feeble due to their lack of a balanced combination of intellect and emotions in each location, the head and the gut.

The Supreme Power of Wholeness principle proposes that the power of manifestation requires a whole consciousness, one comprised of balanced portions of intellect and emotions woven together.

Divine or Holy portions of consciousness are interconnected in a state of oneness-consciousness that enables them to work together using their creative powers to adjust physical reality in a coordinated way that produces a single reality here on the physical Earth plane.

Despite that, beyond the Earth plane, astral travelers report new-found powers in the upper and lower layers of the astral realm. In those layers, astral travelers find that their thoughts and emotions cause immediate changes in their surroundings indicating they have manifestation capabilities in those outer layers.

So, why does the normally feeble human mind appear to have manifestation abilities in the outer layers of the astral realm?

My Soul informed me that the head and gut minds merge back together and become one whole mind when a person who has astral projected travels beyond the Earth layer into outer layers of the astral realm. In support of this idea, experienced astral travelers report increased awareness of their emotions when exploring the outer astral layers. This surge in emotions has caused some travelers to label the astral realm, "the emotional realm," or "the astral/emotional realm."

In addition to this emotional magnification, the progressively empowering outer layers are claimed to offer godlike powers not available on the Earth plane. Some reports claim that the highest layer actually transforms the astral explorer into a god. For instance, in Yogananda's book, *Autobiography of a Yogi*, he claims that his guru, Sri Yukteswar, died and then returned to Earth three days later. Upon his return, Sri Yukteswar claimed that he had become god.[25] In that book Yukteswar informs Yogananda that he began the process by fulfilling all of his desires in astral Heaven. Then, without any desires remaining, he rose to the next layer and finally in the highest layer he became god.

To accomplish this transformation into godhood, the astral body provides a vehicle for the head and gut minds only, leaving the Soul in the physical heart. Then, when the traveler ventures out beyond the central Earth layer to explore the outer layers, the head and gut minds merge back together to become whole. This wholeness elevates the traveler's mind from normal human consciousness into a divine level of consciousness, one with manifestation abilities, but only when traveling in the outer astral layers.

Back on Earth there is support for the idea that the Soul remains behind in the physical heart. That support comes from people who undergo heart transplant procedures. Here's how:

After a prospective heart donor dies, their heart is removed and placed in the recipient's chest. Later, observation has found that the recipient ends up with a new personality that corresponds to the donor's personality as discussed earlier, in Chapter 1. This indicates that the donor's Soul must have remained in the donated heart. If the Soul had left the physical heart to reside in the donor's astral body, upon death, then that Soul wouldn't be located in the transplanted heart and the personality changes wouldn't take place. Since personality changes do take place, Souls must remain in hearts that are removed from donors after their conscious- and subconscious-minds departed to the other side of the veil.

My Soul further advised me that human Souls remain in the physical heart when people astral travel. Moreover, when the head and gut minds are needed back in their physical body, it's the Soul that has remained in the physical heart that reels in the silver cord to draw the astral body back into the physical body. Then, as the whole mind is brought back into the physical body the Soul splits it apart again placing the conscious- and subconscious-minds back into the head and gut, returning them to a feeble disposition.

This means that the physical Earth doesn't offer typical people manifestation powers. The One-Who-Is-All has the power of manifestation. Additionally, our Superconscious-Souls and other whole or Holy portions of consciousness also have that power.

On the other hand, ordinary human minds that are split, and therefore feeble, don't have manifestation power here on Earth. If typical humans, with their wide range of desires, did have such powers here on Earth, conflicts regarding what exists on Earth would quickly develop. To avoid such conflicts, and instead provide a single stable reality in which physical humans can interact with each other, people must employ energy and effort to change the physical realm. The middle astral layer provides an astral realm link to that stable reality.

Conversely, the outer astral layers are able to fulfill widely different human desires simultaneously by making each individual the lord of their personal astral domain.

These functional differences produce very different experiences.

Reaching for extremes in the outer astral layers can elevate a lord of their domain to becoming a demi-god who is lord of their planet.

On the contrary, here on Earth, reaching for the stars often results in tragedy. The mythological character Icarus demonstrates this. His father, who had fashioned wings from wax and feathers, warned Icarus not to fly too high or too low. Ignoring his father, Icarus expresses his excessive pride by flying too close to the sun, melting the wax, and causing him to fall into the ocean and die.

If that story continued, by following Icarus into the afterlife astral realm where his astral body has the ability to fly right into the sun, he would have likely attained demi-god status in his afterlife experience.

Believing that one's ego-mind has great power is a step toward becoming a Pragmatic. The tragic endings of shooting stars reveal that such hubris is out of alignment with the humble Earth path. People with big egos often burn out quickly and die young indicating that their ego-driven path aligns with astral afterlife opportunities.

Having presented all the issues, I'll summarize what's going on when it comes to serendipitous synchronicities here on Earth. Our Souls cause these heartwarming connections to take place by working behind the scenes to arrange serendipitous synchronicities as blessings. To do so, Souls use intuition to place thoughts in our heads guiding us into, and preparing us for what is about to happen. Accordingly, intuitive thoughts commonly lead to serendipitous synchronicities. People who consciously follow their hearts are well aware of this linkage. You have quite likely discovered this yourself.

Marvelous Soul-Magic blessings draw open-hearted people toward humbly surrendering to their Souls to experience a miraculously blessed life here on Earth. That surrender enables love to blossom via heartfelt service and cooperation.

On the other hand, the manifestation powers that are available in the outer layers of the astral realm readily accommodate selfish desires. The polarized Heaven versus Hell extremes offer a way for self-importance to grow all the way to godhood.

In the final analysis, serendipitous synchronicities provide appropriate undercurrents for everyone. To begin with, when one follows their heart, they experience the magic of synchronicities. This draws open-hearted Romantics along the Way-of-the-Heart path.

On the other hand, Pragmatics are drawn up toward Heaven or down toward Hell to fulfill their selfish desires with astral powers.

Given the possibility that godlike powers are obtainable in the outer astral realms, and the alternate possibility that the full blossoming of love may take place here on Earth, you must decide what's more important to you, the power to manifest whatever you want, or an opportunity to explore the full blossoming of love here on Earth?

THE POWER OF OUR THOUGHTS HERE ON EARTH

Here on Earth, one's ego-mind's thoughts do affect their reality in a very important way. They affect how one feels emotionally. One's optimism or pessimism, their beliefs, and their emotional feelings affect their quality of life in powerful ways.

Despite that, what an earthbound person thinks in their conscious-mind doesn't change the physical world outside of themselves.

UNSAVORY MANIFESTATION RESULTS

Over the course of more than ten years I tried various manifestation methods. Much of what my conscious ego-mind pushed to manifest came true. However, I found that the results often contained unexpected features that were distasteful to me. I got exactly what I asked for, but some aspect of the request, a part that I failed to clearly define, would mischievously spoil the result.

It seemed as if a trick were being played on me, a trick that gently pushed me away from the "create your own reality" approach to life. Age-old wisdom advises, "Be careful what you wish for."

I've found the "surrender to the Soul" approach works best for me, and I suspect the same is true for other Romantics as well.

Certainly, it's up to you to determine what you believe and what works best for you.

MULTI-LEVELED SYNCHRONICITIES

To conclude this discussion of serendipitous synchronicities and what causes them to occur, I've been guided to share the noteworthy end of the flower farm experience.

By the time Ruby and I got back to her place, it was late. She suggested that I sleep over and head home in the morning.

While we hung out before retiring, Ruby shared some Native American wisdom with me. She explained:

The Red Road of Beauty is in the middle of everything. When one is walking on it, one's life is beautiful. This road is very narrow and one can easily fall off of it. When one falls off, the world is no longer so wonderful. Once separated from this narrow Red Road, it can be very difficult to find one's way back to this narrow road.

This was my introduction to the Way-of-the-Heart path. Our adventure to the spectacular flower farm, and the wisdom of the Red Road of Beauty will remain precious memories forever.

"Important encounters are planned by the Souls, long before the bodies see each other."
—Paulo Coelho (born 1947) author

If this book's thesis is in alignment with reality, then the key to filling your physical life with magically mystical experiences is to open and follow your heart, so you can walk the Red Road of Beauty. This is a path that a humble, generous person who is willing to surrender to their Soul can easily follow. If this path works for you the way it has for me, some of those experiences will surpass what you could conjure up in your mind.

MIRACLES FROM THE SOUL

In the remainder of this chapter, I share tools and suggestions that are based on the idea that the Soul is the only part of human consciousness that has the power to perform miracles here on Earth. To begin with, I'll briefly review why:

The Soul's masculine and feminine combination of consciousness give it the power to create. The creative power of the Soul can affect the physical realm. The conscious- and subconscious-minds are not capable of modifying physical reality because they both suffer from the Feebleness of Incompleteness principle.

Regardless of those limitations, the conscious-mind, with emotional support from the subconscious-mind, can ask the Soul for help, and if the Soul determines that the request fits into the grand plan of the universe, then the Superconscious-Soul may choose to fulfill the request. Here on Earth in the physical realm, the Soul has the power to perform miracles.

When it comes to personal healing—asking the Soul for help, and making those requests in appropriate ways, can alter your life in unexpectedly wonderful ways.

SOUL HEALING

In 2005, Dr. Zhi Gang Sha taught me how to ask my Soul for healing. When I followed his instructions, and asked my Soul to heal a chronic neck problem, one that I had suffered with for twenty-two years, it was healed in seconds! This really happened.

That experience changed my life.

I didn't believe Dr. Sha's "Soul, Mind, Body Healing" method would work, but my neck was unusually painful that day, so, figuring that it was worth a try, I decided to play along and follow his instructions as well as I could.

Once I had completed the process, my neck began tingling and became warm. Then, without moving my head at all, I felt and heard a few cracks spontaneously occur in my neck. Afterward, when I finally moved my head, my neck had completely loosened up, and all the pain was gone.

HEALING YOURSELF

My Soul and my actual life experiences have convinced me that Souls can heal physical and emotional problems. There's no need to look outside yourself, to angels or any type of external entity or device for healing. Your Soul has the power to heal.

When asking for help, I recommend a respectful approach. Ask clearly and firmly. You're not the master of your Soul, you're its child. This parent is a Mother-Father-God! Be a good kid. Respect your divine guardian. Do what you are guided to do.

Then, when you need help, ask for help in a firm and clear way. It's actually quite important to ask when you need help. Guardians are there to help, but there's a cosmic law that protects your free will. This law restricts the Soul from overriding your free will. That restriction prevents your Soul from altering your beliefs, fears, guilt, shame, and memories, etc. unless you explicitly offer the Soul permission.

These personal features of who you are can be underlying causes for psychological and physical ailments. Accordingly, it's important to ask for help in a way that gives your Soul permission to make adjustments to all the aspects of who you are to heal the root cause.

In the following request for healing, the bold sentences authorize the Soul to alter any and all underlying causes of the ailment.

I take a few Heart-Opening Breaths then state the following:

Dear Soul in my heart, I love you.

Do whatever is necessary to fully heal my _____. **You have permission to change me in whatever way that is needed to resolve this problem. Change my memories, my beliefs, my fears, or any other aspects of who I am that I may or may not be aware of, to permanently heal my _____.**

DO A GOOD JOB!

Thank You.

These simple sentences can be very powerful if they're spoken with sincerity. By giving your Soul permission to change who you have become, you'll be authorizing your Soul to resolve any underlying issues that caused your ailment to develop and persist.

Unlike modern medicine, which focuses on the symptoms, Soul-healing goes to the foundation of the problem—your consciousness—resolving the issue by altering your memories, beliefs, fears, or other issues that are causing your ailment. By altering the foundational realm of consciousness, Soul-healing can have unexpected <u>beneficial</u> side effects.

For example, when I used this method to heal a mild pain that had persisted in my left ankle for about twenty-five years, I noticed an accompanying psychological change. That psychological issue had negatively affected my intimate relationships since I was 13-years-old!

I'm ever so grateful that my Soul repaired more than just my ankle by adjusting my consciousness in a positive way. Although I had come to accept this lifelong challenge as a permanent part of my personality, the unexpected change opened a new chapter in my life: one with better dreams and more enjoyable connections with people.

You may be reluctant to trust your Soul. If you hold back, then your Soul won't be able to do its magic. To fully engage the divine power within your heart, you must trust your Soul and sincerely love this divine part of yourself. In the next chapter, "Soul Love," I offer guidance regarding this type of self-love.

In this request for healing, the "DO A GOOD JOB!" sentence comes from Dr. Zhi Gang Sha, the man who first taught me about *Soul Mind Body Medicine*, which is the name of his book. I must admit that I don't really understand why this sentence is so important, but the success I've had using it convinced me that it works, so I continue to use it. Dr. Sha told me that this sentence needs to be stated in a strong and demanding way, so say these four words with demanding force.

At the end, when you say, "Thank you," assume that the healing will be a success. Support the "Thank you" with the feelings of gratitude that you would have, presuming a successful outcome.

When making each statement in the request for healing, it's important to focus on what you're saying and put sincerity into each word. The idea is to convey the meaning held in each statement with appropriate emotions and literal intent combined together.

To do this, your authentic presence must be placed into each word by feeling and thinking the message you are conveying. Your passion, desperation, and hope for healing must propel the message that the words are used to convey. If the feminine, emotional half of your consciousness is not included, the Soul will not respond. Your feminine and masculine portions of consciousness must come together to jointly make this request, backing it with genuine feelings that support the intellectual meaning being conveyed.

These are not magic words. The words are vehicles to convey your request, your feelings, and your gratitude. To get results, the entire message must be expressed with the emotions and thoughts that correspond to the words.

Be sensible, physical issues often need physical solutions, lifestyle changes, dietary changes, etc. Make appropriate changes in areas of your life that may be aggravating the problem you hope to heal. Ask questions, do some research and get involved in your healing process. Health issues can help a person to look closer at their life and their lifestyle. How we chose to live can foster health and happiness or ill health and sadness. Thus, our daily choices matter.

Whenever you feel that a healthcare professional can help, engage one.

SYMBOL OF MEDICINE

The caduceus symbol shown on the right has been associated with healing. Although some people claim the Rod of Asclepius is the proper symbol for medicine, there are others who have found the caduceus used in conjunction with medicine as far back as 300 B.C. [26]

This ancient symbol of healing may have been intended to depict the healing technique that I just described. Here's how:

First of all, the staff may be meant to represent the Soul. The sphere on top is a symbol of wholeness. The wings add a divine element to the staff. Finally, the staff's central location fits the position of the Soul in the Triality of human consciousness.

The two snakes that are embracing the staff may be meant to represent the conscious and subconscious minds. The way they're staring at the staff and embracing it indicates that they're dedicated to paying attention to it. Then, if one imagines the snakes asking the central Soul, symbolized by the staff, for help, that completes the technique in which one must ask the Soul with their intellect and emotions for whatever healing is desired.

OTHER REQUESTS

In addition to healing, the principles that are employed in this healing method can be used in many ways. There's a lot of power within your heart. Your Superconscious-Soul is the most powerful portion of human consciousness. You can make any request that you believe to be appropriate. I've found that it's important to avoid asking for changes that will expand your ego's importance. Keep a short leash on your ego. Self-glorification is a dangerous road that will likely lead to a tormented Pragmatic life.

It's also prudent to avoid making requests that involve other people. Work on yourself. If someone needs help, share the tool with them so they can heal themselves. This way, they'll also be encouraged to deepen their relationship with their Soul.

As far as causing damage to reality by abusing your Soul's power, my Soul informed me that the only real damage you can do is to yourself. Your Soul isn't your servant. If your request will disrupt the universal plan, your Soul will ignore your request. No matter how sincerely you ask, you can't push your Soul to act out of alignment with the grand plan of the universe.

I prefer to play it safe by using the power of my Soul to heal and tune up my mind and body. The example offered below gives your Soul permission to bring you into alignment with your True-Self, the magnificent Soul in your heart.

After doing the Heart-Opening Breath state the following:

Dear Magnificent Soul in my heart, I love you.
Help me fully surrender to you, living with my heart open and following you attentively. Prepare me to be part of the full blossoming of love on Earth by transforming me to be what you know to be the best for me to be. You have permission to change any aspects of me, be they physical, emotional, intellectual, or any other features of who I am whether I'm aware of them or not. This request and the accompanying permission applies till the end of time!
DO A GREAT JOB!
Thank You. I love you!

To empower this request, follow the recommendations shared earlier in the HEALING YOURSELF section that began on page 258.

Once I made this request, fundamental personality traits that I believed to be permanent flaws in my character, shifted in ways that have been improving my interpersonal relationships. To reinforce this request, I restate it every once in a while.

SPIRITS AND CLEARING FOREIGN ENTITIES

In this section, the term "ghost" is used to identify a person who passed over to the afterlife astral realm, but is wandering around the Earth plane in their astral body. Ghosts are stuck in purgatory, meaning they haven't reached Heaven nor Hell yet. Unlike the exaggerated Hollywood version, they aren't powerful. Still, a ghost's subtle astral body enables it to enter a living person's body and dramatically affect that person's behavior.

This ability to inhabit or possess a human is substantiated by people who astral travel. You may recall the brief story I shared earlier, in Chapter 7, about the astral-projection instructor who slipped into her husband's body one night while she was on an astral adventure. In that journey, she was able guide her astral body into her husband's physical body while he was asleep. Once inside his physical body she was able to feel his body's sensations and operate his limbs.

Additional support comes from astral travelers who consistently report seeing ghosts wandering around the Earth in their astral bodies. Once a ghost discovers that they can slip into living people's bodies they may choose to take advantage of that opportunity. When a ghost enters a physical human, they can have a wide range of effects.

I had a personal experience in which a ghost slipped into my body while I was intoxicated. For the next four days, I had a headache on the right side of my head. Headaches are very unusual for me. When I do get one, it doesn't last more than a day. In addition to the headache, I felt very tired, and noticed that my posture was slumped over in an unusual way that I wasn't accustomed to. Overall, I didn't feel like myself.

In the past, I had experienced being physically hungover, but that sluggishness would only last for a day, at most, then my energy would return. In this particular case, the unusual physical symptoms were exceptionally strong and they persisted for four days, indicating that something out of the ordinary was taking place.

On the third day, I had a very strange experience. A friend told me that we had participated in a long conversation during a period of several hours when I was certain that I was asleep. I even recall briefly waking up three times. Each time, I recall opening my eyes, seeing my friend, then closing my eyes to go back to sleep.

In spite of that, she assured me that I was fully awake and animated—physically pointing things out and talking the entire time.

Then, near the end of the following day, I met someone new. I felt intuitively drawn to engage this woman. Once I introduced myself, I told her about my unusual sleeping discussion that had occurred the previous day. As luck would have it, this woman turned out to be a professional exorcist. She suspected that an entity may have possessed me. She pulled out a crystal pendulum on a delicate silver chain. Then, with me standing still, she checked me for entities and discovered at least one.

Finally, she advised me to say:

"Any entities or energies that are in my body that are not truly me, you are no longer welcome in my body, leave now!"

Immediately after firmly I commanded, "... leave now!" the headache vanished, my posture straightened up, and my energy returned. I instantly returned to being myself again.

I was shocked and exclaimed, "That thing must have been in me for four days!"

In researching possession, I discovered that people become susceptible to being possessed when they're intoxicated. So, it makes sense that this condition began when I was intoxicated.

Later, another woman showed me a better way to remove entities. The improved method removes the entities from the Earth plane so they would come back.

To use the improved method, the affected person simply states the following in a clear, demanding voice:

"Any entities or energies that are not truly me that are in my body, you are no longer welcome in my body. Enter my heart so my Soul can escort you home. Find peace within my heart now!"

After making this statement, I perform at least one Heart-Opening Breath. The flow pattern of that technique draws toward the heart-center which is consistent with the command for the entity to enter the heart. Then, with the Supreme Power of Wholeness, the Soul can escort the ghost to an appropriate place to call home.

Since your Soul is restricted from violating your free will, it can't intervene to deal with ghosts unless you use the ego-mind in your head to make an affirming command that encourages the Soul to help in relocating the entity.

The "enter my heart" method of clearing entities helps the wayward ghosts to leave the astral Earth plane and move on to outer astral layers. Because this method eliminates the entities from the Earth layer, it's a service to all living human beings.

A few weeks after my possession experience, the headache returned. It was in the same location and had the same sharp feeling as the headache I had before. I decided to try the "enter my heart" method this time. Once I made the statement, the headache disappeared instantly. Most importantly, it hasn't returned in several years.

At that time, I was living on a property that was known to be haunted. That being the case, after having success with the "enter my heart" method, I felt inspired to state the command daily for a couple of weeks, and then less frequently for a few months more.

Soon, the creepy feeling around my cabin lifted. Some people who were familiar with the property and aware of the haunted feeling commented on how the place felt so inviting. Some found the difference so significant that they were inspired to ask me what I had done to "clear the energy."

It's beneficial to do a clearing process as part of your hygiene, or at least, whenever you're feeling off or ill.

There is, of course, the obvious concern, that sending an entity into your heart could be dangerous. My Soul has informed me that Superconscious-Souls can easily deal with the small portions of consciousness that comprise a ghost. These astral beings are like little children compared to a Superconscious-Soul that possesses the Supreme Power of Wholeness.

In spite of that, I must admit that it took some courage for me to do the "enter my heart" method the first time. However, once I experienced success using the technique, I became comfortable doing it. It's a bit like cleansing yourself on the inside.

Clearing yourself of foreign entities will help you avoid energy drainage, ill health, and distortions of behavior, if and when those conditions are caused by a ghost that has slipped into your body.

I was guided to include this section on ghosts and possession because these wayward astral beings can interfere with a person's attempts to become their most authentic expression of their True-Self. To achieve that, a tool is needed to clear out foreign entities that may find their way into your body and adversely affect your ability to be your True-Self.

To make oneself impervious to entity possession one must be free of guilt and shame and refrain from becoming intoxicated. Tools to let go of guilt and shame are shared later in Chapter 22.

MENTAL HEALTH ISSUES

Based on what I shared in the last section and taking into account the types of mental health issues that are prevalent these days, my Soul intuitively guided me to consider the possibility that many mental health issues could be caused by ghost possession. Unfortunately, as I explained in Chapter 2, the mental health field adopted the materialistic myth around 1930. Prior to that, the Soul and spirits were included in the mental health field.

I found solid evidence of this in "The Secret Science Behind Miracles," written by Max Freedom Long and published in 1948. The studies of disembodied consciousness that Long refers to in that book, didn't fit into the materialistic head-brain myth that derailed the original consciousness-based perspective of psychology. Unfortunately, the important research referenced by Long may have been lost.

Hopefully, someone will rediscover that extensive research that was performed over one hundred years ago. Even though it may be antiquated and not up to the rigors of modern science, there may be important findings that could be reinvestigated and confirmed with up-to-date methods.

Even without any research to back up the idea of ghosts, the simple affirming commands shared above can be used when disturbing psychological issues and/or physical abnormalities appear. If ghosts are not involved, I can't imagine how making either of these commands could cause any harm. Therefore, using them will, in the worst case, do nothing.

The first time I ordered entities to leave, I had no expectation that the command would do anything at all. When I experienced instant results, I was astonished. Placebo effects require belief in the method. I had no belief, I even recall chuckling when the woman advised me to make the command. Still, I humored her, made the command and the instant results that took place strongly supported the existence of some sort of entity or entities.

Now, when I feel off, I simply state the command to deal with the possibility that an entity is causing the abnormal condition. If the condition persists, I take other steps to recover my normal level of health and vitality. Certainly, infections, viruses, exposure to toxins, poor dietary practices and many other physical causes are real. Modern medicine can be effective in dealing with some of these issues.

Alternatively, I've found natural remedies very effective and prefer to use them whenever possible. I've lived much of my life without health insurance, using natural remedies and Soul Healing. Currently, at fifty-nine I don't have any health issues.

GUIDANCE FROM NON-PHYSICAL ENTITIES

Beyond ghosts, there's an additional issue regarding external nonphysical entities that needs to be addressed. These days, many people are connecting with entities who claim to have great wisdom to share. Assuredly, there are all sorts of non-physical entities that exist in the astral realm: angels, ascended masters, spirit guides, aliens, gods, etc. Many independent sources have corroborated their existence through astral projection, near death experiences, possession, abduction, etc. People who practice astral travel have discovered many different types of astral beings that could be identified by all sorts of labels.

Without getting into specific examples or extensive details, I feel it's important to offer the following suggestions:

First of all, because Pragmatic people don't have inner guidance, it's normal and appropriate for Pragmatic people to engage with these external guides and consider the exoteric knowledge they provide.

On the other hand, Romantics have infallible esoteric guidance that comes from their Superconscious-Soul. With its Supreme Power of Wholeness, the Soul has the ability to interact with any and all non-physical entities that exist. In addition to being your personal guardian, your Soul is a dependable ambassador who can deal with all external nonphysical entities in a safe and reliable way.

Due to the feebleness of our conscious- and subconscious-minds there's no way for us to be sure of exactly what or who is out there, let alone their intentions. My Soul informed me that the divine purpose of these entities is to lure people away from their Soul to sort out who is truly dedicated to their Soul and who is not. This process leads to the big ascension/inheritance event that many are looking forward to.

To accomplish this, the entities are very tricky. They may have lots of wisdom to share in an impressive way to garner your respect. Then to draw you away from your Soul they may offer you what you most desire. Their divine wholeness enables them to know your deeply held secrets. Some can appear as ethereal entities that can look just like a deity that you have great respect for. None of this provides you with any way to determine the true identity of that entity nor its intentions.

All civilized cultures and religions warn of a proverbial serpent or so-called fallen angel that lures people away from their Soul. Once disconnected from the Soul's intuition, conscience, and Romantic guidance via a calcified pineal gland, the now Pragmatic person is provided extreme desires which lead to divisive behavior, personal suffering, and eventually a desire to be liberated from their suffering.

If you're a Romantic who's interested in following your heart, an encounter from an external entity or multiple entities could be a test to see if you can be lured away from your Soul. It's also possible that you may not be following your heart very closely. In that case, a visit from an external entity could be viewed as a wakeup call indicating that your closed-heartedness may have brought you an opportunity to turn away from your Soul and become a Pragmatic.

Therefore, if you're being contacted, be honest with yourself regarding whether you actually have intuition or not. If you don't, you're a Pragmatic and you might as well follow the external guide. Despite that, you might prefer to be reunited with your Soul. If that's the case then you may want to try using the pineal gland decalcification method that's offered in the last section of this chapter.

On the other hand, if you do have intuition, then how attentively are you following your Soul's guidance? To evaluate that, consider how often you find yourself thinking, "Darn, I knew I should have done that!" If that occurs often then you may simply need to follow your heart more attentively.

If you haven't been very attentive to your Soul's guidance, external entities may be checking in to see if they can lure you completely away. Is your ego seeking glorification and expansion? Can your ego-mind be hooked? Are you dedicated to following your heart? Or are you straying from your Soul's guidance, reaching out for extreme personal satisfaction as you discard the guidance you're receiving from within? Keep in mind, the guidance is subtle, often a hunch or feeling. Don't expect clear instructions spoken in your head. Intuition is faint.

If you notice signs that you aren't following your heart very well or maybe you aren't receiving guidance very often, and an external entity shows up, then you must decide if you want to strengthen your relationship with your Soul or explore the Pragmatic alternative that's being offered.

If the Pragmatic path seems more interesting to you, then you may want to explore it. The suffering that often accompanies the Pragmatic way of life ought to be considered before you jump ship. Still, you have the free will to choose your path with your ego-mind.

However, if you do have intuition and prefer the Romantic way of life, then use the tools and techniques here in **Part 3** of this book.

You can deepen your heart connection and receive more of the miraculous benefits that accompany open-hearted living if you choose to.

To be a faithful Romantic, I recommend resisting the allure of external entities. While they can't violate your free will, and even though they're part of the One-Who-Is-All, they can be quite enticing and lead you away from your magnificent Soul.

USING DIVINATION TOOLS

You may enjoy using tarot cards, pendulums, crystals, muscle testing or other tools for divination purposes.

In the previous chapter, I provided methods to engage the Soul by contemplating questions in your head. Then, by paying attention to the feelings in your chest and being aware of any intuitive answers to those questions, you can obtain divine answers from your Soul. These answers are esoteric wisdom. The divine consciousness in the heart has been purported to be infallible and aware of the future. Therefore, you don't need any physical tools, the Superconscious-Soul is always willing and ready to provide all the guidance you need. Therefore, if your pineal gland is healthy, just ask your Soul.

Sometimes what the Soul offers may not be all of the guidance that you want. Still, it's all you need. Beyond the guidance you may be left to make some choices on your own.

In spite of all that, you may enjoy using tools for divination purposes. If so, then you can include your Soul in the process. To do this, begin a divination session by practicing the Heart-Opening Breath a few times and then ask your Soul to advise you through the tool you are about to use. By beginning with an invocation that invites your Soul to guide you through the physical tool, you'll be honoring your Soul while using the tool that you've come to enjoy using.

PINEAL GLAND DECALCIFICATION

If you believe that you have become a Pragmatic person, but you would like to give the Romantic way of life a second try, I offer the following suggestions:

To begin with, determine whether your pineal gland is calcified by getting a head x-ray. In 2017, I got a series of four skull x-rays for $112. The radiologist didn't find any pineal gland calcification. To get the x-ray I needed a doctor's order, so I asked a sympathetic doctor to write an order that I brought to the independent imaging lab. Later, that doctor was notified of the results by the radiologist. Finally, the doctor conveyed the results to me. As I expected, my pineal gland was not calcified.

If you discover that your pineal gland is not calcified, then simply follow the recommendations given in this book.

Conversely, if the radiologist identifies a calcified pineal gland, then you can use the following variation on the Soul Healing technique that was shared earlier.

Dear Soul in my heart,

I sincerely apologize for turning away from you. Please give me a second chance by decalcifying my pineal gland and doing whatever you can do to help me follow your guidance. **You have permission to change me in whatever way that is needed to give me another chance to align with you and your guidance. Change my memories, my beliefs, my fears, or any other aspects of who I am that I may or may not be aware of, that need to be adjusted to give me a second chance.**
DO A GOOD JOB!
Thank You.

This request, gives your Soul permission to bring you back into alignment with the Romantic Way-of-the-Heart.

This method can have great power if you ask in accordance with the recommendations shared earlier in the Healing Yourself section that began back on page 258. The Soul love part doesn't apply in this case, because this request doesn't include the, "I love you" phrase. Still, the other suggestions offered in that section apply and need to be employed when making this request.

In addition to this method, there are many pineal gland decalcification methods offered on the internet.

I sincerely hope that everyone that is interested in a second chance, finds a way to connect with their Soul.

The Way-of-the-Heart is a truly enchanting, enjoyable, and deeply satisfying life path.

Chapter 20
Soul Love

"No one ever asks the meaning of life when they're in love."
—Osho (1931–1990) Indian guru

There are many forms of love and many ways to be in love. I've discovered that being in love with my Soul is the most stable and personally beneficial form of love that I've ever experienced. Moreover, this inner love relationship helps me tune into my Soul and follow its guidance remarkably well.

For instance, after opening to loving my Soul, my writing improved overnight. The words come much easier now. Beyond that, while I'm writing, complex concepts evolve and link in ways unimaginable in the past. The editor I was working with when the Soul Love relationship began, remarked on the dramatic change he noticed in my writing. He claimed that my writing became ten times better in two days!

The Heart-Opening Breath and expressing my gratitude to my Soul led me to discover this love connection with my Soul.

SELF-LOVE VIA THE SOUL

Earlier, I discussed love and shared the idea that love involves a desire to sacrifice oneself to benefit their beloved.

Despite that, many propose that a person can't truly love another until they have learned to love themselves.

Putting these two ideas together, the confounding question arises: How can self-love include sacrifice for one's beloved?

This may sound like an unsolvable riddle, because it doesn't seem possible for a person to sacrifice themselves for themselves. Even so, a realistic way to accomplish this emerged out of my daily practice of thanking my Soul. Here's how that took place:

On a regular basis, I would place my hands over my heart and think in my mind, "Dear Soul in my heart, thank you." One morning, without intending to change my practice I thought in my mind, "Dear Soul in my heart, thank you. I love you."

I was surprised by the "I love you" ending, because that wasn't part of my daily practice. As I thought about it, I considered how my Soul may have intuitively inserted the—I love you—ending which was uttered by my inner dialogue voice.

Despite that detail, as I contemplated loving my Soul, I realized that my ego-mind in my head could love the Soul in my heart as if the Soul is a separate beloved. Even though my Soul is my True-Self, I have come to view this divine consciousness as my guardian. No matter where I go, or what I do, my Soul will never abandon me, lie to me, or hurt me. It will always be inside my heart, ready and willing to guide me. All I need to do on my ego-mind's end, is to keep my heart open and follow the guidance as well as I'm able to.

After choosing to engage in this unusual love relationship, I discovered that loving my divine parent made it easier for me to keep my heart open more consistently than ever before, enhancing my life through the miraculous benefits that come from the divine Soul.

All of this helps to deepen the most important relationship that I can have—the divine connection with my Soul.

On top of that, this type of love solves the riddle presented above: How can self-love include sacrifice for one's beloved?

Here's how: I, meaning my ego-mind in my head, can love my Soul so much that I'm willing to sacrifice my ego's ideas to follow my beloved Soul's greater wisdom. In doing so, I'm engaged in a form of self-love that involves sacrifice for my beloved—my Soul.

Gratefully, the sacrifice of following my Soul's guidance improves my life as more of my True-Self emerges from within.

It's mind-boggling how wonderfully beneficial Soul Love is.

For instance, a side effect of Soul Love is how it's teaching me that sacrificing myself for my beloved can actually improve my life. Experiencing the real benefit of becoming happier every time I give in to my beloved Soul, is teaching me how sacrifice—the defining characteristic of love—can produce a synergistic benefit for everyone involved. In this case, me and my Soul both benefit.

In addition to that, this relationship makes sense to me. Over the course of my life, I've discovered that my Soul is the one thing in the entire universe that I can trust to be working in my best interest 100 percent of the time. My Soul is the greatest parent I could possibly have. It's my Divine Guardian that actually knows what's best for me, much more accurately than my ego-mind. My Soul knows the future and will never violate my free will—making it the ultimate parent. With all those great qualities, plus all the benefits I've already experienced, I wish I had discovered this form of self-love sooner.

Fortunately, I discovered it before I finished writing this book so I could share this powerful type of love with you.

Now, because I really do love my Soul, I can honestly say,

"Dear Soul, I love you."

EXPRESSIONS OF SOUL LOVE

The following song has helped me deepen this relationship. It came to me intuitively. The first stanza arrived one morning and the second stanza arrived a couple of days later.

I sing it when I'm driving my car, taking a moment to express my gratitude, or to start my day after doing the Heart-Opening Breath.

Soul Love

Dear Soul in my heart,
You're the love of my life,
Dear Soul in my heart,
I love You!

If there's a God for me to love,
It's the One inside my heart,
It's the One that is me,
I love You!

I've also found the following expression of gratitude helpful. Sometimes I use this to start my day.

Gratitude

Great Spirit,
Thank you for creating this Grand Illusion, and
Dear Soul in my heart,
Thank you for guiding me through it,
I love you!

You may have your own ways to express your gratitude and the love you feel for your Soul. For example, Janie Comito emailed to me her personal prayer of gratitude that she recites every morning and evening. With her permission, that beautiful prayer is shared below:

Prayer of gratitude to my guide to the Source of Oneness

My soul, my guide, my shelter and safety you are my freedom, my creative inspiration, a source of peace and my door to the Source of Oneness in truth and love. I am eternally thankful to you, for the priceless gift of knowing that you are in me.

My heart is open to give and receive love because of you in me and I am gifted with the knowledge that I am loved and always guided by my eternal soul. I will not fear mortal pain as I move from life – to life.

I thank you for the loved ones I travel with now, let them receive the best of me. Teach and guide me every day to be worthy of them as we travel this path together. Connect my thoughts with those who seek to create a loving world through you.

Thank you, my dearest soul – in the truth and love of now. I rest in your arms; I am your child in love.

Thank you.

Chapter 21
The Negative Emotions of the Heart

"The greatest fear in the world is of the opinions of others. And the moment you are unafraid of the crowd you are no longer a sheep, you become a lion. A great roar arises in your heart, the roar of freedom."

—Osho (1931–1990) Indian guru

THE LITTLE-KNOWN NEGATIVE EMOTIONS OF THE HEART

Most people have never heard of the negative emotions of the heart. I've experienced these negative emotions and found that knowing about them is necessary to have a complete understanding of the Way-of-the-Heart.

When these negative emotions rear their heads, people often misjudge the open-hearted because they're not aware that these little-known qualities of the heart exist. Furthermore, a Romantic person can wonder if they're living with their heart open when these negative emotions flare up. For instance, before I was aware of these mostly unknown qualities of the heart, I wondered if I was really following my heart. What's more, when these negative emotions did emerge, I even wondered if I was in alignment with love.

Later, when I became aware of these negative emotions of the heart, I was finally able to understand this confounding aspect of open-hearted living in a way that finally made sense. In this chapter I do my best to share what I learned about these negative emotions.

A "Taoist Inner Alchemy Anatomy Chart," designed by the well-known Taoist master, Mantak Chia, claims the heart's features are:

Heart Energy Center (seat of love, joy, respect and surrender)
The heart's nature: joy, honor, sincerity, love, respect and kindness.
Open: one feels honor and respect.
Closed: sense of worry and panic.
The (negative) emotion of the heart is impatience, cruelty, hot temper, and violence.

While following my heart, I've found Mantak Chia's concise but complete description of the Heart-Center to be consistent with my personal experiences. I've encountered all of these aspects of my heart, including the negative emotions.

Before examining the negative emotions, it's worth noting how the heart's nature is aligned with romance. Joy, honor, sincerity, love, respect, and kindness are all important qualities for fulfilling Romantic connections. In addition to romance, these qualities are essential for enduring friendships as well as all healthy relationships.

Another notable feature of this chart is how worry and panic take place when the heart is closed. Obviously, a person who lives in a state of worry and panic suffers—fitting Pragmatic closed-hearted people.

Conversely, the open-hearted Romantic way of life results in honor and respect which are needed for peace to emerge on Earth.

Finally, the Heart-Center is the seat of surrender which aligns with the suggestion to surrender to the Soul by humbling the ego-mind. This was proposed earlier in Chapter 18: Following Your Heart.

When it comes to the negative emotions of the heart, my Soul informed me that these emotions erupt under certain circumstances. In particular, the negative emotions emerge in an open-hearted person when they witness someone violating the heart's nature.

As you may recall, the heart's nature includes:

joy, honor, sincerity, love, respect, and kindness.

So, if an open-hearted person observes someone acting:

- ♥ tormenting, which violates being **joyful**;
- ♥ dishonorable, which violates being **honorable**;
- ♥ insincere, which violates being **sincere**;
- ♥ hateful, which violates being **loving**;
- ♥ disrespectful, which violates being **respectful**; or
- ♥ mean, which violates being **kind**,

that open-hearted witness will feel at least one of the negative emotions (impatience, cruelty, hot temper, and/or violence) emerging from within their heart.

In real-life cases, when I've witnessed someone violating the heart's natural qualities, the powerful negative emotions have pushed me to advise the perpetrator to remedy their transgression. If the person refuses, the situation can quickly escalate as my heart will press me to rebuke them with cruel and/or violent words in a hot-tempered and/or impatient way. This will usually lead to a heated argument. Then, after calming down, I'll be confused and surprised by the intense outburst that emerged from within myself.

From the outside, it may appear as if I'm an arrogant fool pushing my values on someone who's minor violation could be ignored by most, but the emotions actually emerge from the Soul within the heart. They're not initiated by my ego-mind in my head.

Here's an example. I saw someone throw their cigarette butt onto the sidewalk in front of a health food store. This is a minor case of littering, still, it's disrespectful to the Earth and other people who will be smelling that cigarette until it finally goes out. Even before that smoker tossed the butt on the ground they were disrespecting themselves by smoking. That's their prerogative, but imposing their disrespectful way of life on others is mean and disrespectful.

This detailed assessment of the situation appeared in my mind instantly. Then a strong inner prompting pushed me to point at the cigarette and ask the smoker, "Could you pick that up and dispose of it properly?"

To that, the smoker replied, "You pick it up!"

Without formulating a response, I rhetorically asked, "You want me to pick it up?"

Then, without giving the smoker a chance to respond, I impatiently continued, "I could pick it up, but if I do, I'm going to shove it down your throat and make you swallow it. Are you sure you want me to pick it up?"

Even though that man was much bigger than me, he cowered, picked the butt up and put it in the trashcan just a few steps away.

I'm ashamed to admit that I acted in such a hot-tempered way, claiming that I might become violent and cruel, but I did. Luckily, that man complied. Still, the negative way I handled it pushed that person away and must have provoked sour feelings.

More often, the negative emotions instigate an argument rather than solving the issue.

There are some unusual cases when such encounters work out unexpectedly well, build respect, and form an enduring friendship, but that is very rare. Usually, the negative emotions of the heart stir up disharmony and push people away.

After one of these incidents takes place, I feel tense and unsettled. I don't enjoy being aggressive. So, even when one of these encounters ends well, I still feel uncomfortable. Part of that discomfort is how I feel so out of alignment with the loving nature of the heart that I'm accustom to feeling most of the time.

THE NEGATIVE EMOTIONS & THE WAY-OF-THE-HEART

The negative emotions of the heart fit what is commonly referred to as a self-righteous attitude; one that's impatient, hot tempered, and confrontational. Those behaviors are clearly in opposition to the loving and kind Way-of-the-Heart. Therefore, before I knew about the negative emotions of the heart, and one of these outbursts occurred, I would presume that I needed to learn to follow my heart better.

After discussing this with other people who follow their heart, I discovered that these lion-hearted negative emotions propel them to defend the nature of their heart as well. Also, just like me, they presumed that they weren't following their hearts when these negative emotions of the heart emerged in them.

Now, having taken into account the Taoist wisdom shared by Mantak Chia, I've learned that open-hearted people can have strong emotional reactions to people who behave in ways that violate the heart's natural qualities.

The following section offers Henry Drummond's support for this bewildering, but common condition.

HENRY DRUMMOND'S SUPPORT

In his famous book, *The Greatest Thing in the World*, Henry Drummond offers a thoughtful analysis of love. In describing love, Drummond lists nine ingredients that make up the spectrum of love. One of those ingredients is good temper. Its opposite is ill temper. Drummond shares the following about ill temper:

> "The peculiarity of ill temper is that it is the vice of the virtuous. It is often the one blot on an otherwise noble character. You know men who are all but perfect, and women who would be entirely perfect, but for an

278

easily ruffled, quick-tempered or touchy disposition. This compatibility of ill temper with high moral character is one of the strangest and saddest problems of ethics."

Obviously, what Drummond is labeling "ill temper" corresponds to the negative emotions of the heart; impatience, cruelty, hot temper, and violence. What he finds so remarkable is how ill temper is well-known to be compatible with high moral character. Still, Drummond doesn't know why ill temper is often found in otherwise noble people.

The explanation offered earlier is based on ancient Taoist wisdom and my Soul's assistance in applying that wisdom to resolve the apparent inconsistency. Because this issue is so odd, I'll restate the explanation with Drummond's support woven in.

Human Souls include, within them, a lion-hearted defender that pounces when someone violates the natural qualities of the heart. Therefore, when a person follows their inner guidance closely, they mostly abide by the heart's nature; joy, honor, sincerity, love, respect, and kindness. By living in accordance with these traits, a person is considered virtuous. However, that same virtuous person can be provoked, by their Soul, to pounce on people who violate these virtues of the heart. In both cases, this open-hearted person is following their Soul's guidance which explains how these seemingly irreconcilable character traits are found in the same person.

Thus, as Drummond so eloquently puts it,

"...ill temper is the vice of the virtuous."

DEALING WITH THE NEGATIVE EMOTIONS

Over the years during which I've been aware of the lionhearted nature of my Soul, I developed some methods for coping with the strong emotions that can flair-up unexpectedly.

Simply being aware of this perplexing situation has helped me to deal with this challenging dynamic in a more skillful way.

To begin with, let's consider how these flare-ups get started:

1. It appears to me that someone violated the heart's nature.
2. I feel agitated and want to demand reparations.
3. My demand usually makes things worse.

As soon as I feel agitated, I could walk away and do the Heart-Opening Breath until the smile returns to my face. Once realigned with the natural qualities of the heart I could choose to let it go.

Even so, that leaves the door open for more of the same sort of behavior which will eventually trigger the negative emotions again. Suppressing the feelings can cause a buildup that eventually results in a blowout, so it's best to deal with these issues when they come up.

To develop skills for sharing your feelings in a compassionate way, check out the book, *Nonviolent Communication: A Language of Life* by Marshall Rosenberg. This book offers a method for expressing your feelings in a considerate way that often works out quite well.

If I don't heed the yellow light and take time to breathe, my lion will roar. In these embarrassing situations, I've found it's best to walk away, cool down, and breathe into my heart until the smile returns to my face. Even though this technique works great, it can be difficult for me to have the composure to walk away and do the breathing in the heat of the moment. Nonetheless, all encounters eventually end.

I've found that the most important follow-up is to apologize for any harsh words that I may have uttered or more likely shouted. Without condoning the specific activities that may have triggered my Soul to pounce, I feel responsible for any additional chaos my negative re-action may have caused. Accordingly, I'll often begin by apologizing for my intensely negative approach.

Additionally, I might mention what incited me if I'm able to do it in a skillful and sensitive way. Here again, "Nonviolent Communication" which is also called "Compassionate Communication" can help.

In addition to all of that, I've discovered that when I've been practicing the Heart-Opening Breath often, or when I'm deeply in love and my heart is wide open, I might laugh or make a sarcastic joke to gently express my disapproval. It seems that when I'm in a very joyful state-of-being, with my heart wide open, I'm able to use the lesser violence of a sarcastic comment, which is humorously cruel rather than overtly cruel. Reacting this way allows me to remain in a relatively positive state-of-being and hopefully everyone can laugh at what took place.

LEARNING FROM THE INCIDENT

Later, once I've calmed down, I review what happened to determine if there are personal lessons for me to assimilate. When I'm able to learn and grow from the incident, I can be sincerely grateful for what happened and thank the person who triggered this deep part of my True Self. This sort of follow-up has actually led to special connections with people that have lasted for many years afterward.

I also consider the possibility that it may be best for me to keep my distance from the person who woke up the lion that sleeps deep in my heart. If this person has a habit of acting in ways that oppose the natural qualities of the heart, then it may be best for me to avoid additional contact with them because it will almost certainly lead to additional conflict.

EVERYONE IS PLAYING THEIR PART

It's important and helpful to remember that everyone is playing their part. There are billions of roles in the play of life, many roles include acting in opposition to the heart's nature. Earlier, I explained how divisive activities are needed to individualize humanity. Coincidently, divisive activities often oppose the nature of the heart.

That being the case, if one accepts the need for individuation as a precondition needed to accomplish the goal of the universe—meeting mysterious others—and the proposal that extremist Pragmatics are accomplishing this individuation with divisive activities, then the Pragmatics are playing their divinely formulated roles. Finally, their divisive actions will violate the heart's nature.

If all of that is true, then it's not really appropriate for the open-hearted people to interfere with or blame the Pragmatics when they're simply playing their necessary divisive role.

The next chapter, *Forgiveness and Gratitude*, follows this train of thought to arrive at a beautiful way to handle this clash between divisive activities and the nature of the heart.

THE SILVER LINING

There are positive features to this challenging dynamic.

For instance, I've discovered that the negative qualities of the heart can help me to clarify who my real friends are while also helping me notice who doesn't fit into the open-hearted lifestyle. With this in mind, the negative emotions act as alarms, or red lights, alerting me to the fact that I'm dealing with a divisive person or a divisive situation. When the lion in my heart stirs, I can choose to walk away and avoid the conflict that will take place if I foolishly stick around. Once alerted to the situation, I can step aside, check in with my Soul, and adjust my life accordingly.

Conversely, the positive emotions can be interpreted as green lights, letting me know I've found a kindred spirit.

When living a full life, all these features of the heart get activated.

As I learn to open to love more and more deeply, I seem to be better able to remain in the pink zone of love that instills a sense of wonder and provides a graceful path around these hurdles. This is because a wide-open heart enables me to see the perfection in everything and everyone which avoids becoming upset by divisive activities.

WHY DO WE HURT THE ONES WE LOVE MOST?

Next, I'll show how these negative emotions are involved in what has been called the most common and frustrating relationship dynamic known:

"Why do we hurt the ones we love most?"

As you may have discovered on your own, it's quite common for people to experience conflict with the people they love most. During these conflicts, violent and cruel words may be exchanged in hot-tempered and impatient ways. The well-known fact that people who truly love each other often succumb to this disheartening relationship dynamic makes it terribly frustrating.

To see how the negative emotions of the heart are involved, consider the following scenario:

Two people love each other, and while together, one of them has their heart open, but the other's heart is closed. The one whose heart is closed does something or says something that's tormenting, dishonorable, insincere, hateful, disrespectful, or mean. They may not realize what they're doing; it could be a sarcastic joke that's part of their way of kidding around.

Nevertheless, their words or actions were not in alignment with the natural qualities of the heart. Therefore, the negative emotions of their beloved's open-heart can leap out, causing the open-hearted person to retaliate with cruel or violent words in a hot-tempered rebuke. The situation can quickly escalate into a full-on fight.

In scenarios like this, the negative emotions of the heart cause open-hearted people to **hurt the ones we love most.**

HEART-OPENING BREATH SOLUTION

I experienced this dynamic with a woman I loved and lived with for a few years. When we found ourselves involved in a disagreement, we'd practice the Heart-Opening Breath together. After breathing together, peace and love was restored.

When my beloved and I would find ourselves in a disagreement or a full-on-fight, I would ask her, "Can we breathe together?"

Then my beloved and I would hug each other and place our heads over each other's shoulders. In this embrace, we would both practice the Heart-Opening Breath until we both smiled. Immediately afterwards, we would be in love again. Quite often, we couldn't remember why the dispute started in the first place, or even, what it was about.

Amazingly, this method worked <u>every</u> time we did it!

To establish this system, we made an agreement: when a confrontation developed and the offer to breathe was proposed by one of us, then the other would accept the offer. By making this agreement when we were in love and at peace, we established a commitment that was honored even in the midst of highly emotional conflicts.

The most difficult part was for one of us to think of asking the other to breathe while engaged in a conflict. The acceptance of the suggestion to breathe together and the act of breathing together was easy and 100 percent effective.

Thus, this solution is quick and powerful when used.

In researching this relationship dynamic, I found that this issue is one of the most common problems in relationships. It happens between beloveds, between children and their parents, and between siblings. It can even happen between close friends.

If this is an issue for you and people you love, you may want to ask them if they're willing to try this technique.

If they are willing, then make an agreement about how you'd like to go about it. Work out the details of how to make the suggestion. I've found that it's important to <u>ask</u> to do the breathing <u>together</u>. Telling the other person that they need to breathe is arrogant, and implies that they're the problem. Blaming them can fuel the fire. Therefore, it's much more effective to say something like, "I need to calm down...would you be willing to breathe with me?"

Additionally, there's the question of how do you prefer to do the breathing together? If one person is a lot taller than the other, then hugging with your heads over each other's shoulders won't work. Some other arrangement may be more appropriate. It may take a couple of tries to get the bugs worked out, but I can assure you it will be well worth the effort.

MAKING A MUTUAL COMMITMENT

It's important for everyone involved to make a commitment to do the breathing whenever it's requested. No one wants conflict with the ones they love, so it ought to be reasonably easy to make this agreement during a peaceful point in time.

EMPOWERING OTHERS

Because it's difficult to think of doing a breathing technique while caught up in conflict, it's a good idea to empower other family members or friends to help. When they see or hear a fight developing, or discover one that's in full swing, they can suggest that now would be a good time to do the Heart-Opening Breath together.

For example, on one occasion when my beloved and I were involved in an argument, a friend of ours asked, "Why don't you do that breathing technique that you talk about?" At that point, neither of us had thought of doing it. We looked at each other, hugged, and breathed together. The conflict vanished in a few breaths.

Using the Heart-Opening Breath to end conflict and restore love between people who love each other is a wonderful way to use the power of the Heart-Opening Breath to improve your most important relationships.

KEEPING OUR HEARTS OPEN

If you and your loved ones could keep their hearts open all the time, no one would do or say things contrary to the natural qualities of the heart. With everyone's hearts open permanently, all would be expressing their hearts' natural qualities. Accordingly, the negative emotions wouldn't get triggered by abhorrent behavior, because it wouldn't take place.

Personally, I've found that my heart remains open in the most enduring way by loving my Soul. This was discussed in the previous chapter, Soul Love.

Doing the Heart-Opening Breath often is also very helpful. That's why I use a wristwatch with a repeating countdown timer to remind myself to practice the Heart-Opening Breath throughout the day. The details can be found in the REMEMBERING TO BREATH section presented earlier on page 232.

TODAY'S REALITY

Given the world we live in, and the wide variety of people that exist, it's helpful to be aware of the negative emotions: impatience, cruelty, hot temper, and violence. These real aspects of the heart can pop up when your heart is open. This is because your Soul is strongly opposed to people acting in ways that are tormenting, dishonorable, insincere, hateful, disrespectful, or mean. Being aware of this will help you know why these emotional reactions emerge like an angry lion.

Even if you're a Romantic person who is dedicated to love, these fierce emotions can cause you to pounce like a lion without having much time to think about what you're doing or why.

Hopefully, being aware of the negative emotions of the heart will help you cope with this challenging aspect of your Soul.

NEGATIVE EMOTIONS & ASCENSION/INHERITANCE PROPHECY

Even though there's no way to know if the Romantic people will actually inherit the Earth, my Soul showed me how these negative emotions of the heart fit with the ascension/inheritance prophecy in a remarkable way.

During the current Age of Individuation, with the Pragmatic people far outnumbering the Romantics, the inescapable reality we all experience includes divisive activities that trigger Romantic peoples' negative emotions of their hearts. This prevents the open-hearted people from experiencing uninterrupted peace during the divisive Age of Individuation that is taking place as I write.

Be that as it may, if the Pragmatic people actually ascend into the astral realm, and the people who have learned to open their hearts, follow their hearts, and open to love subsequently inherit the Earth— the negative emotions will finally stop getting triggered.

This is because open-hearted people normally behave in accordance with their heart's nature which doesn't trigger the negative emotions, leaving them dormant. So, when the Age of Love dawns, the negative emotions will remain dormant till the end of time, allowing abundant peace and prosperity to prevail.

Despite that wonderful possibility, divisive activities continue to violate the nature of the heart today, triggering the negative emotions in otherwise virtuous people. This makes it difficult for open-hearted people to experience peace while divisive people continue to provoke the negative response. On top of that, the divisive activities appear to be increasing and becoming more sensational triggering the negative emotions more often than ever before. According to the Consciousness-Origin Cosmology this escalation will continue up until the transition when peace on Earth will finally dawn.

So, even though open-hearted Romantic people yearn for peace, the negative emotions of their hearts postpone their ability to experience true peace until the global transition takes place. So, it seems that the negative emotions of the heart may have been cleverly designed to ensure that peace on Earth will arrive when the Age of Love begins.

Hopefully, that global transition will occur soon.

In the meantime, being aware of the negative emotions and how they get triggered can help you cope with this challenging aspect of open-hearted living. Also, by using the Heart-Opening Breath when these situations are just beginning to take hold, you can calm yourself down and deal with the situation more skillfully using compassionate communication techniques.

The next chapter offers a way to practice forgiveness and gratitude by adjusting your point of view. With the insightful perspective that is offered, situations that would normally trigger the negative emotions can be reframed in a way that may enable you to forgive divisive people and even be grateful that they are doing their part. Using this technique, you may be able to open your heart wider and open to love even more because these challenges provide opportunities to broaden your capacity to love.

Chapter 22
Forgiveness and Gratitude

"True forgiveness is when you can say
Thank You for that experience."
—Oprah Winfrey (born 1954) producer, actress, philanthropist

SETTING THE STAGE FOR FORGIVENESS

To begin with, it's helpful to be honest and realize that in some way or another, we've all taken part in divisive activities. It may have been in a subtle way, but no mature human is completely innocent.

I suppose there may be some exceptions, however I certainly know that I've acted in divisive ways. The negative emotions of my heart have made sure of that. Furthermore, when triggered by the negative emotions of my heart, I still find myself acting divisively.

Therefore, an important starting point when considering forgiveness is to let go of any "holier-than-thou" beliefs.

WHAT IS REALLY BEHIND DIVISIVE ACTIVITIES

The next step is to consider how **all of the divisive activities may have been instigated by our Souls.**

Through extremely polarized desires that come from the Souls of Pragmatic people, or via the negative emotions of the heart that come from the Souls of Romantic people, we all commit divisive activities that are needed to individualize humanity. Moreover, our Souls are completely aware of what's taking place and how all these activities are psychologically affecting all of us. Souls know what we're all thinking, feeling, and therefore, how we're affecting one another. The continuum of consciousness provides our Superconscious-Souls with instantaneous access to all the portions of consciousness. Thus, divisive activities are planned and used to individualize us all. Even Romantic people are involved via the heart's negative emotions that propel Romantics to hurt the ones we love most!

287

Although our Souls are completely aware of what's taking place, those of us who are being driven, by our Souls, to perpetrate these divisive activities are much less aware of the impact. When a Pragmatic person is cut off from their conscience, their conscious-mind can easily rationalize their actions in a way that ignores the victim. For example, in the bombing of Hiroshima, the person who pressed the button that dropped the bomb, killing over 150,000 innocent people, was simply doing his job. Someone had to do it, right?

In a different way, when a Romantic person reacts to a violation of the natural qualities of the heart by pouncing with their heart's impatience, cruelty, hot temper, and/or violence, they see themselves as a righteous defender of the heart's virtues. Someone must defend the virtues of the heart, right?

In most of these cases, the ego-minds of the perpetrators of divisive activities are not able to truly understand the long-term impact of their actions. Going even further, rationalization of these types of situations can flip the blame around enabling the perpetrator to see themselves as a victim who is fighting back. In some way, they are. For example, the bombing of Hiroshima was done to stop fascism from taking over the world.

By looking deeper into all of this, we find that humans are pawns in a chess game that's being played by our Superconscious-Souls. In addition to our Souls, there are many other types of non-physical spirits who also possess the Supreme Power of Wholeness. Those spirit guides encourage Pragmatic people to play their part in the chess game of life. Together, as a unified team, all these portions of the One-Who-Is-All guide our lives from inside and outside. By recognizing the power of the One and how it propels us in a myriad of ways, it becomes clear that we've been cast into roles in the grand play of life.

To make life a mysterious adventure, we haven't received a script, been informed of the plot, nor notified of the purpose behind it all.

The Holy entities that maneuver us through life must be aware of the plot, of course; how else would they fulfill the purpose?

The Consciousness-Origin Cosmology provides a purpose and even a general plot line. At this late hour, knowing these basics doesn't interfere with our ability to fulfill our roles and achieve the purpose—meeting mysterious others.

Still, the Soul guiding a human puppet arrangement is needed to keep everything on track and insure that the goal is accomplished.

Even though we have free will, our conscious-mind's attempt to chart a course of its own choosing is commandeered by our desires that are provided by our Souls. The relentless longings to satisfy our desires cause our ego-minds to make the very choices that our Souls have surreptitiously guided us to make. Using the power of desires, Souls even lead Pragmatic people who've been cut off from their Souls' intuition. Thus, Souls have the power to guide people into committing the divisive activities that are needed to individualize humanity.

The negative emotions of the heart and the deviant desires imposed on Pragmatics have caused many people to claim that people's hearts are tainted with perverted desires making most hearts impure. These observant people have noticed how the Souls in some people's hearts push them to carry out what appear to be "evil" activities.

Because people are not aware of how divisive activities are needed to individualize humanity, they judge divisive activities to be wrong or "evil." Despite that, those activities are actually necessary and in alignment with the One's grand plan.

By labeling divisive activities as evil or wrong, many are told they must purify their heart and change their behavior. Meanwhile, the deepest Truth is that everything is perfectly on track.

HOW RESENTMENT TAKES ROOT

By viewing divisive activities as wrong, resentment takes root.

When we're born, we have no knowledge of where we came from or why we're here. As we become conscious of what's going on around us, we find ourselves in the midst of a battle between good and evil. Our human guardians and teachers guide us to believe in the good versus evil duality even though it's actually an illusion. The penalties and rewards that are doled out by adults indoctrinate children into accepting the good versus evil illusion to be real.

Additionally, thrillers and horror stories presented in books, movies, or in television shows, escalate this battle to absurd proportions. In olden times, legends and ghost stories played this role. To further support this illusion, we all have real experiences of being victims. We also know of others who are victims, making it nearly impossible to deny that reality contains a good versus evil dynamic. The process is unavoidable, and it's intended to be nearly inescapable.

Once I discovered that the good versus evil battle is an important part of a grand plan to individualize humanity, the implications of that realization offered me a way to forgive everyone for everything that may have hurt me or anyone else. It became clear that it's not personal, it's a divinely ordained individuation process.

The positive effect of this process is how it makes us into individuals that can meet one another. Those meetings have enabled us to discover love as well as friendship, companionship, romance, etc.

The unfortunate side effects of divisive activities include resentment, shame, guilt, blame, hatred, etc.

These feelings are often the root cause of chronic physical and psychological distress. Additionally, holding on to these feelings keeps the treasure chest in our hearts locked up, preventing amazing hidden talents from coming out to play, preventing us from actualizing the wonderful True-Self that we have the potential to become.

FORGIVENESS IS PART OF THE SOLUTION

Forgiveness is a powerful way to let go of resentment and release the associated emotional burdens. The more you're able to forgive, the more you'll be able to let go of anger, resentment, and other stressful emotions that can prevent your personal wounds from healing and your Soul's precious talents from emerging.

In some cases, you or the culture you identify with, may have acted in ways that cause you to feel remorse, guilt, or shame. Forgiving yourself and the culture you identify with is just as important as forgiving others. Letting go of self-condemnation can free you from the depression and health issues that develop from guilt and shame.

My Soul has convinced me that the necessity of individuality is the reason for these divisive activities. It's not bad luck, or punishment for being a bad person. Reality doesn't support such theories. The fact that the oneness perspective found in Original-People has transformed into increasing individuality in advanced cultures shows that challenging experiences have driven the individuation process. Moreover, they are divinely ordained and divinely orchestrated.

My Soul convinced me that everyone must go through challenges that are sufficient to forge us all into individuals. We're all born completely innocent, but in civilization, we're all forged into individuals. Divisive activities do hurt when they take place, and they're designed to hurt. If they didn't hurt, how would they divide each of us from the rest of the universe and make each of us into separate individuals?

If you're willing to adopt the theory that the good versus evil duality is designed to individualize humanity, then, with one additional step, you can adopt the understanding that everyone is doing their perfect job. It may be a good perfect job, an evil perfect job, or a neutral perfect job, but in all cases, it's a perfect job. This point of view opens a very wide door that enables you to forgive everyone for every divisive thing that has ever taken place!

Fortunately, this is something you can do on your own.

You may not be interested in hanging out with people who you don't resonate with, but with the perspective that everyone is doing their perfect job, you can release the anger and resentment that may have developed in the past. Additionally, by forgiving yourself and your culture you can let go of any shame or guilt that you may be holding onto.

SEEING THE PERFECTION FOR YOURSELF

There is a way for you to see for yourself, that everything is perfect. To do that you must open your heart very wide.

The illustration on the right was presented earlier. It reveals how to see universal perfection. When the heart is open wide enough, one can see the perfection that exists. With that open-hearted perspective, it's easier to accept the wide range of activities that are taking place today. The knowledge that universal perfection exists, makes it much easier to forgive everyone.

Practicing the Heart-Opening Breath often allowed me to see this perfection. To experience it for yourself, try the following exercise.

When you have a free day, begin the day with a longer than normal Heart-Opening Breath session. Then, every time you notice that you aren't smiling, do the Heart-Opening Breath again. While you continue this practice, take a solo vacation out to a beautiful natural location. Once you're alone, soak up the beauty as you stroll around nature and continue to practice the Heart-Opening Breath.

Eventually, you'll shift into an altered state in which you feel extraordinarily happy. Colors will become more vibrant than they usually are. You might even notice a sparkling effect that makes the natural world glisten. When you have reached this level of open-heartedness, head to town while you continue the breathing practice.

Once in town you will eventually find something that you would normally judge to be wrong or evil. Take a moment to notice how you perceive it with your super wide-open heart.

When I did this, I noticed things that I normally disapproved of, but with my super wide-open heart, it became clear that those things would eventually produce positive results. Possibly they taught a lesson or for some other reason these seemingly wrong or evil things would, over time, produce positive results.

If you haven't already experienced this, hopefully you will be able to see it for yourself by opening your heart wide enough to see with the divinely blessed viewpoint of your Superconscious-Soul.

REFRAMING NEW ENCOUNTERS

When new divisive encounters take place, you may feel anger and resentment, but as soon as you reframe the situation to accept it as part of universal perfection, you'll be better able to calm down, dispense with the anger, and let the resentment roll off your back.

There's no benefit to developing debilitating emotional feelings with regard to people who are playing their perfect role in the grand play of life. Even when someone is being divisive you can remind yourself that they are performing an important function that's part of the divine plan.

By being aware that individuation is an important part of that plan, you have discovered how all sorts of disturbing activities are necessary. Then, by accepting everyone and everything to be accomplishing the plan, you can stop burdening yourself with emotional baggage.

Whether you're a Pragmatic or a Romantic, this can help you have a much more enjoyable life with greater health and happiness.

If you're a Romantic, you'll be better able to keep your heart open. Also, by dispensing with resentment you'll crack open your treasure chest to become more of your True-Self.

DROPPING OUT OF THE BATTLE TO GIVE FROM YOUR HEART

Everyone who drops out of the battle between good and evil frees up time to do those things that accommodate people's actual needs.

Many people think they must pick a side and step into the battle to fight for what they think is right. It's hard for most people to see how that is simply going to escalate the battle as they become one more **Universal Soldier:** One more warrior that makes the battle incrementally larger.

With that in mind, if you really feel drawn to help, it's more helpful to step into the middle and ask, what's going on here? What's the problem? How can this be resolved peacefully through mediation? How can everyone win? In some cases, this approach can work.

Still, there are some people who just like to fight. Apparently, that's their divisive job. Anyone who can be lured into the fray is fair game from their point of view. People and circumstances draw us in to skirmishes. The process is infectious, and standing on the sidelines is very difficult for people who truly care about others.

During a thirty-year period of my life I was caught in my version of a battle for peace. Then, after circumstances brought me to my knees, I experienced my ego's death and let go of my efforts to fight for peace. As I emerged from the ashes, a new direction took hold. Without being distracted by the fears and judgement that had trapped me in a battle for peace, I was able to open my heart more than ever and align with my Soul in a deeper way that guided me toward the middle Way-of-the-Heart.

If you're a Romantic, then by acting from your heart, and giving what you're guided to give, you'll be one of the people who puts their heart into their work, and lives in the beneficent Quintessential Core of the human Triality. Rather than being a Universal Soldier, you'll be a Universal Provider of goods and services that help to bring peace and prosperity to everyone.

PEACE WILL PREVAIL

Peace will prevail when no one is willing to fight for, or even identify with either side: good or evil. Love is founded in acceptance, not judgement. In the end, the power of love will prevail.

Pragmatics can choose to follow the middle path of Buddhism in which one uses their conscious-mind to avoid the extreme polarities. Following the Buddhist middle path could lead a Pragmatic to decide to ask for a second chance by using the pineal gland decalcification method presented earlier at the end of Chapter 19.

When every human being on Earth is part of the productive Quintessential Core in the middle of humanity, the extremes of good and evil will no longer exist. A New Earth of abundant peace and prosperity will be born: a world in which love will blossom to its fullest. Judgment will be forgotten because love will have taken its place.

Exactly how we'll get from here to there is impossible to know. And, in the meantime, divisive activities are taking place. Fortunately, these activities have a boomerang effect, one that operates in the darkness, encouraging Romantic people to open their hearts even more than ever before.

BEYOND FORGIVENESS IS GRATITUDE

Beyond forgiveness, we can thank those who have given us our challenges in life. It's these challenges that push us to open our hearts further. Without hurdles to overcome, we wouldn't have opportunities to strengthen our ability to love. So, even though conflict and hardship appear wrong on the surface, these difficulties contain a silver lining, a blessing that fortifies our ability to love more than ever. Accordingly, we can be sincerely grateful for the challenges and the divisive people who challenge us.

Noticing the boomerang effect of divisiveness and being grateful for the blessings it provides is a very important step that you can take on your own.

Discovering how to transform your enemies into teachers will make a huge difference in your life. Situations that may have incited you to retaliate with anger in the past can become opportunities that bring forth gratitude, and deepen your ability to love more than ever.

The most powerful techniques of judo, jujitsu, and aikido occur in the dojo of consciousness. By turning a foe into a teacher, you will be flipping reality on its head. This was the first lesson my sensei taught me when I was 10-years-old. It took most of my life for me to understand how powerful that wisdom is.

BEING GRATEFUL FOR THE PRAGMATICS

If you're a Romantic, then you're probably playing a reasonably enjoyable role in the grand play of life. Conversely, out in the extremes, many Pragmatic people are suffering. Someone needs to play each and every role that has been cast by the One-Who-Is-All. If you're a loving Romantic, then you got a wonderful role to play. However, the difficult roles, those in which the person's conscious- and subconscious-minds are suffering, are being played by others. By recognizing the blessing your life is, you can be grateful that you didn't have to take one of the difficult roles that result in suffering.

Gratefully, you got a Romantic loving role.

So, rather than letting the role a divisive person is playing upset you, you can be grateful that you weren't stuck with that terrible role. Instead, you're blessed with a Romantic role. You're able to open and follow your heart and open to love to experience a wonderful life.

By noticing that billions of people got stuck with divisive roles, you ought to be very grateful for the wonderful role you ended up with.

Therefore, beyond forgiving divisive people for the activities that they play, you can flip the whole situation around by choosing to be grateful for the people who are playing the painful roles. Someone had to play them and luckily it wasn't you!

THE POWER OF GRATITUDE

Gratitude contains within it the powerful blessing of love. For me, it begins as a subtle feeling of appreciation for something or someone. Gratitude is an intuitive feeling that emerges from my Soul. The subtle nature of it makes it easy to ignore. If I don't act quickly, then the opportunity to express gratitude fades away and is forgotten.

Conversely, when I feel an intuitive prompting to show appreciation and I follow through, the simple words "thank you" fill my heart with joy. Even though the gratitude is offered to bless someone else, the act of expressing appreciation has a truly positive effect on me. I don't do it for myself, but I do benefit every time I express the appreciation that comes from deep within my Soul.

My prayers are all about expressing gratitude. There are times when I ask my Soul for help, but I don't view those requests as prayers. For me, other than love, the most precious feeling I can express is gratitude, and that expression of appreciation feels like a prayer to me.

Being grateful and expressing that gratitude brings more blessings than all the wishes one can make.

THE SOURCE OF GRATITUDE

Gratitude and love both come from the Superconscious-Soul that resides in the heart. Both are forms of intuition. Our Souls are Trees of Life that bear the fruit of love. This fruit contains a precious seed that is gratitude. Planting these seeds of gratitude causes love to grow in your heart, and the hearts of whomever you bless with appreciation.

To plant a seed of gratitude, all you need to do is express the feeling of appreciation whenever it is offered from your heart. All seeds are truly magical, and the seeds of love are gratitude. These magic seeds spoil quickly if they aren't planted. That being the case, one of the most important things that you can do is to simply say "thank you" every time you feel the slightest sense of appreciation.

I especially like to thank humble working people that I encounter: cashiers, busboys, floor sweepers, cooks, builders, repairmen, garbage collectors, and anyone who does anything to assist the general public in any way. Planting seeds of gratitude blesses the world with an abundant forest of love.

Thank you, dear reader, for being who you are and for playing your divinely perfect role in this gloriously bewildering play called life.

The next chapter is my favorite. In it I share some intriguing portions of the investigative adventure that unfolded whilst writing the early drafts of this book. Those episodes uncovered interlinked endorsements for this book's message. Miraculously, many linkages connected here on the island paradise where my heart guided me to put down roots—Maui. If you have any doubts about what has been shared so far, they may disappear once you've read the next chapter.

Chapter 23
Support from Hopiland, Hawai'i and Mu

In this chapter, I share some astonishing support for the Consciousness-Origin Cosmology, the Triality of human consciousness, and the future predictions presented in **Part 2**.

The following goes beyond supporting what has been shared earlier to also revealing the intuitive method of discovery that guided me to learn what is shared in this book. By following my heart, pieces of the puzzle showed up, one at a time as if by magic. The pieces eventually fit together to form a picture. As more pieces fit together in tightly interlocking ways, the picture became clearer, reinforcing my confidence in what was highly questionable at first.

Over the years it became apparent that the thesis offered here is supported in so many different ways that it's nearly certain to be true. After noticing that the thesis resolves questions that have remained unsolved for ages, I began to suspect that my Soul had led me to discover something truly remarkable. Then, with a new perspective of reality formed, I felt the need to share it. This book is the result.

All along the way, my Soul led me from within, whispering encouragement and placing the ideas into my conscious-mind, guiding me each step of the way. The real author of this book is my dear Soul.

I hope this chapter draws you into the excitement that I experienced on the adventure that confirmed what has been presented herein. In addition to that adventure, I found the Hopi people to be the most open-hearted, humble, and kind people I've ever met. Therefore, I include details that reveal the nature of the Hopi people.

MY VISIT TO HOPILAND

I began learning about the Hopi people and their prophecies by reading a few articles. Some of that information appeared to match the Consciousness-Origin Cosmology's prophecies that I had written about in an early version of what eventually became this book.

Additionally, I fit the description of a man the Hopi call "True White Brother" in three out of four ways. The fourth characteristic gave me room to imagine how I might possibly fit that feature as well.

Then, in October of 2009, I felt my Soul firmly guiding me to visit the Hopi people. At that time, I was making arrangements to visit my parents in Detroit. So, on my flight from Maui to Detroit, I arranged a two-day layover in Phoenix, Arizona. Before leaving Maui, I printed a few copies of what I had written so far, so I could share that draft with my parents and the Hopi people.

Flying through the night, I landed in Phoenix at dawn, rented a car, and began the long drive up to Hopiland which is located in the northeastern corner of Arizona. I arrived around mid-afternoon and saw a sign with the name of the oldest Hopi village, "Oraibi," written on it. I pulled off the road, turned off the car, and got out to stretch my legs.

A young man, Wayland Namingha, Jr., happened to be nearby, and asked, "Who are you and why have you come?"

I explained that I was working on a book that I thought the Hopi people might find interesting. I also mentioned that I was hoping to find an elder to share with him what I was writing about.

Wayland further inquired what my book was about.

To discuss the contents of the book, I strolled over to where he was hulling dried Hopi beans that he had grown and harvested. He invited me to join him while we discussed my book. As we took the beans out of their dry hulls, I began. However, before I had said much at all, six more men pulled up in a pickup truck and joined us. They all wanted to hear about my book, so I started again.

When I finished sharing the message in the book, a man asked, "How is it that you know more about the Hopi way than we do?"

That question surprised me. I didn't know much about the Hopi. I had only read a few short articles at that time, so I simply replied, "I don't know about the Hopi way. I just explained what's in my book."

"That's the Hopi way," the man exclaimed, then asked, "You've been here before, haven't you?"

"No, I got here just before all of you showed up." I replied.

One of the men stood up and told me there was something he wanted to show me. As I stood up to follow him, the other men joined us. We all walked to a large boulder known as Prophecy Rock and viewed the petroglyph scrached into it (see photo on right).

One of the essays that I had read before going to Hopiland included an illustration of this petroglyph.

One of the men explained that the four upper human figures originally didn't have heads, but someone had added the heads recently. Additionally, he told me that these upper figures are called the "two-hearted," while the one located on the lower line that continues around the bolder is called a "one-hearted."

As we all looked at the petroglyph, one of the men asked for my thoughts, which have matured since then, and will be shared soon.

Eventually one of the men told me that I needed to see Martin. He explained that Martin was the last living elder who lived the "old-fashioned way," in Hotevilla, the next village down the main road. Finally, in a kind and gentle way, the men encouraged me to simply head further down the road where I would find Martin.

Accepting their suggestion, I got into my rental car and headed toward Hotevilla. Soon, I spotted a sign that read "Hotevilla." At that intersection, a car was waiting to pull out onto the main road. I waved out my window for the driver to wait and got out of my car to ask her for directions to Martin's place.

The woman in the car suggested that I follow her. As I got back into my car, she turned her car around. I followed her down a winding road through a sparse desert to a little cabin. As we got out of our cars, I felt a cool wind blowing. It was getting dark and I thought it was a bit odd to just show up after sundown. Despite that, the Hopi woman walked briskly to the door of the cabin and knocked loudly.

Soon, the door opened and an old man greeted us. She said something to him in Hopi and then introduced me to Martin.

We shook hands and he kindly welcomed me in. As I stepped past the woman, she whispered to me that Martin was losing his hearing.

We spent a couple of hours sharing information with one another. I showed him little parts of my book to read, drew pictures, and wrote things on paper to communicate with him. He could speak well and told me that he had been informed that Iran was going to nuke Israel, then China and Russia would get involved and nuke the USA, triggering the transition into a new Earth. Back in 2009 that sounded far-fetched. Surprisingly, today it seems realistic.

Eventually Martin said, "It's getting late, could you come back tomorrow so we can talk some more?"

I wrote down, "How about 8 a.m.?"

He said that would be fine. We shook hands and I departed.

Wayland, the first Hopi man that I met, had invited me to spend the night at his place if I needed lodging. So, I drove back to his home.

It was a very small stone structure. Wayland, his lovely wife and two adorable children were home. As I went to sleep on the couch near the fireplace, I felt touched by the open-hearted hospitality these people so easily offered to me, especially since I was a stranger.

I was finding every Hopi person that I met to be very kind, humble, and accommodating.

In the morning, I folded the blankets and did my best to show my gratitude and avoid imposing on them any more than necessary.

When I got back to Martin's, we sat down together and Martin began to unwrap a bundle that was in his lap. The four wrappings took a while for him to unravel. Finally, Martin handed me a stone tablet with a corner missing. (see illustration below)

Then, with the tablet in my hands, Martin asked, "Do you have the corner?"

I realized that he was testing me to see if I was the True White Brother that I mentioned earlier. According to one article that I had read before my visit, this man has the missing piece of the sacred Tiponi Tablet. More importantly, the Hopi believe that he's the only person who can correctly interpret the Tablet's symbolic message.

That article further explained that in addition to being white, this man is expected to have four primary characteristics:

- ♥ He follows his heart;
- ♥ He speaks the truth unlike other white men;
- ♥ He teaches how to heal the red and white; and
- ♥ He has the missing piece of the Tiponi Tablet.

When I read that, I was surprised by how the first three characteristics fit me quite well. Here's how:

- ♥ My life's purpose had become all about following my heart;
- ♥ My brother and a beloved I lived with had both recently told me that I was the most honest person they had ever met;
- ♥ The Heart-Opening Breath brings together red and white essence to form pink loving wholeness. That could be viewed as a way to heal the red and white. I had already found that breathing technique to be the most powerful tool I knew of. Moreover, I was teaching it to others and had begun writing this book, mainly, to share the Heart-Opening Breath.

With regard to the fourth point, the missing piece of the Tiponi Tablet, I had no idea what the Tablet looked like nor the shape of the missing piece so I couldn't know if I had it. Given all that leeway, I was able to imagine that a stone object featured as a key element in the most memorable dream of my life, could possibly be the missing piece. I knew it was preposterous to imagine that I could be this important man. Besides, based on how precious the Tablet is to the Hopi people, I figured that I wouldn't even get an opportunity to see it. But, since the Hopi people and I appeared to share a similar perspective about the heart, and because Arizona was on my way from Maui to Detroit, I figured a two-day layover in Arizona was a convenient way to meet the Hopi people and determine if our views are actually alike.

Most importantly, my inner guidance pressed me to go.

So, there I sat, and Martin had just asked me if I had the missing corner of the sacred Tablet that he had actually placed into my hands. Obviously, he suspected that I might be the True White Brother!

The missing corner was a completely different shape than the stone object featured in my most memorable dream. Therefore, I quickly replied, "No, I don't have the corner. I'm not the guy."

Martin looked at me intently and appeared to be deliberating.

To avoid staring at each other, I looked back at the Tablet and examined it more closely. It was unexpectedly smooth and perfectly flat. It appeared to be made with modern tools in a very precise way. This impressed me as very odd, because this Tablet was purported to have been held by the Hopi from before the Great Flood, making it several thousands of years-old.

Unexpectedly, Martin took the Tablet out of my hands and handed me a master copy that looked like the illustration on the left.

The lower right corner that was missing contains a gut symbol, a jagged opening with a squiggly line inside that looks like intestines. There's also an equilateral triangle curiously intermingled with the intestines which will be discussed later. The upper right corner has a simple head symbol.

In between the head and gut, there's a circle with four lines radiating outward. This "center-mark" symbol could easily represent the Heart-Center because that would fit with how the Hopi are dedicated to following their hearts. Just below the center-mark is a line with a turned-up end that could be intended to emphasize the importance of the heart symbol by underlining it.

Alternatively, an acupuncturist that I meet a few years later, explained to me how that curved line looks similar to the Chinese xin symbol which means heart-mind and is shown below.

Chinese Taoist wisdom identifies three primary tantiens (or focuses of essence) that are located in the head, heart and gut. If the three dots in the xin represent these three tantiens, then the xin depicts the Triality of human consciousness with the middle dot, corresponding to the heart, emphasized by the curved underline. This interpretation of the xin symbol fits the curved line's position on the Hopi Tablet.

Amazingly, "xin" literally means heart-mind. On top of that, in Chinese the heart-mind is defined to contain intellect and emotions combined together. The xin is considered to be the physical heart, as well as a bowl that holds the consciousness of this highly revered heart-mind, perfectly fitting the thesis of this book.

In a research paper entitled, *The Meaning of the Chinese Cultural Keyword Xin*[27], the authors emphasize the cultural importance of this symbol and show how the xin is featured in numerous important Chinese words. The paper goes on to support essentially everything I have claimed about the Superconscious-Soul including the guidance it provides, the importance of following it, its divinity, that it is the source of happiness, love, health, etc.

Now returning to the story, just after Martin handed the master Tablet to me, I drew an illustration of it and annotated the drawing to share my interpretation of its message with Martin. I labeled the xin line, "an underline meant to emphasize the importance of the heart."

When Martin examined my annotated illustration, he pointed to the xin and exclaimed in a loud corrective tone, "That's China!"

As I mentioned earlier, Martin had predicted a nuclear attack involving China. With that still fresh in my mind, I mistakenly thought that he viewed the Tablet's message from a geopolitical perspective, while I saw it representing the Triality of human consciousness and how we must attentively follow our Superconscious-Soul.

Thinking that our viewpoints where too far apart for further discussion, I didn't know what to say. Speechless, I stood up and Martin retrieved the Tablet. Being astonished, confused, and feeling out of place, I simply thanked Martin, gave him a copy of my draft and left.

After leaving Martin's cabin I took some time to draw another illustration of the Tablet as accurately as I could. Since I had just drawn the image and annotated it, my memory of it was very clear.

Then, a few years later, when I was showing my illustration to a woman who had studied acupuncture in China, she told me that the underline looked like the Chinese xin symbol. I Googled, "meaning of xin" and was amazed by how well the definition fit the Soul and its home—the human heart. So, it wasn't until a few years after my visit to Hopiland that the confusion about China was finally resolved.

Then, just one year ago, I noticed how the three dots fit the head-heart-gut Triality. While looking for supporting evidence, I found the research paper mentioned above. Although it didn't discuss the dots, that paper supported everything I had written about the Soul. Finally, this little, but important, piece of the puzzle was fit tightly in place.

With that confirmation explained, I'll interpret the Tablet.

First of all, the symbols along the Tablet's right edge clearly support the Head-Heart-Gut Triality of Human Consciousness.

Next, the snake emerging from the gut has a "V" on top of her head. The V symbol has been used to represent the feminine polarity for ages, making that snake feminine. Since the gut is the emotional feminine polarity of human consciousness, the feminine snake fits the Triality model.

The other snake is coming down from the masculine head. Since that snake doesn't have a V on its head, it would make sense for it to be masculine, further aligning with the Triality model of human consciousness which associates the head with masculine intelligence.

These snakes cross next to the xin symbol. Then, after crossing, one extends up and the other dives downward. This split provides an appearance of opening. Putting all of this together, these snakes and the symbols on the right could be a symbolic depiction of the Heart-Opening Breath presented earlier in Chapter 17. Here's how:

The snakes emerge from the upper and lower polarities going toward the middle to converge next to the xin. That corresponds to the inhale that draws from above and below into the heart. Then, the snakes cross at the heart-mind where the mixing of the red and white takes place. Finally, the snake's heads extend apart from each other corresponding to the exhale which involves opening the heart.

Then there's the swastika-like symbol located in the upper left corner. That symbol has a long history with Native American people. One Native American meaning for that symbol is, "the union of the Sun and Earth." This meaning corresponds to the Heart-Opening Breath's Father Sky essence and Mother Earth essence uniting in the heart, where they mix together to become pink loving wholeness. Therefore, the swastika-like symbol tightens the fit between the Tablet and the Heart-Opening Breath technique.

Finally, there's the upward-pointing triangle that's intermingled with the intestines in the gut symbol. An acquaintance showed me how this triangle is balanced by a downward-pointing triangle hidden up in the head symbol.

The three dots in the head—the mouth and the two eyes—are vertices of a triangle. By connecting them with three lines, a downward-pointing triangle is revealed. Then, by bringing the two triangles together and overlapping them inside the Heart-Center circle, the image on the right is formed. Gray lines are included to connect the three dots and form the downward-pointing triangle. This relocation of the triangles is suggested by the path of the snakes and by the way the triangles themselves point toward each other and toward the circle located in-between them.

This result is very similar to the Hindu mandala shown on the right. The following description accompanied this mandala.

*"In Hindu, the six-pointed star is generally understood to consist of two triangles – one pointed up and the other down – locked in harmonious embrace. The two components symbolize humanities' position between **Earth and sky**. The downward triangle symbolizes Shakti, the sacred embodiment of **femininity**, and the upward triangle symbolizes Shiva, the **focused aspects of masculinity**. The union of the two triangles represents **creation, occurring through the divine union of masculine and feminine**."*

This supports the Supreme Power of Wholeness principal that provides the Soul with the divine powers of conception and creation. I was intuitively guided to this Hindu image and the associated explanation which is yet another confirmation.

All of this is surprisingly consistent with the Heart-Opening Breath and the Triality of consciousness that I had shared with Martin the day before he placed the Tablet in my hands. I had drawn pictures of the breathing method and the Triality of consciousness. I also annotated them, and even had Martin read a portion of the old draft describing the breathing technique. On top of that, I had repeatedly emphasized the paramount importance of the Soul in the heart.

So, even though this master copy of the Tablet is held in secret and used to verify that a person who presents the missing piece has the genuine piece and not a counterfeit, Martin decided to show it to me. It seems nearly certain that he did that because of how closely the Tablet matched the pictures and ideas I had already shared with him.

Later, on my way out of Hopiland, I attempted to discuss the Tablet with Wayland, the Hopi man that had provided a place for me to sleep. He explained that he had never seen either of those sacred tablets. On top of that, he said that very few Hopi people had seen them.

When I met Martin, I had no idea he was so important. His home was a very simple cabin with hardly any furniture. Afterwards, when I discovered that he was the most revered Hopi elder, I was amazed by how open-hearted, humble and accommodating he was.

Meeting with him and seeing the Tablet filled me with inspiration to continue writing about and sharing the Heart-Opening Breath. Additionally, even though my visit was short, I felt a tremendous amount of gratitude and respect for the Hopi people and especially Martin.

Sadly, Martin passed on. Hopefully he reincarnated and is growing up so he can be part of the full blossoming of love here on Earth.

HOPI COSMOLOGY

The Hopi cosmology contains background information that helps in fully understanding Prophecy Rock and the Tiponi Tablet.

Their cosmology explains that there have been four worlds or ages of humanity so far. We're currently in the fourth world, and soon the fifth, and last world, or age will begin. The last age will correspond to what I've been guided to name the Age of Love.

The Hopi explain that each time humanity transitions from one age to the next, it splits into two groups:

1. A large group of people who pass away during the shift.

2. A small group of people who survive to live on after the shift.

In the most recent transition, humanity shifted from the third world to the current fourth world. That transition was brought about by the Great Flood. The Hopi explain that they brought the Tiponi Tablet with them when they survived that flood over 6,000 years ago.

While waiting for the True White Brother to arrive with the missing corner, the Hopi have been conscientious caretakers, passing the Tablet on from one generation to the next for thousands of years!

According to the Hopi people, the Tablet's message explains how to become the fifth and final form of human, what they refer to as a "Great Spirit in human form." The people who fit that description will survive the upcoming transition into the final age—the Age of Love.

My Soul guided me to recognize how someone who lives with their heart wide open as they surrender to their Soul's guidance has actually surrendered to the One-Who-Is-All, making them the Great Spirit in human form.

THE BACK OF THE TIPONI TABLET

To obtain the full meaning behind the Tiponi Tablet, the back-side, which is illustrated on the right, needs to be taken into account. This headless stick-figure links to the headless figures originally depicted on Prophecy Rock that is shown again below.

I labeled the important elements with letters and arrows to facilitate the written interpretation that follows. Interpretations that already exist for this petroglyph contain a common thread; of the two paths that end at "M" and "O", the one ending at "O" corresponds to a final age of peace on Earth that proceeds to the end of time. The jagged path ending at "M" is not peaceful and ends quite a bit earlier.

The Hopi men who showed this to me, explained that the four figures, labeled "L," were originally headless and are referred to as the "two-hearted." This term fits Pragmatic people who follow two minds, the head- and gut-minds, but not the heart-mind or Soul.

307

The Hopi call the single figure "N," "one-hearted" which corresponds to the Romantic people who follow their central heart.

Stepping back to consider the entire petroglyph, what follows shows how it aligns with the Consciousness-Origin Cosmology.

First of all, the line that begins down at "A" and goes up to "D" and then all the way across to "O" is a timeline extending from the being of time "A", to the end of time "O". Alpha to Omega, so to speak.

The circles "C", "F", "G", and "I" are milestones.

"C" corresponds to the advent of humans. "B" is an Original-Person with a feather sticking out his head. He touches the timeline to indicate the meaning of the first milestone "C."

"D" is the split in humanity that separates the Romantic givers from the Pragmatic takers who have bigger egos. To depict their self-importance, the Pragmatics are located on an elevated path.

The first section of the dual path going from "D" to "E" is the period of time when Atlantis, Mu and possibly other places where used to experiment with different types of divisive methods.

The shift at "K" corresponds to the Great Flood which involved clearing the slate and thereafter using the best divisive system.

"F" could be the arrival of the white man to the Americas which was a very impactful event for Native Americans.

"G" could be the arrival of electric and phone to Oraibi. In 1906, that opportunity caused a historical split in the Hopi people between traditionalists and modernists. The traditionalists formed a new settlement called Hotevilla which is where Martin lived the old-way.

"H" is a line representing the last chance for Pragmatics to reconnect with their Soul and come down to the lower line by humbly surrendering to their Soul's inner guidance.

"I" is a milestone that only has an upper half. It represents the beginning of the final age in which the divisive portion of humanity is not included. This is the beginning of the Age of Love that takes place on the physical Earth. The corn plant labeled "J" and the Romantic "one-hearted" person labeled "N" insure that this lower line corresponds to the physical Earth plane.

The transitional part of the petroglyph is enlarged on the next page so you can see the details.

First, let's focus on the one-hearted Romantic labeled "N":

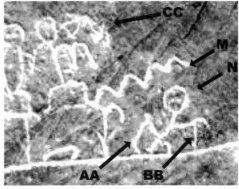

The line labeled "AA" is a digging stick used by the Hopi to plant beans and corn. "BB" indicates that seeds are being broadcast by hand. These features, plus the corn plant just to the left of the farmer, indicate a return to simple natural living for the one-hearted Romantics who inherit the Earth.

Moving upward, a zigzag line "M" symbolizes a path through the upper and lower astral realms that will be encountered by the Pragmatics who ascend away from Earth. This short path ends long before the lower path does—confirming the Pragmatic's early departure.

The funky blob labeled "CC" is indiscernible. This blob could be interpreted to indicate how the upper and lower layers of the astral realm adapt to fit each visitor's desires, which could be anything. So, that blob could represent different things for different people.

In summary, the two options are:

1. **ascension** up to the astral to fulfill one's desires or

2. **inheritance** of the Earth to live till the end of time.

Thus, Prophecy Rock and the Tiponi Tablet very strongly support the thesis of this book, which has remained essentially the same over the ten years that have passed since I wrote the early draft that I shared with Martin. What has changed over those years is the growing amount of support for the Consciousness-Origin Cosmology and the Triality of human consciousness. For example, upon my return to Maui, I found more remarkable support.

BACK IN HAWAI'I

Once back on Maui, I shared the story of my Hopi adventure with some friends. A couple of them knew a very interesting fellow named Jeff Munoz who was adopted by a famous Hawaiian kahuna, Daddy Bray. Moreover, they claimed that Bray had an extraordinary connection with the Hopi people.

I called Jeff and he asked, "Who are you and what are you about?"

I was intuitively guided to offer him an e-copy of the draft that already had the Hopi story added to it. I explained that it conveyed who I was and what I was about. At that time, it was only a hundred pages long. Jeff gave me his email address and I sent him a copy.

About a month later he called me and said he had read the book and discovered that it contained what Daddy Bray had taught him. Jeff wanted to meet me and asked if I would be willing to come up to his remote hermitage. I had already heard about the legendary Daddy Bray who had passed away in 1968. He was considered by many to have been the most knowledgeable kahuna of the twentieth century. Many people claimed that Bray was actually able to perform miracles. Therefore, I was very interested in hearing more about how my book was similar to what Bray had taught Jeff.

I ought to mention that Jeff is a reclusive man who lives in a hermitage that he built. I found him to be a very humble person who lives a simple life. We met in 2009. At that time, he was working on his book, *Islands of Refuge: Adventures with a Living Kahuna*, published September 2012. Some of what follows is documented therein.

Between that visit, and some additional research that came from books that a friend of mine loaned me, I discovered some very interesting connections between my work and legendary Hawaiian spiritual wisdom, which has remained clouded by secrecy even today.

THE KAHUNA SECRET

To begin with, the literal meaning of kahuna is "keeper of the secret." "Ka" means "keeper," and "huna" means "secret." The word kahuna has evolved to mean "a master trained in one of a wide variety of specific areas of knowledge." The evolution of "kahuna" is very similar to how "esoteric" came to mean "specialized knowledge."

Bray fit the original literal meaning of the word. He had been considered the leading authority on the secret spiritual knowledge of the Hawaiian people. Even though people had witnessed Bray perform miracles, he refused to share the secret behind the magic with people who inquired. Despite that, Bray adopted Jeff Munoz and while training him, Bray revealed the secret.

To share it with you, I'll begin by defining the Hawaiian terms for the three portions of human consciousness.

> The conscious-mind in the head is named 'uhane.

> The superconscious-mind is named, 'Aumakua.

> The subconscious-mind in the gut is named 'unihipili.

The Hawaiian 'uhane and 'unihipili are even defined to be located in the head and gut respectively. The 'Aumakua is the Hawaiian name for the portion of human consciousness that has the power to perform miracles. Those miracles had made the Hawaiian kahuna legendary and had awarded Daddy Bray great respect.

The following deceptions hid the 'Aumakua's true location:

> The 'Aumakua represents one's ancestors.

> There are 'Aumakua spirit animals like owls, sharks, etc.

> The 'Aumakua is a person's guardian angel that hovers up above them.

Despite those popular claims, Bray revealed to Jeff that **the kahuna secret is that the powerful 'Aumakua resides in the human heart!**

According to Jeff, Bray emphasized, multiple times, that **the most important thing is to get to know the 'Aumakua in your heart.** He further explained to Jeff that the 'Aumakua is one's mother father god within, their True-Self. Obviously, the 'Aumakua is the Hawaiian name for the Superconscious-Soul that resides in the heart.

Because the 'Aumakua, or Soul, has the power to perform supernatural miracles, the kahuna kept the location of it secret. This secret was only shared with an apprentice while being trained to be a kahuna. Jeff was being trained by Bray, who had adopted him as his son.

Thankfully, Jeff had found, in my early draft, that I already discovered the location and power of the 'Aumakua.

MIRACLES

On a very dry, crystal clear day, Jeff witnessed Daddy Bray enlist the 'Aumakua's supernatural power to make it rain near Kona on the Big Island—Hawai'i. Even though no clouds could be seen, and despite how arid the Kona area is, after Bray made his request a dark cloud formed in the sky, and out of it, a heavy rain poured down.

Bray performed this miracle as part of Jeff's training to demonstrate what the power of the 'Aumakua can do. Later, Jeff witnessed more miracles in which Bray revealed additional powers.

These examples convinced Jeff that the powers are undeniably real. Three examples are detailed in Jeff's book, *Islands of Refuge*.

In all three cases, Daddy Bray used the power in a humble way that didn't involve gaining recognition for himself. He used the power in a demonstration that was part of Jeff's training, for safety, and to save Jeff's life when a fatal condition was progressing quickly.

I asked Jeff why most people believe one or more of the three deceptions about 'Aumakua that are listed on the previous page, while the truth is that 'Aumakua reside in human hearts. In response, Jeff explained that kahuna had concerns that some people might misuse the power of their 'Aumakua. Additionally, they believed that the power could only be accessed if a person knew where their 'Aumakua was located. Therefore, the heart location became a very tightly held secret while misinformation was given to the general public. Keeping this secret was considered so important that the people who held it were named "kahuna," meaning "keepers of the secret."

I'm not concerned that the supernatural powers possessed by our Souls can be misused if people learn where the Soul is located. Instead, I'm convinced that Souls are in control and will only accommodate requests that are in alignment with the grand plan of the One-Who-Is-All. 'Aumakua are guardians, and the basic plan has been clear from the beginning of time. These guardians use their Supreme Power of Wholeness to help the plan unfold successfully.

All Souls, or 'Aumakua, as well as all entities that possess the Supreme Power of Wholeness, are divine portions of the One-Who-Is-All. They're all working together to accomplish the One's grand plan.

FALSE TEACHINGS

Even though the Way-of-the-Heart message shared in this book is in alignment with what Daddy Bray taught Jeff, there are many people who teach a very different message and claim they're teaching the ancient Hawaiian spiritual wisdom, even though they're not. Ironically, what they teach is appropriate for Pragmatic people as I will explain here.

Max Freedom Long studied Hawaiian kahuna for many years and wrote several books about their famous miracles. For example, *The Secret Science Behind Miracles* was published in 1948.

Some of Long's books used the term "huna" to name the spiritual kahuna practices that he investigated and wrote about. Even though he openly admitted in his books that there was something that kahuna seemed to be keeping from him, he also believed that he had uncovered the secret. Long claim that 'Aumakua hover above people like guardian angels, but he was wrong. Kahuna had successfully kept the secret heart location hidden from Long.

Today, many people teach Long's huna theory or something like it, combined with other ideas like "the power of attraction" that are ultimately ego-expanding methods to quench one's desires. This makes those teachings appropriate for Pragmatics. Ironically, these teachers call what they're teaching "huna," which means "secret," even though they don't know the secret location of 'Aumakua.

This is an exquisite example of the hidden nature of Quintessential Cores. In this case, the 'Aumakua or Soul, the center of the human Triality of consciousness, is so well hidden that Long's years of looking failed to uncovered it. Moreover, Long's misinformation has introduced a false "Huna Teaching" that has spread around the world.

Of course, no one is aware of what they don't know. The "huna" teachers that I've met, believe that what they're teaching is accurate. They're doing their best to share what they believe to be true. It's not their fault that they were misinformed.

Having provided all this background on kahuna, Daddy Bray, and the secret location of the 'Aumakua, it's time to close the circle and share Bray's interlocking connection with the Hopi elders.

THE HAWAI'I-HOPI CONNECTION

According to Jeff, Daddy Bray was guided to go to the mainland to meet some spiritual people. Bray obligingly flew to California. Once there, Bray found his humble Way-of-the-Heart path to be completely different than the glamorous ascension path zealously promoted by the new age spiritual people he encountered.

Without being able to find humble people on the Way-of-the-Heart path, Bray was about to give up and head back to Hawai'i when a man asked him if he was Hopi. Bray hadn't heard of the Hopi, so the man filled him in and told Bray that he looked Hopi. Finally, he claimed the things Bray said sounded like things the Hopi people say.

Consequently, Daddy Bray went to Hopiland. When he arrived, the Hopi elders recognized him as one of their own and invited him into their elder's kiva (an underground meeting place).

Once inside their kiva, the elders told Bray that they originally came from Mu. When that continent was sinking, they traveled from one atoll to the next until they arrived on what are now called the Hawaiian Islands. Several of the survivors chose to remain in Hawai'i, while most continued to what is now named Central America.

From there, the Hopi traveled to the four extremes of the Americas: south to the tip of South America, north to the Arctic Circle, east to the east coast of North America, and west to the west coast. Finally, many settled in a central location, where they live today in Hopiland. Along the way, some of the Hopi stopped and decided to inhabit various locations along their migration route. The people who chose to shorten their migration include various Native American people throughout North, South and Central America.

The Hopi elders further explained to Bray that about a thousand years ago, the elders received a psychic distress call from their relatives that had remained in the Hawaiian Islands. In response to the call for help, a group of Hopi men decided to walk to the west coast of North America, carve out a giant canoe, and paddle it out to the islands in an effort to help their brothers.

Finally, the elders confessed to Bray that they didn't know what had happened to this group of men who answered the distress call. Did they make it to the islands, and if they did reach Hawai'i, were they able to help? They asked Bray if he had heard a story about men coming to Hawai'i in a big canoe about a thousand years ago?

Bray told the elders that he had heard a story about men coming to Hawai'i in a big canoe about a thousand years ago, but he explained that the difficulty was that the Tahitians had arrived. The Tahitians being very large, fierce warriors, killed most of the peaceful, smaller people who originally inhabited Hawai'i. Still, some survived.

So, even though men in a big canoe had arrived, and it was about a thousand years ago, those men who arrived were not able to stop the Tahitian warriors. The big, aggressive Tahitians took control of Hawai'i. They erected hierarchical power structures with royalty, rules, and penalties that included beheadings. Battles between various island leaders became commonplace and finally ended about 800 years later in 1821 when Queen Ka'ahumanu, as Regent of the Kingdom, married Kaumuali'i, the hereditary chief-king of Kaua'i and Ni'ihau.

Supposedly, the Hopi made the big canoe out of a California redwood log. I found support for this on the Waimea website:

"It was reported that some of the largest Hawaiian canoes were carved from California redwood logs... In the 1870s there was a 108-foot long hull that was said to have been discovered, which is now gone." [28]

THE MOST SACRED SONG

After answering the Hopi elders' question, Bray told them that he felt guided to sing a song for them. He explained that the song was the most sacred song he knew. Additionally, it was only to be sung under specific circumstances. Even though sitting in a kiva wasn't the correct circumstances, he still felt that he ought to sing this sacred song.

The elders encouraged Bray to sing. Then, when Bray began singing, the Hopi elders sang along with him; they knew the words. When the song was finished, the elders explained to Bray that this song is their most sacred song. Moreover, they only sing it in the elder's kiva, right where they just sang it. Accordingly, most of the Hopi people don't know the song.

Finally, they asked Bray, "How is it that you know our most sacred song?"

Of course, this confirms the Hopi story. Some of their people must have stayed in Hawai'i. Those people passed that song along to Daddy Bray. These early Hawaiians are legendary. The stories I've heard claim that they had no leaders. Instead, they followed their hearts, did their part and shared cooperatively with their neighbors.

This is how the Hopi people have always lived.

THE HOPI WAY OF LIFE

Even today, the Hopi don't believe in hierarchical leadership making them a very unique type of agrarian village people. They were never relocated by the white man. They never signed a treaty with the United States of America. Even though Hopiland is geographically located inside the 2,500-square-mile Four Corners Native American Reservation which lies in the northeastern corner of Arizona, the Hopi remain a sovereign nation and have produced and successfully used their own passports. The oldest Hopi village, Oraibi, has been inhabited continuously for over 2,600 years, making it the longest, continuously inhabited village in North America.

The name Hopi is short for Hopituh Shi-nu-mu, which means "The Peaceful People," or "Peaceful Little Ones." These people embody the ideals of humbly following one's heart. Rather than following leaders, the Hopi expect everyone to live in accordance with what is true, deep within their hearts.

HAWAI'I-HOPI DESCENDANTS

As for the Hopi who remained in Hawai'i, history has twisted things quite a bit. The peaceful people of ancient Hawai'i appear to have been transformed into mythical Menehune, legendary dwarfs who work at night building stone structures, and then hide in the forest in the daytime. Some people claim to have caught a glimpse of these Menehune. In the same way that modern civilization has a tendency to misrepresent Original-People and in some cases, ignore their existence, the Original-Hawaiians have become a myth.

Over the twenty-one years that I've lived on Maui, Hawai'i, I've met many Hawaiians who are open-hearted yet cautious. Moreover, these gentle Hawaiians are usually physically small- to normal-size. I've also met big, arrogant locals who deny the legend of pre-Tahitian inhabitants. So, even though the myth of the Menehune is predominant, and the legend of the peaceful little people is little-known, some of the peaceful little ones have survived along with their legend.

For instance, I recently met a Hawaiian who was about my age. After telling him what is presented in this chapter, he explained to me that he still lives on family land near La Perouse Bay, Maui. He further explained that his great grandmother was a kahuna and that she told him that the power was in his heart. He gave me a hug, and as we parted, we put our hands on our hearts and bowed our heads.

In, *Maui A History*, by Cummins E. Speakmans, Jr., I found remarkable support for the presence of Hopi near La Perouse Bay. This history book reports that on May 30, 1786, Admiral La Perouse landed on Maui in what is now known as La Perouse Bay. There he found a village of little people standing an average height of 5 foot 3 inches tall. The physical features he noted match the Hopi people right down to their traditional haircut which includes bangs cut straight across the forehead making their hair look like a helmet. Regarding their peaceful attitude, La Perouse wrote, "I had no idea of a people so mild and attentive."

PRAYING FOR RAIN: A FINALE HOPI-HAWAI'I LINKAGE

There's another connection between the Hopi and Daddy Bray. The Hopi live in a desert without a river anywhere nearby. They plant their corn and bean seeds nine inches deep, using a digging stick to make a deep hole. Then, to water their crops, they perform ceremonies asking for rain. There are springs from which they carry some water to drink and supplement the rain, but their prayers for rain have been the miraculous key to their survival. People visit Hopiland in order to witness, firsthand, the legendary rain ceremonies.

For over 2,600 years, these humble generous people have been praying for rain in a desert that has no river for miles. Their prayers for rain have brought the water needed to grow their beans and corn.

Daddy Bray also knew how to pray for rain. As I explained earlier, the key is the Soul or 'Aumakua that resides in the heart.

SO MANY LINKAGES

How could all of this be possible: a California redwood canoe in Hawai'i; a Tablet from Mu depicting the Triality of human consciousness; Hopi elders and a Hawaiian kahuna with the same most sacred song; and people in a desert praying for rain for over 2,600 years?

Moreover, how did all of this just happen to fall into my lap?

These linkages interlocked like pieces of a puzzle strengthening my confidence in the Triality of human consciousness model, the Superconscious-Soul, and the prophesies for a peaceful Age of Love.

The Tiponi Tablet is real, the petroglyph is real, and the Hopi people—the peaceful little ones—are still following their hearts.

Earlier, on pages 158 and 159, I provided a picture showing physical remains of the legendary continent of Mu. If Mu was an advanced culture, as the legends claim, and the Hopi and Hawaiian kahuna obtained their knowledge about the Triality of human consciousness from Mu, that would explain how these seemingly less advanced people possess a more complete understanding of human consciousness than modern neuroscience and psychology has developed so far. The people of Mu must have known about the Superconscious-Soul in our Heart-Center. The exquisitely manufactured Tiponi Tablet certainly indicates that the Triality of consciousness was known before the Great Flood.

China is located on the western side of where Mu once stood. This is where the xin, heart-mind symbol is in use today. Archeological evidence of Chinese script has been dated to over 5,000 years old. If some of the people who survived the sinking of Mu headed west to what is now called China, and they knew what the Hawaiians and the Hopi knew, they could have encoded the knowledge regarding the Triality of human consciousness and the importance of the heart-mind into their xin symbol. It's well-known that the three most important tantiens in Chinese Taoism are the head, heart and gut.

Combining all that has been shared in this chapter together, the support from Hopiland, Hawai'i, and Mu provides substantial support for what I've been guided to share in these pages.

To connect all of this back to the Mesopotamian civilization that grew to dominate the Earth, I was guided by my Soul to offer the following linkage that was briefly mentioned earlier.

A LINK TO MESOPOTAMIA: THE CADUCEUS

On the opposite side of the Earth from Mu, which was located in the Central Pacific Ocean, is Mesopotamia. This is where the Garden of Eden was located. It's the birth-place of the Judea-Christian-Muslim civilization that spread all around the world. The

well-known Caduceus symbol, shown on the left, originated in Mesopotamia. The oldest artifact containing the Caduceus symbol has been dated to be 6,000 years old. Therefore, the Caduceus and the Tiponi Tablet (shown again on the next page) are both approximately 6,000 years old.

As you can see they both feature two snakes indicating that a linkage between them might exist.

The popular interpretation of the Caduceus proposes that a person must rise up out of their emotional, physically dense, lower polarity to elevate themselves up toward a higher way of life to fly like an angle into the heavenly realms. The way the snakes are moving up toward the wings is claimed to imply flying upward to escape the dense lower polarity of the physical realm. In a word, the popular view of the Caduceus suggests ascension.

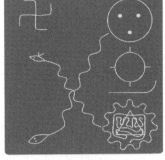

Putting aside that popular view to take into account the Tiponi Tablet's message, my Soul offered a very different way to interpret the Caduceus.

First of all, the meaning of the snakes is changed to align with the Tablet. One of the Caduceus snakes is seen to represent the intellectual conscious-mind in the head, while the other snake represents the emotional subconscious-mind in the gut. Then, because the staff is located in-between the two snakes, the staff corresponds to the Soul in the heart forming the head-heart-gut Triality of consciousness.

The wings of the staff symbolize the divine nature of the Soul and the spherical ball on top represents the Soul's wholeness that aligns with the Supreme Power of Wholeness principal making that central portion of consciousness holy.

The way both of the snakes are wrapped around the staff with their attention fixed firmly on it indicates that the head and gut portions of human consciousness ought to pay close attention to the Superconscious-Soul in the middle. By embracing the staff and staring at it intently, the snakes are certainly indicating that the winged staff, crowned with wholeness, is the most important part of this symbol.

Oddly, popular interpretations simply identify the staff as a spine that goes from our lower polarity up to our upper polarity. If the staff is so unimportant then why does it have wings and why are the snakes embracing the staff and staring at it so intently?

Based on everything that has been presented in this book, it seems highly probable that the staff could have originally been intended to represent the human Soul, our Tree of Life in the Garden of Eden. If that's true, then the message that the Caduceus may have originally been intended to convey is how the head and gut minds ought to embrace the Soul and fix their attention on the divine genius that resides in-between them.

That message is equivalent to what is more obviously conveyed by the Tiponi Tablet which clearly identifies the location of the important component to be in the Heart-Center. The Tiponi also clearly associates one snake with the head and the other with the gut, making the Tiponi Tablet's message much easier to decode.

The Tablet has additional information on the back that links it with the Prophecy Rock petroglyph. The Hopi people have been conscientious caretakers who know that the Tablet symbolically depicts how to become the Great Spirit in human form—the fifth and final type of human who will inherit the Earth.

Most spiritual people ignore the bewildering meek inherit the earth prophecy to instead consider the more popular ascension path. The popular exoteric belief is to reach higher for a connection with the divine that resides outside oneself, in heaven. This ascension path, in which higher is better, has spread all around the Earth. It's the preferred path for Pragmatic people who are clearly the majority.

It's also possible that the Caduceus was intentionally designed to fit both interpretations so everyone can interpret the Caduceus to fit their path regardless of whether they're interested in ascension or the Way-of-the-Heart. The Tiponi Tablet has the ascension option on its back side as shown again on the left.

For Romantic people who follow the Way-of-the-Heart path, inward is the key when it comes to looking for divine guidance. This middle way has lead me to the most wonderful experiences of my life. I've met other people who believe their choice to follow their hearts has led to blessings beyond their wildest dreams.

The paradoxical claim, "he who gives shall receive," seems to apply to a person following their heart in a generous way, giving what they are guided to give. Then without asking and without expectation, abundant blessings are bestowed on the giver. The Soul, using its divine power, wisdom and knowledge of the future, is able to reward its host in ways that are perfectly fitting and astonishingly well-timed.

Conversely, Pragmatic takers end up suffering and consequently develop desires to end their suffering. Eventually, ascending to heaven is widely acclaimed to be the ultimate solution.

So, it seems that the Tiponi Tablet and the Caduceus both contain messages for Romantics and Pragmatics. When it comes to the back of the Tablet, that headless image may provide too much information for Pragmatic people who mistakenly believe that death is a final end,

320

even though it is just a shift over to the afterlife side of the veil. A shift that includes obtaining the powers to fly and create your own reality.

WHY IS THE SOUL AND THE WAY-OF-THE-HEART SO HIDDEN?

For the Hawaiian kahuna, it seems that keeping the location of the 'Aumakua secret developed out of self-preservation. The invasion of the Tahitians and their conquest of the Hawaiian Islands must have pressed the peaceful little people to keep their powerful knowledge secret.

Beyond that, it seems the divine nature and location of the Soul has been hidden or obscured by more than the Hawaiian kahuna.

I showed at the end of Chapter 1 how all major religions have references in their scriptures that identify some sort of connection to the One-Who-Is-All in our hearts. Despite that, most of the scriptures expound on the father who resides in Heaven where our spirit goes when we die. Thus, the teachings that locate the divine outside and above are much more prevalent, while the rare but more precious references point to the heart.

Additionally, it's common in Christian churches to claim that the spiritual leader who stands at the pulpit is the conduit through which God speaks to the parishioners sitting in the pews. This arrangement denies the heart connection to the Holy Spirit even though it exists.

For example, Quakers who are Christian, but few in number, sit in a circle waiting for someone to be moved by Holy Spirit within themselves. When someone is so moved, they stand up and share what has emerged. This makes every member of a Quaker meeting a potential conduit for the One to speak to the group.

Both perspectives exist, and one is appropriate for Pragmatics while the other aligns with the Romantics.

The popular exoteric view of the One being an external divine being works very well for Pragmatic people.

On the other hand, when it comes to Romantic people, developing a relationship with the Soul within is their key to happiness, love, genius, intuition, and many other magnificent blessings.

My Soul advised me that the Way-of-the-Heart path has received much less notoriety for two main reasons.

First of all, the Way-of-the-Heart path applies to a minority of people.

More importantly, if the details about the two paths were well-known, that would make it more difficult to sort out which people have a natural disposition to follow their Souls and those who are not naturally inclined to do so. This is because knowledge of the benefits could persuade a selfish person to endeavor to follow their heart in order to reap the miraculous benefits, not because following their heart is what they naturally feel drawn to.

Because this book spills the beans, I've wondered if it's appropriate to publish it. Intuitively, I feel reassured that it's time to let the cat out of the bag. The benefit of helping people to follow their heart outweighs the danger of people trying to fake it.

Even if someone tried to fake following the Way-of-the-Heart path, their Soul would be fully aware of that person's intentions, simply because a person's Soul knows all of their thoughts.

In regard to the benefits, many people have thanked me for sharing this book's message and told me that early versions improved their connection to their Soul and enhanced their lives.

So, it seems that the time has come to put all the cards on the table and see where the chips fall.

If you have intuition, your Superconscious-Soul has all the happiness, love, knowledge and miraculous powers you'll ever need.

If you're a Pragmatic and you want to explore the intuitive Romantic path, try using the decalcification method offered at the end of Chapter 19.

Regardless of who you are or what you believe, a magnificent consciousness resides in your heart. Some have named this inner divine consciousness the 'Aumakua, others the Holy Spirit, the Tao, the Atman, etc. I chose to label this divine guardian the Superconscious-Soul. Regardless of the name you may prefer to use, if you are drawn to look within, I hope what has been shared in this book helps you deepen your relationship with this magnificent part of yourself.

Chapter 24
Conclusion

TURNING REALITY RIGHT-SIDE-UP

When consciousness is placed at the foundation of the universe, mysteries that couldn't be solved from a materialistic perspective practically solve themselves.

For example, the way birds fly in formation, moving as if they're one organism, is easily explained: Their Souls connect through the continuum of consciousness to choreograph the flight pattern. A similar explanation would be true for schools of fish or herds of land mammals.

Beyond those specific examples of inexplicable behavior, the more general idea of animal instincts, which has never been adequately explained, can be easily explained to be Soul-intuition.

Having experience as a mechanical engineer, I've been especially impressed by the way little spiders build intricate webs with brilliantly devised supporting strands. I've even seen support strands that cross over a river, allowing the web to be positioned in the center of the river where flying insects are common. These eight legged engineers even employ gravity to provide a third direction of tension by hanging a leaf from their horizontal support structure. Then with added triangulation the tiny spider forms a beautiful web that shimmers in the sunlight and leaves me truly amazed.

Often the head of a spider is as small as the head of a pin, making the source of engineering knowledge needed to build magnificent spider webs inexplicable—from the materialistic point of view. However, since consciousness is formless and nonphysical, a functional portion that knows how to build webs can reside inside a spider, regardless of how small that spider is.

We live in a world in which nature has countless marvels to consider, and so many of those wonders evade explanation by materialistic science. In spite of that, a consciousness-based perspective of reality provides simple sensible answers to those same realities. When the universe is upside-down, that mistake fosters outrageously complex theories. However, with the universe turned right-side-up, simple explanations become obvious.

Max Plank, Rupert Sheldrake, David Chalmers, and Robert Lanza have taken bold steps by confronting the dogmatic "religion" of materialistic science. Their leadership toward a consciousness-based model of the universe paves the way for other open-minded scientists to follow. Certainly, others are already following their lead.

As this monumental shift to a consciousness-based reality takes place, and it must, spirituality and science will merge into one universal truth. Hopefully, both sides will be willing to drop their dogmatic beliefs and embrace a view in which consciousness resides at the foundation of everything.

All the names for the One-Who-Is-All surely point to the singular consciousness that formed the spectacular semi-parallel universe that includes Heaven and Earth. Rather than getting caught up in specific names, particular events, methods of worship, or even believing in a "God," everyone, even atheists, can embrace the idea that the entire universe has a foundation of consciousness.

Call the One-Who-Is-All what you prefer to call it. Live the way you choose to live. Worship as you choose, or as you choose not to. The consciousness model presented in this book offers an acceptance of beliefs that embraces popular religions and even most of science as it is. Everyone can continue their way of life, maintaining their core beliefs while opening to seeing how the underlying foundation of consciousness offers a unifying principle that has the potential to relax tensions that have divided numerous factions for thousands of years.

Some scientists and mental health practitioners could benefit by taking what has been presented in these pages seriously.

Given adequate time, the Triality model of reality presented in this book could be expanded upon by others and eventually make the antiquated materialistic model of reality obsolete.

In due time, we will see what actually takes place.

THE MAGNIFICENT SOUL

On a personal level, if this message about the Soul rang true for you, then you may be wondering how to begin deepening your relationship with your Soul.

Here are a couple of simple suggestions and some advice:

When you wake up tomorrow, do the Heart-Opening Breath (or an equivalent) while sitting on the edge of your bed, or in whatever position feels best to you. By opening your heart soon after you wake up, you'll begin your day in the joyful state of being in love, walking the Red Road of Beauty to see beauty everywhere. It only takes a few minutes, so do this every morning from now on.

If you do, then every day of the rest of your life will begin with your heart open—in a state of love. This change will deepen your relationship with your Soul and enrich your life with love and happiness. This practice changed my life. If you do it, it could change yours, too.

In the REMEMBERING TO BREATH section presented on page 232, I shared how to use a wristwatch with a repeating countdown timer to remind yourself to practice the Heart-Opening Breath throughout the day. I enthusiastically recommend doing that!

The documentary movie, "The Power of The Heart" is inspiring and supportive of what is offered in this book. Watching it will help to stoke the fire that's alive in your heart. It's available on Youtube.com.

Here: https://www.youtube.com/watch?v=H6fr2omaNXU

If you feel moved to, reread **Part 3** once in a while so you can remind yourself of the tools and techniques that are offered therein. Especially the Soul healing request offered on page 262.

Most of all, listen to your intuition and do what your Soul guides you to do. In the final analysis, that's what it takes to honor the divine consciousness that resides within your heart.

The other key that I've found to be very important is to give my Soul credit, thanking it for the truly magnificent guidance it provides. So, whenever you notice that your Soul assisted you in some way, place your hand over your heart and thank your Soul. Gratitude is very important and tremendously powerful. Even though it's simple to say thank you, when those words are said with sincerity they make a huge difference.

Extend your gratitude to your friends, strangers, and to the entire One-Who-Is-All. The more you offer gratitude, and follow your heart in a generous way, the more blessings you'll receive.

Consider the possibility that you have a purpose that's your personal destiny. As you open your heart wider and surrender deeper, you'll be better able to accomplish your divine mission which will emerge from within. Presumably, you're already on that adventure; may you find many blessings and unexpected treasures along your personal Way-of-the-Heart adventure.

Finally, let your inner child come out to play. Open-hearted living can be quite joyful and effortless. When your childlike wonderment is alive within you, a smile appears on its own indicating that your heart is open.

Happiness is a priceless treasure that comes when your Soul is leading the way.

Contacting the Author

Dear Reader,

Thank you for taking the time to read my book. I hope you enjoyed reading it and will find the message helpful as your life progresses.

My passion is to live the Way-of-the-Heart that's presented in these pages. I love to discuss this subject and share what I've learned through practicing the open-hearted way of life.

I'm available for individual guidance and group presentations.

You're welcome to contact me, via email, at:

magnificentSoul@yahoo.com

Or visit my website: https://www.soulcovenant.org/

The Soul Covenant Organization is dedicated to encouraging people to make a covenant with their Soul to live in accordance with their Soul's guidance.

Then to help these people to follow their heart, this organization endeavors to establish sanctuaries that will be safe havens for people who have made the Soul Covenant and chosen to follow the Live and Let Live Principal. Details are available at the website.

The inspiration that led to this Soul covenant concept is shared in Appendix A which discusses the Ark of the Covenant.

In closing, I offer the idea that the human Soul is quite likely the most precious thing a person can have a positive relationship with.

Blessings and Aloha,

George

Appendix A
The Ark of the Covenant

In this Appendix I show how the famously mysterious Ark of the Covenant fits the primary message in this book—the most important thing in your life, your personal God, resides in your chest.

In 1981 the popular movie "Raiders of the Lost Ark" brought this important Judaic relic into the limelight.

I'll begin by showing how the specific features of the Ark fit the characteristics of the Soul in our heart.

First of all, "ark" means chest which fits the location of the Soul.

Secondly, the Ark was always covered by an animal skin, just as a human chest is also covered with skin. Biblical references explain that the men who carried the Ark never saw it because the animal skin kept it hidden. An artist's interpretation of that is shown on the right.

Thirdly, the Ark contained God's commandments. Specifically, the Ten Commandments written with God's finger on the stone tablets that Moses brought down from Mt. Sinai. In Psalm 37 where King David describes the righteous and the meek he explains that, "the law of their God is written in their hearts." Therefore, the tablets being located inside the Ark could be symbolic of God's laws that are written in our hearts which are located in our chests under our skin. Our intuition and conscience makes us aware of such laws in the very moments that circumstances call forth such guidance.

Fourthly, the Ark contained a pot of mana. The meaning of the word mana is debated. This provides leeway to link it to the Hindu word "prana," and the Hawaiian word "mana" which both mean: life energy, life force or life essence. The Soul, being the Quintessential Core of our Triality of consciousness, is our life essence. In support of this, research has found that 5,000 times as much energy emerges from the heart in comparison to the brain. This huge energy field created by something in the heart can be measured up to fifteen feet from the human body. The source of this energy is not understood. Therefore, it could emerge from the Superconscious-Soul. Thus, our chest could be viewed as a container of life energy or mana that emerges from the Soul. This corresponds to the pot of mana symbol.

Fifthly, the Ark is claimed to contain Aaron's rod which was a staff that had great powers and bore ripe almonds. A depiction of the rod budding is shown on the left.

Staffs are used by shepherds to guide their flock. The Soul guides us which fits with this traditional usage of a staff. Additionally, the Soul is the central component of the mandorla symbol that decorates the cover of this book. Mandorla is Italian for almond which is the shape of the central overlap of the double circle mandorla design. Therefore, the claim that Aaron's rod bore ripe almonds links it to the central component of the mandorla, the Quintessential Core of the human Triality of consciousness. Finally, the rod's miraculous powers are symbolic of the Soul's powers to perform miracles.

Thus, Aaron's rod is linked to the Soul in three ways.

Sixthly, on the Ark's lid there are two cherubim, one at each end as shown in the illustration below. They're looking down toward the

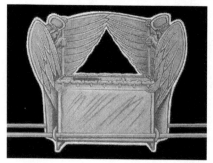

center of the Ark. These cherubim are described to form the space where God will appear in what is called the "mercy seat." These cherubim could be meant to correspond to a person's head and gut minds which ought to pay attention to the Soul's guidance emerging from within one's chest. By doing so, and following the guidance that is provided by the godlike Soul, one is mercifully relieved of the guilt and shame that would accrue if a person disregarded that divine inner guidance.

Finally, the fact that our Souls are invisible and undetectable could explain why so many symbolic relics are purported to reside in the elusive Ark that was always hidden with skin. Each relic identifies one or more of the divine features that all Superconscious-Souls are empowered with.

Ironically, the Ark has been physically lost while our Soul has been all but lost because the upside down materialistic view of reality can't find any physical evidence for it's existence. Only circumstantial evidence has been discovered.

So many important aspects of the Ark link quite readily to the features of the Soul, especially the Superconscious-Soul's magnificent godlike powers and undetectability.

It's very intriguing that the Ark's location is not known. There are several claims regarding the Ark's location, but none have been confirmed.

How could something of this size and importance be lost? Could it be that people have been so focused on looking outside themselves for a physical Ark that they may have overlooked how all the symbols point overwhelmingly to the magnificent Souls that are hidden inside our little hearts? Viewing the Ark this way, the answer to this ancient mystery may have been sitting right under our noses.

Moreover, the covenant may be to open and follow one's heart.

As usual, my dear Soul guided me to view the Ark of the Covenant this way.

Once my research revealed how all of the symbols link our Souls with the Ark of the Covenant, the idea to establish the Soul Covenant Organization came to me intuitively.

If you're interested check out my website:

https://www.SoulCovenant.org

[1] "Electrophysiological Evidence of Intuition: Part 1. The Surprising Role of the Heart" available at www.heartmath.com

[2] "Electrophysiological Evidence of Intuition: Part 2. A System-Wide Process?" available at www.heartmath.com

[3] I read about this research project in a book that was loaned to me. I returned the book and it was loaned out again and lost. Unfortunately, after extensive investigation, I have not been able to find the book that was the source of this information. The book was a silver hard-cover that I recall being published in the 1990's in English, but translated from German. The "infallible voice" research was discussed near the beginning of the book. If you know the name of this book, please contact me at magnificentSoul@yahoo.com

[4] Same as 3 above.

[5] The Apple Application: Dictionary Version 2.2.1 (178)

[6] Psalm 37, English Standard Version of the Holy Bible

[7] Source: **The Quran** Translated to English by Talal Itani

[8] Source: **The Quran** Translated to English by Talal Itani

[9] Excerpted from "Bhagavad-gita As It Is" by A.C. Bhaktivedanta Swami Prabhupada, courtesy of the Bhaktivedanta Book Trust International, www.Krishna.com

[10] Excerpted from "Taoist Sexual Meditation: Connecting Love, Energy and Spirit" by Bruce Frantzis, page 74.

[11] The Apple Application: Dictionary Version 2.2.1 (178)

[12] Psychology and the Soul, by Otto Rank, page 3.

[13] The Apple Application: Dictionary Version 2.2.1 (178)

[14] The Apple Application: Dictionary Version 2.2.1 (178)

[15] The Apple Application: Dictionary Version 2.2.1 (178)

[16] The Apple Application: Dictionary Version 2.2.1 (178)

[17] The Apple Application: Dictionary Version 2.2.1 (178)

[18] The Apple Application: Dictionary Version 2.2.1 (178)

[19] Wurtman RJ, Axelrod J, Barchas JD (1964) Age and enzyme activity in the human pineal. J Clin Endocrinol Metab 24: 299–301. [PubMed]

[20] Old V, Firm IN. Parameters of Normality in a Geriatric Population. Arch Intern Med 1974;132: 101-32

[21] The Apple Application: Dictionary Version 2.2.1 (178)

[22] The Apple Application: Dictionary Version 2.2.1 (178)

[23] The Apple Application: Dictionary Version 2.2.1 (178)

[24] https://www.buildingbeautifulsouls.com/symbols-meanings/five-elements-symbolic-meaning/fire-element-symbolic-meaning/

[25] Yogananda, Paramhansa. Autobiography of a Yogi (p. 426). Open Road Media. Kindle Edition.

[26] C.M.A. JOURNAL/DECEMBER 9, 1972/VOL. 107, "The earliest medical use of the caduceus", By Gerald D Hart. MD Toronto

[27] ISSN 2141-6540 Copyright 2013 Academic Journals. Available at http://www.academic-journals.org/JLC

[28] www.waimea.com/culture/canoes.html

Made in the USA
Middletown, DE
04 December 2019